D1617342

Evolution of the Judicial Opinion

Evolution of the Judicial Opinion

Institutional and Individual Styles

William D. Popkin

NEW YORK UNIVERSITY PRESS
New York and London

NEW YORK UNIVERSITY PRESS
New York and London
www.nyupress.org

Library of Congress Cataloging-in-Publication Data
Popkin, William D.
Evolution of the judicial opinion : institutional and individual
styles / William D. Popkin.
p.   cm.
Includes bibliographical references and index.
ISBN-13: 978-0-8147-6726-9 (cloth : acid-free paper)
ISBN-10: 0-8147-6726-5 (cloth : acid-free paper)
1. Judicial opinions—United States—History. 2. Judicial opinions—
United States—Language—History. 3. Judicial process—United
States—History.   I. Title.
KF8990.P67 2007
347.73'12—dc22   2007015409

New York University Press books are printed on acid-free paper,
and their binding materials are chosen for strength and durability.

Manufactured in the United States of America

10 9 8 7 6 5 4 3 2 1

To my wife
Prema

Contents

Introduction

The judicial opinion is the public face of the judiciary, in much the same way that a statute is the public face of the legislature. In the United States we assume that judges (at least on collegial appellate courts) will accompany their decisions with a written, signed, and (except in unimportant cases) publicly reported opinion that speaks for the court, with dissents and concurrences at the discretion of each judge. But the way judges present their decisions should not be taken for granted. Judicial practice has varied in different legal cultures and at different times within a legal culture. And, given current concerns about the role of judging, it is time to consider how contemporary practice should adjust to a changing legal culture.

The central theme of this book is that the way judges present their decisions in judicial opinions is a response to the following descending chain of concerns: (1) at the top of the chain, judging serves *political goals*; (2) these political goals are achieved through a *legal culture*; and (3) the legal culture expresses itself through a *style* of judging suited to that culture. Each of these ideas—political goals, legal culture, and styles of judging—bristles with complexities that will be developed later in this book, but some further introductory material will lay the groundwork.

Political goals

The most fundamental problem for judging is how to satisfy two political goals: (1) the need to project judicial authority to the external public and (2) the need to perform the difficult task, internal to the profession, of applying the law to decide cases (especially to adapt to change). These external and internal political goals are often in tension. When judges try to do their professional job well—by explaining the uncertainties of the law that they apply—they run the risk that the public will doubt judicial authority. Judges are especially concerned with such perceptions because they often lack the conventional source of authority in a modern democracy—political election—and even when elected, judges are reluctant to ground their authority on an electoral base because doing so would encourage popular review of their work.

Legal culture

The political goals served by judging work themselves out through the legal culture, which consists of: (1) the source of law, and (2) an understanding of who judges are.

(1) The source of law can be: (a) substantive—such as custom or a legal landscape, working itself pure through particular cases; or (b) an institution—such as the judiciary, the legislature, or the people; or (c) some combination of substantive and institutional sources.

(2) Judges can be: (a) experts in the law, (b) passive civil servants, (c) political officials, or (d) some combination thereof.

Style

Finally, the judge's role in the legal culture is expressed through the two components of judicial style: (1) institutional style (the way judicial opinions are presented to the relevant audience); and (2) individual style (the way the individual judge explains the decision). The following outline suggests the complexity of institutional and individual styles.

(1) Institutional style depends on answers to the following questions:
  (a) whether the judge states his or her own individual opinion or submerges judicial individuality in a court opinion;
  (b) whether an opinion of the court (if that is the choice) is signed or anonymous and whether any such opinion of the court is unanimous or can be accompanied by dissents and/or concurrences;

(c) whether an opinion includes more or less elaborate reasoning, or only a relatively bare-bones presentation of reasons;

(d) whether an opinion is written or oral; and

(e) whether an opinion is officially or unofficially reported.

(2) Individual style refers to the (a) voice and (b) tone of the judge's opinion.

(a) Judicial voice is a function of the relationship between the judge and the source of law, and can be either (i) impersonal or (ii) personal:

(i) An impersonal voice transmits meaning from a source external to the judge and can be either:

(A) magisterial—calling upon a distant, grand, even mysterious source of law, or

(B) professional/technical—relying on an expert body of technical legal knowledge;

(ii) A personal voice locates the source of law in the nonprofessional community, with the judge speaking as a fellow member of that community (often presenting conclusions as "common sense").

(b) Judicial tone is a function of the relationship between the judge and the audience, and can be either (i) authoritative (speaking down to the audience), or (ii) exploratory (drawing the audience into a participatory effort to determine the law).

Each legal system must decide how best to achieve an optimal balance of its political goals (both externally projecting judicial authority and internally accomplishing professional objectives) through its legal culture and through the institutional and individual judicial styles it adopts. Not surprisingly, the decisions vary among legal cultures. For example, the problem of adapting the law to change is addressed by the French through extensive reliance on academic commentary rather than, as in the Anglo-American tradition, a flexible conception of judicial precedent and the issuance of either seriatim opinions or dissents and concurrences. Sometimes, the same institutional style has different significance in different legal cultures—for example, the unanimous judicial opinion implements the notion of passive judging in France but is an assertion of judicial power for the English Privy Council.

There is, however, a dominant theme across legal cultures that has influenced the evolution of judicial styles in presenting judicial opinions.

Judging has, at least since the end of the 18th Century, been forced to work out its relationship to legislation in response to the rise of statutes as the dominant source of law. The rivalry with legislation became especially important when the expanding democratization of the electorate made legislatures a formidable alternative to judicial authority, and legislatures and judges often had different substantive goals, with judges leaning toward the preservation of a private economic sphere free of legislative regulation. This evolving relationship between the judiciary and the legislature forced courts to adopt new methods of presenting opinions—namely, the shift in England from unofficially reported, oral opinions to written semi-official reports; and the adoption in the U.S. Supreme Court of mostly unanimous opinions of the court in the early 19th Century. These shifts in style signaled a transition from judging as the product of a group of professional experts with access to a specialized body of legal knowledge to judging as something more analogous to legislation—the articulate voice of a government institution.

But (I will argue) the shift in judicial style toward an institutional source of law never completely displaced grounding judicial law in a substantive source of law that exists outside of the government institution that gives it voice. Although an institutional source has given judging the foundation it required in an age of legislation, a substantive source of law remains a necessary feature of judging (at least in the Anglo-American tradition). It is this persistent effort to identify and rely on a substantive source of law in the contemporary legal culture that bedevils judging in a modern democracy.

This book deals with these issues in the following order. Chapter 1 recounts the early English tradition and its evolution—from unofficial reports of oral seriatim opinions delivered by judges who were not located in a single government institution toward a system of semi-official reports that present the written opinion of judges who speak through something like an opinion of the court (at least among the Law Lords). It also includes a brief comparison of the English and French experiences. Chapters 2 through 4 deal with the historical evolution of U.S. practice, at both the federal and state level. Chapter 2 traces the shift between the Revolutionary period and the time of the Founding toward locating judges in a government institution. Chapters 3 and 4 discuss the development of an institutional style of presenting judicial opinions in the U.S. Supreme Court and state courts respectively during the 19th Century.

Chapters 5 and 6 deal with contemporary judicial practice in the United States. Chapter 5 explains how, once judging established a firm institutional foundation, modern U.S. practice has reverted toward something more closely approximating seriatim practice (in the form of increased use of separate opinions), though without abandoning the opinion of the court. Chapter 6 discusses which individual judicial style for writing judicial opinions is best suited to the contemporary U.S. legal culture—that is, the voice and tone used to convey an opinion to the judicial audience. I suggest that modern U.S. judges should make greater use of the personal voice and exploratory tone, which honestly explains the complexities and uncertainties of their decisions—what I call "democratic judging." Whatever may have been appropriate in an earlier period or in other legal cultures, this personal/exploratory style responds to a widely held view (associated with Legal Realism) that judges necessarily rely on a substantive, as well as an institutional, source of law, and are not simply legal experts but also government officials concerned with political values. In today's political environment, judges who employ a personal/exploratory style are more, rather than less, likely to accommodate the twin political goals of projecting judicial authority and performing the difficult professional task of deciding cases, at least in the United States.

My focus on the institutional and individual styles of presenting judicial opinions is not a common theme in the literature. There has been some discussion of the English and U.S. law reporting systems and the development of an opinion of the court practice in the U.S. Supreme Court; and some judges (most recently Judge Posner) have written about individual judicial styles and their relationship to the U.S. legal culture. But there is no comprehensive study of the evolution of judicial styles among English, U.S. federal, and U.S. state judges that integrates various concerns—about an opinion of the court practice, official law reports, the writing of judicial opinions, and the voice and tone used by judges when they write opinions—into a broad picture of the changing legal culture and the political goals of judging. This book should, therefore, be of interest to those curious about legal history, comparative law, and the evolution of legal and political institutions, as well as a professional audience of legal scholars, judges, and practitioners; and it should also be of interest to those concerned with how constitutional courts and supranational tribunals in Europe and courts in the former colonies should write and report opinions.

1

The English Tradition and Its Evolution

A. *Introduction*

The evolution of the English style of presenting judicial opinions falls into three periods, marking a transition from judging as the product of a professional bench and bar in search of legal principle toward an as yet incomplete conception of judging as located in an institutional branch of government. The impact of these changing conceptions of judging on the institutional style of writing opinions has been a shift from oral opinions issued seriatim (that is, each judge giving his individual opinion) and reported unofficially and unreliably, to a semi-official and reliable system of reporting written opinions in the mid-19th Century, to a significant increase in the use of a single opinion of the court with dissents (in practice, if not in form) in the late 20th Century.

The first period (up to the 1750s) is one in which the common law reigned as the preeminent source of law, expounded by a self-confident, expert, and close-knit bench and bar. This conception of law and its professional elaboration was associated with an institutional style in which each individual judge delivered an oral opinion, in effect conversing with his fellow professionals, and in which judicial opinions were (sometimes) reported unofficially, accompanied by edited arguments of counsel and (occasionally) learned commentary. There were, to be sure, sporadic rival claims from other sources of law—from King James I (in the early 17th Century), and from Parliament (in practice, during the Interregnum from 1642 to 1660 and, in theory, after the Glorious Revolution of 1688)—but the common law and its professional caretakers prevailed.

The second period (from the 1750s to the 1960s) covers the rise of legislation from a time when Parliament was theoretically sovereign after the Glorious Revolution of 1688 to its practical dominance as the preeminent source of law. This period is divided into two parts, characterized by different defensive judicial responses to the challenge of legislation to common law supremacy. From the 1750s to the 1860s, the bench and bar developed a public image of judging as a parallel and legitimate form of law, side by side with statutes. They did this primarily through the evolution of a semi-official reporting system, which gave the judicial opinion a written status similar to legislation. Thereafter, from the 1860s to the 1960s, the growing dominance of legislation created a tension between the judge's external public and internal professional role. This tension led the judiciary to react defensively, embracing an external public image of legislative supremacy and judicial passivity, while retaining a significant amount of power, internal to the profession, to develop the law. The doctrines of binding precedent in case law and literalism in statutory interpretation publicly depicted judges as passively yielding to the legislature's legal authority while, at the same time, judges exercised power to develop the law through a flexible application of these doctrines.

Third, from the 1960s to the present, English judges have adopted a new realism about their role, publicly acknowledging that they make law. This change was marked by the 1966 Law Lords Practice Statement rejecting the doctrine of binding precedent and by the abandonment of an ostensibly passive but manipulable literalism in statutory interpretation in favor of a purposive approach to determining statutory meaning, including a willingness in 1992 (contrary to centuries of practice) to consider legislative history. Initially, the judges' new realism was prompted by an effort to prevent judicial marginalization as a result of hostile scrutiny from the political Left, which explains why it was accompanied by a public acceptance of a junior lawmaking role. More recently, the effort to define a new judicial role has been complicated by England's participation in the European legal system (especially the protection it accords to human rights), and by the introduction of "federal" principles through the devolution of political power to Scotland, Wales, and Northern Ireland. Both of these developments have the potential to override a sovereign Parliament in practice, if not in theory, and could make English judges something more than junior lawmaking partners.

It remains unclear what institutional changes will follow from the new realism. One change might be to alter the institutional relationship of judging to legislating by relocating a final appeals court in an institu-

tionally separate Supreme Court (not the House of Lords). Such a proposal was made by the Labour government in June 2003, but its implementation has been shelved for the present in light of more pressing political business. Another change might be for judges to continue a shift
in their opinion-writing style, which has in recent years begun to rely in
practice on something approximating a single opinion of the court, and
to abandon the form as well as the substance of seriatim opinions by
explicitly adopting an "opinion of the court." These changes would give
judging a more secure institutional base, a step that seems necessary after the decline of the older tradition of relying on an expert bench and
bar to make judicial law and after the demise of the fiction of judicial
passivity.

B. To the 1750s: Professional collaboration between bench and bar

1. Source of law: The substantive common law

The historical source of English law was the common law, not legislation. For Coke, who served as Chief Justice of Common Pleas and the
King's Bench in the early 17th Century, the common law was immemo-
rial custom, discovered by the judges. For Hale, Chief Justice of the
King's Bench after the Restoration in 1660, the common law was an
adaptable set of customs worked out in the process of judging cases.
Hale's image of an adaptable common law was vividly described by the
metaphor of the Argonauts' ship, which had every plank replaced during a long voyage, and yet returned to its home port retaining its identity. But whatever the specific conception of the common law, there was
a unifying vision of the law as existing outside of any single judge or
government institution. Government institutions, rather than being a
source of law, were themselves a creature of law. Parliament derived its
authority from the common law; and, according to Coke, the King was
protected by the law.[1]
Nothing, of course, is quite that simple. Parliament achieved significant institutional status—first, during the Commonwealth period (from
1642 to 1660) and then as the sovereign constitutional authority after
the Glorious Revolution in 1688. But parliamentary sovereignty mani-

fested itself primarily in laws dealing with what we would consider constitutional structure (the relationships among Parliament, judges, and Crown), reflecting the fact that most parliamentary disputes were with the Crown, not the courts. Parliament did not routinely speak about most substantive English law, except (by its lights) to improve the common law. As Posner notes, Blackstone "assigned a limited role to statutory law: its proper office was to resolve conflicts between common law precedents and otherwise to supplement and patch common law doctrine";[2] consequently, parliamentary sovereignty "was . . . more apparent than real, for the common law reigned supreme. . . ."[3] David Lieberman says that the courts' attitude toward parliamentary lawmaking was not "fully disclosed in . . . formal doctrines of constitutional sovereignty."[4] The common law, therefore, retained its preeminence over legislative law in practice because Parliament was not, at this time, the vital democratic institution that it was to become in later centuries. The Glorious Revolution was not the French Revolution; it was not even the American Revolution.

The absence of a powerful legislative rival to the common law was not, however, associated with a judiciary located in a powerful government institution. In England, there was no single judicial branch of government. There was only a variety of courts, arising at different times, with different jurisdictions, and with different legal roles. The common law emerged originally from the Court of Common Pleas, later from the King's Bench, and was subsequently complemented by the Chancellor's equity courts to alleviate common law rigidities. In addition, there were Exchequer, Ecclesiastical, and Admiralty courts, and the Star Chamber. There was nothing like a supreme court at the apex of an independent judicial system. The House of Lords, the upper chamber of Parliament, acted as the final appeals tribunal, but it did not professionalize its legal work by relying only on the Law Lords until the 19th Century.

The fact that England did not have a unified court system did not mean that English judges lacked confidence. Quite the contrary. They were experts in discerning the substantive common law. This claim of special expertise was clearly apparent in Coke's assertion of artificial reason against the monarch's reliance on natural reason, a claim that relied on the special training and education by which lawyers understood and expounded the common law.[5] Hale also relied on legal learning as the foundation of the judge's role, even as to statutory interpretation: "As to exposition of Acts of Parliament and written laws certainly he that hath been educated in the study of the law hath a great advantage over those that have been otherwise exercised. . . ."[6] This expertise was, moreover, the province of both bench and bar, who were few in number and who shared a common social class and legal training in the Inns of Court. Nor was there any academic, university legal education to rival the teaching in the Inns of Court and the preeminence of what judges and lawyers said and did.

2. Institutional style

a. Institutional presentation: Seriatim opinions by named judges

The English judicial practice was (and, formally, still is) for each named judge to give his individual opinion (seriatim). This made good sense in a system where a close-knit and expert bench and bar collaborated to reach a decision based on their efforts to apply legal principle (the common law) to the individual case. The sense of shared expertise among bench and bar led to an institutional style of judicial opinion writing in which individual judges issued oral opinions, explaining their decisions to their barrister colleagues. There was no unified opinion of the court because courts were not the institutional source of law; judges were only "oracles" of the law.[7]

It is not that England was unfamiliar with an "opinion of the court." Before 1966, the Privy Council issued a unanimous opinion as the final court of appeals from the colonies; dissents were not published.[8] (Although the Privy Council was not a common law court, English judges would certainly have been familiar with this practice. Judges were included on the Privy Council before the Judicial Committee Act of 1833;[9] and the 1833 Act provided that most of the members who would perform judicial tasks would be judges.)[10] The doctrinal fiction supporting Privy Council unanimity was that the Council merely advised the Crown about the law; and, because the Crown could only speak with one voice, the Council likewise should speak as one and without individual identity. In fact, the political imperative that supported Privy Council practice was the need to project the court's legal authority to the colonies through unanimous judging. The Privy Council could not rely on the long English tradition of a professionally expert bench and bar to sustain judicial authority; for the colonies, something more was needed.[11]

b. Writing and reporting opinions

The early system of reporting judicial decisions—the Yearbooks and the law reports—was well suited to a conception of law as common law principle expounded by individual judges speaking to a close-knit bench and bar. Beginning in the 13th Century, the Yearbooks presented information about what went on in the courts. At one time, it was thought that these were official government reports (Plowden had made this assertion in the late 16th Century), but the contemporary view is that they were produced privately.

The Yearbooks varied greatly in what they included. Substantive law was often neglected; instead the Yearbooks often provided information about how to plead a case, which was critical when adherence to the proper procedure meant the difference between success and failure in court. When the Yearbooks discussed substantive law, it was not always clear whether the discussions were about hypotheticals used to educate students of the law, whether they were lawyers' arguments in actual cases, or whether they were judicial statements. Sometimes, the results of a case were not even reported. With the advent of written pleadings in the reign of Edward IV (in the second half of the 15th Century), more information about substantive law was provided, although it was still not necessarily tied to the decision of a particular case. The Yearbooks' brevity and specialized language bear all the earmarks of authors writing for a specialized audience, intended to educate younger lawyers as well as to provide judges and practitioners with needed information. The overall impression is one of insiders conveying information to other insiders about procedure and substantive law.

In the 1530s, the Yearbooks ceased and were followed by a system of unofficial written reports of oral judicial opinions. Most of these reports consisted of lawyers' or judges' notes originally transcribed for the benefit of their authors and not intended for publication. Plowden published his notes covering the period from 1550 to1580 only when borrowed copies began to appear publicly in pirated versions. Consistent with the idea that the bench and bar collaborated to produce judicial law, Plowden (like most reporters) also included thorough reports of lawyers' arguments.

Plowden was unusual in his detailed reporting of both lawyers' arguments and the judges' opinions, and he had enough concern for accuracy to show the material to judges prior to publication and, frequently, to write down all of what the judges said. His reports also contain material that explains the broader legal context in which the decision appears; for example, his report of Easton v. Studd contains a small essay on statutory interpretation, replete with references to other cases and to Aristotle. But he was almost alone in his efforts to present thorough and accurate reports of cases, lawyers' arguments, and learned commentary.

Even Coke's Reports, which appeared during the first two decades of the 17th Century, were far from accurate. One commentator said that Coke "was too fond of making the law, instead of declaring the law, and of telling untruths to support his own opinions."[12] Another observer said:

> The fact is, Lord Coke [sic] had no authority for what he states, but I am afraid we should get rid of a good deal of what is considered law in Westminster Hall, if what Lord Coke says without authority is not law. He was one of the most eminent lawyers that ever presided as a judge in any Court of Justice, and what is said by such a person is good evidence of what the law is, particularly when it is in conformity with justice and common sense.[13]

In sum, apart from Plowden and a few others, accurate law reporting was rare until Burrow's Reports in 1756. A lot of what judges said was simply not reported, reported inaccurately, or reported late. Some reports were so bad that judges refused to permit their citation.[14]

There was occasional discontent with inadequate public disclosure of what judges did, as part of a general debate over whether more publicity of otherwise esoteric knowledge was desirable.[15] For example, Francis Bacon successfully persuaded James I to assign two official reporters in 1618 to report and publish judicial decisions. There was also an explosion of law reports in the 1640s and 1650s (including many cases decided decades prior to their publication),[16] which was probably the result of democratic impulses associated with the Commonwealth. But the official reporter system advocated by Bacon did not succeed and the Commonwealth was short lived. The legal profession did not respond in any organized way to demands for more publicity about judicial opinions until the mid-19th Century.

3. Blackstone: The beginnings of a transition

Blackstone's Commentaries on the Laws of England (delivered at Oxford in 1753 and published from 1765 to1769) reaffirmed the view of law as existing outside of the judge who issued an opinion. The judge's decision could in fact be wrong, in which case his opinion was not "law"; judicial opinions were only "evidence of the law." But, right or wrong, Blackstone's common law was the embodiment of reason, superior to Parliament's inept efforts to change the law; and his Commentaries were intended to remedy the "defective education of our senators" and to make "the penners of our modern statutes . . . better informed . . . in the knowledge of the common law."[17] However, Blackstone was writing at a time when legislation was beginning to be a real threat to common law dominance and much of his defense of judging carried within it the seeds of the demise of the legal profession's control of the law.

First, Blackstone's public defense of the profession's legal expertise appealed to its knowledge of the science of law. But, as Boorstin has explained,[18] this was risky. Blackstone was forced to explain science in a way that preserved the power of the bench and bar. To that end, he pictured law as a "mysterious science," not accessible to just anyone capable of scientific thought. After all, James I had claimed knowledge of the law through natural reason in opposition to Coke's reliance on the "artificial reason" of the law. And Bentham, Blackstone's great rival for the hearts and minds of the English legal establishment, would soon claim reason as the foundation of his utilitarian approach to law and public policy, favoring legislation and codification over judge-dominated common law. In the 18th Century, the mystery of legal science kept law securely in the hands of the professional bench and bar. But "science" is a genie not easily kept in a professional bottle. The innate conservatism of English legal culture would eventually yield to a more scientific "legislative" approach to lawmaking, just as it did in the United States.[19]

Second, Blackstone asserted a preference for the common law over legislation, but had to publicly acknowledge that, since the late 17th Century, Parliament was sovereign. This led him to explain statutory interpretation in a way that eventually undermined the dominant lawmaking role of courts.[20] "Equitable interpretation" had, for centuries, been the method by which judges, by treating the text as malleable, had molded legislation to suit what the judges thought made the most sense. They often did this to protect the common law from legislative encroachment. However, in the 18th Century, Blackstone had to concede that law over equity was preferable to equity over law, which meant that the statutory text could prevent judges from being too aggressive in statutory interpretation. In Blackstone's time this concession had limited effect; parliamentary sovereignty and the primacy of the statutory text yielded, in practice, to judicial control and interpretation. Blackstone's statements about preferring law to equity appeared in the section of the Commentaries dealing with the "Law in General." In a later section, dealing with English law, Blackstone affirmed the traditional power of judges to work out the relationship of legislation to common law. And Bentham certainly understood Blackstone's not-so-hidden agenda in statutory interpretation as preserving judicial power in practice, whatever his theoretical commitment to the statutory text. Nonetheless, the rhetorical commitment to the statutory text could not easily be limited once the institutional reality of increased legislative power forced judges to pay closer attention to legislative language.

Third, Blackstone's audience included the educated public, thereby implicitly admitting the need to justify the role of the bench and bar to a broader nonprofessional audience.[21] By addressing an audience beyond the bench and bar, Blackstone indirectly foreshadowed the beginning of a decline in professional dominance of the law.

In sum, Blackstone's reliance on science, the statutory text, and his appeal to an educated but nonprofessional audience, all reflected a mid-18th-Century tension about the nature of law and judging that would eventually undermine professional control of a dominant common law. In one respect, however, Blackstone proved not to be a transitional figure. Although he presented his lectures on the common law in an academic setting, he was not the immediate forerunner of a vibrant academic branch of the profession that rivaled or supplemented the contributions of the bench and bar. That development would not occur until the 20th Century.

C. 1750s to 1960s: The rise of legislation as the dominant source of law

If the mid-18th Century witnessed English legislation as a growing threat to common law superiority, by the mid-19th Century Parliament was perceived as a vital and effective democratic institution, not merely as a theoretically sovereign source of law. The legal profession dealt with this reality in several ways, which can be broken down into two periods. First, from the 1750s to the 1860s, judging evolved as a rival source of law to statutes, which culminated in a law reporting system that presented judicial opinions in the same semi-official guise as legislation—that is, as a written document published for both a professional and public audience. Second, from the 1860s to the 1960s, judges formally assumed a passive role, asserting that case law precedent was binding and that the statutory text must be literally applied. These doctrines denied judges the power to make law either by changing prior case law or by interpreting legislation with inadequate attention to the statutory text. Despite these formal doctrines, however, judges retained a significant amount of lawmaking power by applying them in a flexible (many would say, manipulative) manner.

1. 1750s to 1860s: Institutional style: The judicial opinion in "legislative" form

Between the 1750s and the 1860s, Blackstone's concerns about England's growing reliance on legislation became a reality. The profession's primary response was to present the judicial opinion as a rival to legislation. Two individuals in the second half of the 18th Century mark a tentative move in that direction—Lord Mansfield and James Burrrow (the first "modern" law reporter). Mansfield judged as a legislature might legislate—attempting to update and change the common law through unanimous judicial opinions; and Burrow's Reports recorded Mansfield's decisions with an accuracy and thoroughness that proved to be the harbinger of the modern law reporting system.

Thereafter, the increased democratization of the legislative process posed an even greater challenge to judging. The Great Reform Act of 1832 began a process of expanding the franchise so that it would eventually include women and those who did not own property.[22] In this increasingly democratized political environment, it became more and more difficult for the profession to consider legislation as simply supplemental to the common law, although this view still had its proponents as late as 1863.[23] The response—characterized by the fits and starts that we associate with change in English institutions—was to make the law reporting system more reliable. The organized bar took it upon itself to develop a system of semi-official law reports in the 1860s so that the judicial opinion would be published in written form, like legislation.

a. Lord Mansfield and Burrow's Reports

Mansfield began his tenure as Lord Chief Justice in 1756. His judicial opinions were "legislative" in several respects. First, they stated new law. Second, Mansfield wrote decisions with greater emphasis on general principle, reflecting his Scottish bent toward casting judicial law in a more legislative mold. Third, Mansfield decided cases in a self-conscious effort to head off bad legislation with (in his view) more preferable judge-made common law. He was determined to rewrite a great deal of English common law, especially commercial law, to prove that judging was better able to adapt to change than legislation. His famous statement that the common law worked itself pure was only the first part of a claim that finished with the assertion that the common law was *therefore* superior to legislation. Some of his decisions (for example, involving bankruptcy) even responded directly to the inadequacies of legislative reform.[24] On a more formal level, Mansfield projected judicial power as a rival to legislation through unanimous opinions, so that judging would speak with a single voice, like legislation.[25] According to Burrow, a significant number of decisions by the court on which Mansfield sat abandoned the traditional seriatim practice and were decided by "an opinion of the court" delivered by Mansfield.

At the same time that Mansfield began his tenure as Lord Chief Justice, Burrow began his career as a law reporter. His reports marked the first time since Plowden that a lawyer had routinely and accurately recorded the lawyer's arguments in the case and the judge's oral opinion. The link between Burrow and Mansfield was no coincidence. Burrow had originally planned to begin his reports in 1733, when he became Master of the Crown Office with ready access to all the civil and criminal records of the court.[26] But he ended up beginning with the accession of Mansfield as Chief Justice of the King's Bench in 1756, in part because of the legal skill shown by Mansfield.[27] (One author notes that Burrow was in awe of Mansfield,[28] and Burrow's Reports are fashioned as Reports of the King's Bench "during the time of Mansfield's presiding in that court.") Burrow comments in the preface to his reports on the authority and unanimity of King's Bench decisions—specifically, that the "reasoning and opinions of the judges never gave more satisfaction"; and that "[t]he authority of right judgements, upon right principles, given unanimously by magistrates who add weight and dignity to the highest offices . . . is so great, that the direct point determined becomes a rule for ever, and establishes certainty, the mother of fecundity and peace."[29]

It would be a stretch to argue that Burrow developed reliable law reports explicitly to provide a voice for Mansfield's legislation-like opinions or to record judicial opinions so that they would seem like legislation. Burrow probably had not planned to publish his reports.[30] And I am certainly not arguing that Mansfield's approach was accepted by all judges, many of whom objected to what they viewed as his excessive exercise of discretion in common law cases.[31] Nonetheless, it seems more than a coincidence that Burrow was inspired to lay the groundwork for the modern law reporting system by that most legislative of English judges, Mansfield.

b. The Law Reports and the Law Council

Law reporting had a checkered history after Burrow. There was a growing sense that a reliable system of law reports was needed (although the frequent use of juries in many cases reduced that need). From 1785 to 1800, the "term" reports were issued, meaning that they appeared (conveniently) at the end of each term of court.[32] And, around 1800, judges experimented with appointing "authorized" reporters in their courts and limiting citation to those reports. The system of "authorized" reports led some judges to write their opinions or at least examine the reporter's drafts of their oral opinions to assure accuracy. But the reporting of cases continued to be late, inaccurate, incomplete,[33] and expensive, and the experiment with "authorized" reporters lasted only until the 1830s—failing to prevent the publication of multiple reports of the same case.[34]

By the 1840s, there was growing impatience with this arrangement for reporting judicial opinions. Many of the complaints were internal to the profession—focusing on expense, delay, irregularity, multiplicity, and the tendency to pad the privately published reports with unnecessary material to inflate cost. Moreover, there was a gradual (though hard to document) shift during the 19th Century away from a small group of barristers who were familiar with judicial opinions and who shared notes of these opinions among themselves to a less intimate group of advocates, and this shift may have increased the profession's need for a more formal system of law reports.[35]

But a broader complaint dealt with the public image of judging—the discrepancy between officially published legislation and the inadequate arrangements for publishing reports of judicial opinions. An early proposal in 1849 by the Society for Promoting the Amendment of the Law favored government publication of judicial opinions, and emphasized that judicial decisions should be published like legislation: "The judicial decisions of the Superior Courts at Westminster, as reported in the volumes recognized by the Courts, constitute at the present day, almost equally with the statute book, *the law of the land.*" They are "the formal constituents of the common law and yet, by a singular inconsistency, whilst every Act of Parliament . . . [is] communicated to the public in the most authentic form, the law laid down by our tribunals is in no respect *officially* promulgated." The Society's Report notes that "the voice of the Judge who delivers [an opinion on one of the leading principles of common law] may not reach any one beyond the parties immediately interested in the case which gives rise to it."[36] A subsequent Report on "Law Reporting Reform" in 1853 by the same organization makes a similar point:[37]

> The authority of a judicial decision of the Courts of Westminster Hall in practice, at least, equals that of an Act of the Supreme Legislature. . . . Judicial precedents are, therefore, . . . *Judge-made laws,* and, when long acted upon, become of equal force with the express enactments of the Legislature; and if it is the duty of the State to make the Law of the land universally known, there can be no reason why the publication of the Law declared from the Bench should be less formal and less complete than that of the Law declared by the Legislature.
>
> [I]t is *the duty* of the State to undertake the work. The statutes at large have from the time of the first invention of printing been published under a formal arrangement with the State. . . . [And] it is hardly too much to expect that every Court of Justice throughout the empire should at least have authentic volumes of the Law provided at the public cost.

Eventually, a bar-sponsored Council (instead of the government) began the task of publishing the Law Reports in 1865, largely as a result of the initiative of a barrister, W.T.S. Daniel. Many of his arguments relied on the analogy of judging to legislating. A letter by Daniel to the Solicitor-General quoted Douglas's Reports (1779–1785) to the effect that judicial statements "become, in a manner, part of the text of the law" and "Judges . . . consider themselves as bound to adhere to them no less strictly than to the express dictates of the Legislature." He went on to argue that the law consists of written and unwritten law—

> the one to be found in the Acts of the Legislature, the other in the judicial decisions. . . . [I]t would seem to follow . . . that it is as essential to the interests of the community that the judicial decisions of our Courts . . . should be prepared and promulgated with a care and authority not less than those which are bestowed upon the preparation and promulgation of the Acts of the Legislature. . . ."[38]

He concluded that it would be absurd to argue that there was some mistake in the engrossment of a statute and equally absurd to have "a want of authenticity in the reports of judicial decisions."[39] And, in an 1863 paper, he stated: "[T]he proper preparation and publication of those judicial decisions, which are expositions of the law *ex non scripto,* is a public duty, and . . . the public have a right to expect that it will be discharged by a recognized body in the State qualified for the purpose."[40]

The decision to reject official government reports in favor of semi-official reports under bar control was specifically justified by a concern that government appointment of reporters would give the government too much control over the law, a concern that also produced opposition to judges having the legal right to determine which cases were reported.[41] But there is a broader implication to bar control over law reporting, which is the latent (and, I would argue, irresistible) survival of the older view of law as consisting of legal principle accessible to an expert bench and bar, alongside the growing effort to analogize judicial opinions to legislation. This older conception of law also survived (and still survives) in England in the continued publication of lawyers' arguments in the English law reports, a practice that was abandoned for the U.S. Supreme Court reports in the early 1940s.

2. 1860s to 1960s: Passive/aggressive judging

Despite semi-official publication of the Law Reports, there was no way to successfully maintain English judging as a source of law equivalent in weight to legislation. The pace of democratization continued with the Reform Act of 1867 (giving the vote to the working class), and with later expansions of the franchise in 1887, 1918, and 1928, which replaced a property requirement with a residence test and also included women. The power of the House of Lords was severely curtailed during the 20th Century, and the Labour Party victory in 1945, after World War II, sealed the triumph of democratic politics when the House of Lords adopted the so-called Salisbury Convention, agreeing not to block legislation that had formed the basis of an electoral pledge by the present government.[42]

The political reality of a dominant legislature also had important consequences for the judiciary[43] and led to some tentative steps toward locating judges in a judicial institution. First, the House of Lords took measures to make itself more like a court. The year 1834 was the last year it decided a case without a Law Lord; in 1844 the convention that lay lords did not vote was established (in 1883 a lay lord tried to vote and he was disregarded); and, in 1876, the institution of paid Law Lords was adopted and the time for hearing appeals to the Law Lords was no longer tied to the period during which the House of Lords sat. Second, the Privy Council was professionalized in 1833 by the creation of a Judicial Committee of the Privy Council.[44] Third, a Royal Commission on the Judicature was established in the late 1860s, and a Select Committee was formed in the early 1870s to study the judiciary, leading (among other things) to the Judicature Act of 1873, which merged equity and common law courts into a single court of appeals.[45] Finally, serious efforts were made to end the House of Lords as the final court of appeals in the 1870s, but they did not succeed. A law was passed that replaced the House of Lords as the final appeals court with an expanded *en banc* Court of Appeals, but it was never allowed to take effect as the issue became intertwined with the political survival of the House of Lords itself.

A major result of the growing democratization of government was frequent tension between the substantive goals of organized labor and the judges,[46] just as it was in the Lochner era in the United States. Anti-labor decisions in the early 20th Century produced a lasting legacy of mistrust of the English judiciary by the political Left, which helped to bring the labor movement into the Labour Party and to achieve a Lib-Lab parliamentary victory in 1906. As a result, judges were told to stay out of politics. One way the Law Lords responded was to avoid speaking on politically controversial issues in the House of Lords, a practice that began in the early 20th Century, though often breached. Doctrinally, the Law Lords responded to the demand that they avoid politics by ushering in an era of ostensible judicial passivity. They hoped, in this way, to present a publicly apolitical image and to head off political attack, while still retaining considerable internal professional control over the development of the law. As one commentator noted, bad judging had earlier meant reaching unreasonable results, but it now consisted of "making law."[47]

Public judicial passivity was manifest by two doctrines that affirmed deference to the legislature. First, judges insisted that precedent was binding, not just on lower courts but also on the court that issued the decision, so that only Parliament and not the courts could change court-declared law. Second, judges espoused a literal approach to statutory interpretation, so that the courts could not go behind or beyond the words of the statute.[48] Nonetheless, judges maintained control over the law by a flexible application of the doctrines of binding precedent and literal statutory interpretation. Moreover, aside from manipulation of these legal doctrines, the surest indication that judges were not committed to passive judging was their willingness to make controversial common law judgments rather than leave major policy decisions to the legislature.[49] The most famous example is the House of Lords' three-two decision in Donoghue v. Stevenson,[50] which held that a manufacturer of a defective product was liable in negligence to the ultimate consumer. There was some sparring among the judges about how much flexibility they had in light of prior decisions,[51] but the significant feature of the case is that a truly passive judiciary would have left a decision with such significant economic impact to the legislature.

a. Deference to the legislature

i. Binding precedent

There is a lively debate about just how strong the notion of binding precedent was in England before the 19th Century. Judges often referred to prior decisions, frequently finding them persuasive. But this did not amount to a doctrine of binding precedent. For example, Mansfield had a healthy respect for precedent but was still able to question the continuing validity of Shelley's Case, which had established a longstanding rule in that bastion of precedent and legal certainty—property law. In any event, there is a difference between relying on a group of cases and deferring to binding precedent, which parallels the distinction between law as principle and law as contained in a single document (such as legislation). A group of cases can provide evidence of a legal principle that constitutes the law, but a single case can create a binding precedent, similar to a statute. Even French judges rely on the "jurisprudence" found in a line of cases, but would never rely on a particular case as binding precedent.

The doctrine of binding precedent in the sense of a single case having the force of law is a 19th-Century phenomenon. It took root in the 1861 House of Lords case of Beamish v. Beamish,[52] where the Law Lords concluded that only Parliament could override an opinion of the House of Lords; and the doctrine was formally established by the House of Lords in London Tramways Co. v. London County Council in 1898.[53] Prior to these decisions, English legal doctrine did not clearly establish that the House of Lords was bound by its own precedents.[54]

There are a number of possible explanations for the development of a doctrine of binding precedent in the 19th Century. Arguably, reliable law reports created the environment in which binding precedent became possible. Or, conversely, the law reports arose because of the developing doctrine of binding precedent. Undoubtedly, the relationship worked both ways, with the impact of prior case law increasing as law reports became more reliable, and the demand for reliable reports increasing as reliance on prior cases became the norm. But the symbiotic relationship between law reporting and deference to prior cases could have developed without the adoption of a doctrine of binding precedent. The usefulness of law reports would have been apparent if a group of cases established a legal principle, even if a single case was not binding.

It is more likely that the 19th-Century embrace of the doctrine of binding precedent was a reaction to the dominance of legislation as the quintessential form of law. A binding judicial opinion is like legislation, purporting to contain the law within the four corners of a single written document. Indeed, the Lord Chancellor in the 1861 Beamish case stated that it would be "arrogating to [the House of Lords] the right of altering the law, and legislating by its own separate authority" if it could overrule its own decisions.[55] Binding precedent, therefore, had the happy, dual characteristic of asserting judicial power to legislate through the initial declaration of law *and* deferring to the legislature by acknowledging that lawmaking had shifted to Parliament, thereby leaving any change in judge-made law to the sovereign legislature. In this way, courts could lock in judicial law, giving a prior decision the same status as a statute, while asserting that any change in the law rejecting a precedent would improperly arrogate lawmaking power to the courts. The doctrine of binding precedent was, therefore, an example of a shift away from considering law as a set of principles existing outside of the judges who applied them and toward an image of law as a statement issued by a government institution, whether the legislature or the judiciary.

A more substantive explanation for the doctrine of binding precedent stresses the importance of reliance interests (especially for private economic activity), which would be protected by a judicial refusal to override a decision.[56] This substantive rationale is independent of the formal constitutional principle about what is law and who can change it. But protection of reliance interests does not adequately explain the success of the binding precedent doctrine in the 19th Century. Reliance interests were not very well served by the actual application of the binding precedent doctrine because of the threat that judges would distinguish away a prior case. Moreover, reliance interests are a context-specific value, more applicable in some areas of law than others, while the doctrine of binding precedent applies across the board. A legal culture explanation that is not entirely wedded to substantive results—that law was found in a document, whether judicial or legislative—is essential to understanding why the doctrine of binding precedent took firm hold in the 19th Century.

ii. Literal statutory interpretation

Another way in which judges appeared deferential to the legislature was literal statutory interpretation, which ostensibly relied on a "clear" statutory text to determine statutory meaning. This contrasted with the older equitable interpretation approach, in which the text was a jumping off point for speculation about how legislation fit into the broader legal landscape. Equitable interpretation, as explained by Plowden at the end of the 16th Century, emphasized the kernel rather than the shell, the soul rather than the body, the spirit rather than the letter of the law. By the 18th Century, however, judges had begun to place greater emphasis on the statutory text, as I explained in my earlier discussion of Blackstone's Commentaries. Judicial claims to rely on the text became more numerous and finally achieved the status of established doctrine in the 19th Century, tempered only by the Golden Rule that allowed the judge to depart from the text to prevent an absurd (or, sometimes, an unreasonable or inconvenient) result.[57]

b. Judicial power

Despite the public posture that binding precedent and literal statutory interpretation limited judges, these formal doctrines were sufficiently malleable that judges retained considerable power.[58]

i. Determining the "*ratio decidendi*"

Judges used two methods to prevent precedent from being binding in fact, whatever the doctrine. First, the judge was only bound by the *ratio decidendi* of the prior case (that is, the holding or the rationale that was essential to deciding the case) and, as the number of books and articles published on this issue attest,[59] it is not easy to distinguish holding from dictum. Immense intellectual and professional energy went into making that distinction in England, leaving the widespread suspicion that astute judges and lawyers could, when so inclined, find a way to dispose of a prior decision that was "in the way."

Second, the doctrine of binding precedent did not apply to a decision *per incuriam.* This doctrine allowed a court to depart from a prior decision that was erroneous because it rested on obvious errors—such as the failure to take note of an even earlier decision. Although less malleable than the concept of *ratio decidendi,* the *per incuriam* escape valve also gave judges wiggle room.[60]

ii. Flexible literalism

The concept of literal statutory interpretation proved no less malleable in the hands of the astute bench and bar than the doctrine of binding precedent, in large part because the concept of the text and how its meaning should be determined is itself flexible. For example, there is no clear agreement on whether a text consists of one (or a few) word(s) or the entire text; or on whether the various linguistic canons of construction (such as "no surplusage," and *expressio unius est exclusio alterius*) should be applied as strong or weak interpretive presumptions;

or on how the "mischief rule" (taking account of the mischief at which the law was aimed) should interact with the substantive canons of interpretation to influence interpretation of a text. This leaves wide latitude for a judge to claim deference to the text while choosing among various ways to determine textual meaning to reach a particular result—hence, the pejorative terms "literalism" or "manipulative textualism" to describe this interpretive approach. Moreover, in addition to the inherent variability of the concept of the "text," there was a widespread and justified suspicion that judicial literalism was applied by the judges to favor the more wealthy sectors of society,[61] especially in the tax cases that made up a significant percentage of the Law Lords' workload[62] (most famously, in the Duke of Westminster case),[63] and, less clearly, in labor law cases.[64]

This discussion discounts two institutional arguments for English judicial literalism. First, it is often said that parliamentary drafting is very precise in England and that this has encouraged literalist interpretation, which in turn required the draftsmen to be even more precise to achieve legislative goals.[65] But statutory detail, while constraining judges, does not prevent purposive interpretation. Indeed, in the same year (1935) that the Law Lords were adopting a literalist pro-taxpayer approach in the Duke of Westminster case, the U.S. courts were developing a purposive approach in tax cases, involving some of the most densely written sections of the tax code.[66] Second, the ability of a parliamentary system to respond quickly to judicial decisions arguably reduces the need for judges to implement legislative goals through nonliteral interpretation.[67] But, as Lord Scarman said in a 1984 tax case,[68] the solution to tax avoidance was "beyond the power of the blunt instrument of legislation."

D. *1960s to the present*

Beginning in the 1960s, English judges embraced a new realism to publicly explain their work, admitting that they make law through common law decisions and statutory interpretation. But this admission has come at a price—judges have been forced to admit that they are only junior lawmaking partners with the legislature, and to abandon the older tradition of judicial dominance and the more recent fiction of a passive judiciary. This new perspective on judging may also have consequences for the institutional style of presenting judicial opinions, leading to a shift away from seriatim opinions and toward an opinion of the court (in practice, if not in theory). It may even encourage the location of the Law Lords in a separate institution similar to the U.S. Supreme Court.

1. Judicial realism about making law

A new judicial realism was clearly foreshadowed in a 1956 speech in the House of Lords by Lord Chancellor Kilmuir, which purported to reclaim an older view of law and judging, and in which he asserted that the law was not an heirloom but a dynamic force in society capable of helping with the solution of modern problems, though based on historical roots.[69] And, in the early 1960s, Lord Reid described as a "fairy tale" an earlier view that judges "only declare [law]."[70] In a significant shift of rhetoric, Reid argued that "[l]aw is as much an art as a science,"[71] an argument that abandoned the image of "scientific" expertise on which the older view of judicial law had rested. Lord Diplock described the judicial insistence on precedent at the turn of the 19th Century as a loss of judicial courage, arguing that the void created by judicial failure was filled by law reform committees and statutes; in his view, each resulting statute "announces the twentieth-century failure of the judges to show courage and imagination"; he argued that "the old machinery of the judicial process still has a valuable if unspectacular part to play" in law reform.[72]

Some judges insisted that statutory interpretation was different—that judges still did little but defer to what Parliament said.[73] But other judges were equally realistic about judging in both common law and statutory interpretation cases. Lord Diplock wrote: "[T]here are also cases—many more than one would expect—where there is room for dispute as to what the rule of conduct really is. This is so as much with rules laid down by Act of Parliament as with those which have evolved at common law." Diplock's realism, if not his enthusiasm, also extended to tax cases. Although he "would rather do a cross-word puzzle than try a revenue appeal [because it] calls for much the same mental agility and the solution is more rewarding," he insisted that, in deciding whether a particular gain is taxable, judges should not "deceive ourselves with the legal fiction that the Court is only ascertaining and giving effect to what Parliament meant. . . . [W]hoever has final authority to explain what Parliament meant by the words that it used makes law as much as if the explanation it has given were contained in a new Act of Parliament."[74]

The dominant reason for the change in the judge's public posture was concern about judicial marginalization by a dominant political Left. The Labour movement had no illusions about judicial passivity and, after WWII, had no intention of allowing judges to defeat its political agenda.[75] If judges were to retain some power, they would have to abandon the pretense of passivity and acknowledge their lawmaking role. The establishment of the Law Commission in 1965, charged with developing law reform proposals, was a signal that judges might be shunted to one side as a source of legal change. It was probably no accident that, one year after the creation of the Law Commission,[76] the Law Lords issued a Practice Statement that jettisoned the doctrine of binding precedent, and implicitly conceded that they (along with Parliament) can and do change law.[77]

But it was not enough for judges to be more openly honest about lawmaking. It was also necessary that they be genuinely subordinate to Parliament. This required a new approach to statutory interpretation, which now dominated judicial business.[78] Judges would have to shelve a manipulative literalism in favor of being more faithful to legislative intent.[79]

Two doctrinal shifts marked a more realistic and deferential approach to statutory interpretation. The first shift was to explicitly adopt a "mischief" or "purposive" approach, which allows judges to be more faithful to legislative intent without eliminating judicial discretion. This change was explained in a 1969 Law Commission Report, which clearly rejected what it called the "sterile literalism"[80] symbolized by the Duke of Westminster tax decision. Nor did the Report shy away from the broader implications of the mischief/purpose approach to statutory interpretation. It described this approach as requiring reliance on context, and described context broadly—to include "mischief" and "reason and spirit"[81]—noting how hard it might be to identify the legislative purpose and to balance it against substantive legal presumptions about statutory meaning.[82] It also noted the usefulness of purposivism in allowing the court to adapt a statute to change, stating that "excessive emphasis on the words of a provision divorced from their context may be especially inappropriate where it is unlikely that the legislator had in contemplation the particular facts which subsequently arise. . . ."[83] And it even commented favorably on the U.S. judicial transition to purposivism, from the Caminetti to the American Trucking decisions in the first half of the 20th Century.[84]

The Report's rejection of literalism was embraced by several House of Lords tax decisions. The 1981 decision in W.T. Ramsay Ltd. v. I.R.C.[85] dealt with a taxpayer who had created two debt instruments issued by a controlled corporation, with offsetting gains and losses, so that there was no economic risk. Lord Wilberforce repeated the old view that taxpayers were entitled to the letter of the tax law, but then stated that the tax statute was to be interpreted in the light of its context and purpose. He refused to rely solely on Parliament to prevent tax avoidance and made favorable references to U.S. anti-tax-avoidance doctrine, stating: "While the techniques of tax avoidance progress and are technically improved, the courts are not obliged to stand still. Such immobility must result either in loss of tax, to the prejudice of other taxpayers, or to parliamentary congestion or (most likely) to both. . . . The capital gains tax was created to operate in the real world, not that of make believe." And, in the 1984 case of Furniss v. Dawson, Lord Scarman stated that the solution to tax avoidance was "beyond the power of the blunt instrument of legislation,"[86] completely inverting the traditional view that the problem was suited only to legislative solution. By 1992, the Law Lords would affirm that "the ghost of the Duke of Westminster . . . has haunted the administration of this branch of the law for too long."[87]

A second doctrinal shift that signaled a greater judicial effort to defer to Parliament was the 1992 Pepper v. Hart decision, in which the Law Lords changed their longstanding practice and decided to consider legislative history in the form of written materials in parliamentary debates, at least if the statutory text was unclear and the legislative history was clear and authoritative.[88] Perhaps the most telling indication of a shift in judicial approach in Pepper v. Hart is something that was *not* said. In the Black-Clawson case, Lord Diplock had insisted that "Parliament, under our constitution, is sovereign only in respect of what it expresses by the words used in the legislation it has passed."[89] Pepper v. Hart contained no such admonition, even from Lord Chancellor Mackay, the sole dissenter. Mackay expressed only prudential concerns about the relative costs and benefits of searching for legislative history, not an insistence on the sovereignty of the parliamentary text.

It may sound strange to a U.S. observer that purposivism and consideration of legislative history would mark a shift to a more realistic effort to collaborate with the legislature to determine statutory meaning. Recent criticism of U.S. judging stresses how purposivism and the judicial use of legislative history potentially allow judges too much lawmaking discretion.[90] But it is important to remember that purposivism and reliance on legislative history originally flourished in the United States in the first half of the 20th Century as a way to counterbalance judicial hostility to legislation, and as a technique for judges and legislatures to cooperate in making law.[91] Contemporary English judges appear to be responding to similar concerns.

At the same time that English judges openly asserted and accepted a secondary lawmaking role, the development of a vibrant academic branch of the legal profession undermined the bench-bar monopoly on legal learning on which judicial power was traditionally based. This development was a long time coming. Blackstone's successors treated the Vinerian Chair as a sinecure; it was not until Dicey's efforts in the late 19th Century that an increasing role for the university in legal education began to be taken seriously, although it was an uphill battle.[92] Two well-known non-university journals (the Law Quarterly Review and the Modern Law Review) began in 1885 and 1937, respectively, and a growing number of university-based law journals were published in the 20th Century (beginning with the Cambridge Law Journal in 1921; the Oxford Journal of Legal Studies did not begin publishing until 1981). Today, more and more lawyers go to the university for their training. By 1966, there were 17 law faculties, as well as many polytechnics training lawyers; by 1980 there were 34 university and 24 polytechnic law courses.[93] The growing influence of academics has also been reflected in the judicial willingness, contrary to an older tradition, to cite living authors,[94] and even to welcome interchange with academic writers.[95]

Two recent developments may enhance the power of English judges, even to the point of their being senior (rather than junior) lawmaking partners under certain circumstances. The first is the interaction of European law (especially Human Rights law) with parliamentary "sovereignty." Section 3 of the English Human Rights Act 1998 (HRA)[96] provides that "so far as it is possible to do so," legislation shall be interpreted as compatible with the European Convention on Human Rights (ECHR). The HRA enhances English judicial power in two ways. First, by interpreting legislation to avoid incompatibility with the ECHR (whether the legislation precedes or follows passage of the HRA), judges can alter the meaning that would have been reached under prior interpretive approaches—by using an approach similar to what U.S. courts adopt when they interpret a statute to avoid doubts about the constitutionality of legislation. Second, although English courts cannot find a law invalid on the ground of incompatibility with the ECHR— there is, technically, no power of judicial review—a judicial finding of incompatibility will probably result in a proposed amendment of the law by a Minister under the fast track procedures of sec. 10 of the HRA, which then becomes law if it is approved by Parliament within 60 days.[97]

The second development with the potential for enhanced judicial power in England arises from 1998 parliamentary legislation devolving power to Scotland, Wales, and Northern Ireland.[98] This legislation determines the scope of authority that can be exercised by these three jurisdictions and gives English courts a power of judicial review of Scottish, Welsh, and Northern Irish law, analogous to a U.S. court's power to invalidate state legislation as incompatible with federal law.

2. Institutional style: An opinion of the court

The evolution of the judicial role in England toward acknowledging judicial lawmaking and the decline of the professional bench-bar monopoly over law requires a new institutional base to sustain judicial authority. The most dramatic step would locate the judiciary in a separate branch of government apart from the House of Lords (as in the United States),[99] a possibility considered by a recent Royal Commission on the House of Lords[100] and proposed by the Labour government in June 2003. (There is no suggestion that a new institutional home would be accompanied by two other changes that would make the highest court in England more like the U.S. Supreme Court—a shift to *en banc* decisions by all the Law Lords rather than continued reliance on the usual panel of five selected judges, and appointment of a Chief Justice.) This proposal is now moribund, however, so the focus of this section is on a more modest step—a shift in the institutional style of writing judicial opinions, which would enhance judicial authority even without an institutional change. The institutional style suited to this task is an opinion of the court (with or without dissents), which enables judges to project an image of judicial authority as a court rather than as individual legal experts speaking seriatim to fellow professionals.

Some commentary in England suggests that abandoning seriatim opinions would be controversial. These comments have focused on the potential increase in judicial workload—that is, the time and effort required to hammer out a consensus opinion of the court[101]—as well as on more fundamental issues regarding the nature of law. Lord Reid, for example, compares a single judicial opinion to a statute and prefers the legal variety presented by multiple opinions, allowing the "next generation to pick out what they like."[102] Reid thereby makes a virtue of one of the criticisms of multiple opinions—the confusion in the law—echoing another judge's view that "the beauty of the common law . . . [is that] it is a maze and not a motorway."[103]

Nonetheless, Alan Paterson's 1982 study notes a shift of the pendulum away from Reid's enthusiasm for multiple opinions, and David Robertson states that Lord Diplock's leadership as a Law Lord in the early and mid-1980s led to fewer divided opinions.[104] Some commentators have also spoken favorably of an opinion of the court,[105] and there is evidence that the Law Lords occasionally used a single judicial opinion to project judicial authority. For example, in the Heatons Transport case[106]—a controversial decision that went against labor interests—the Law Lords uncharacteristically issued a joint and unanimous decision (naming Wilberforce to deliver the opinion). This unusual joint opinion was meant to assure the public, which was suspicious of the Law Lords as anti-labor, that the decision was not legally in doubt.[107]

My own study of Law Lords opinions identifies a gradual shift toward greater use of the equivalent of an opinion of the court, which is evidenced by the widespread use of the formal seriatim practice of a concurring judge stating "I concur"—with little or nothing more being said. In effect, judges who simply state "I concur" are joining an opinion of the court. The following Table 1.1 summarizes this shift by identifying what I label a decline in the lost potential for an opinion of the court. For example, a decision in which all five judges wrote separate opinions agreeing on the result on more or less similar grounds has a .8 lost potential for an opinion of the court, because four of the five judges could have joined a single opinion. But, if four of the five judges simply stated "I concur," there was a .0 lost potential for an opinion of the

TABLE 1.1
Lost Potential for Opinion of the Court;
Unanimous Opinions

	Total cases	Lost potential for opinion of court	Unanimous opinions Number (%)
1892	28	.46	3 (10.7%)
1902	27	.496	2 (7.4%)
1952	23	.46	0 (0)
1962	15	.62	0 (0)
1972	29	.518	4 (13.8%)
1982	31	.219	14 (45.2%)
1992	37	.16	20 (54.1%)
1993	25	.145	15 (60%)
1994	29	.145	18 (62.1%)
1995	29	.27	11 (37.9%)
1996	26	.161	14 (53.8%)
1997	20	.22	7 (35%)
1998	25	.144	14 (56%)
1999	36	.288	13 (36.1%)
2000	29	.28	8 (27.6%)
2001	36	.36	6 (16.7%)

court; in essence, there was a unanimous opinion of the court despite formal seriatim practice because four judges agreed with a single opinion. The identification of this lost potential is more difficult than these examples let on, and an endnote describes my methodology.[108]

As Table 1.1 indicates, a sharp break in the institutional style of writing judicial opinions occurs between 1972 and 1982 in the direction of greater use of something like an opinion of the court (that is, a decline in the lost potential for an opinion of the court), even to the point of embracing unanimity in a growing number of cases.[109]

It is possible that the prior data suppress variation within different types of cases. Thus, cases involving more technical issues might attract something closer to unanimity as various Law Lords defer to a judge with expertise, but something closer to the older seriatim practice might persist in other cases. I made a stab at unpacking the data by identifying tax cases, using the "Revenue" designation at the front of the Appeals Cases volumes for 1992 to 2001. There were nine such cases. The lost potential for an opinion of the court was .30, and 1/3rd of the cases (three of nine) were unanimous (that is, all but one judge stated "I concur"). Although these figures fell more or less in between those for all of the pre-1982 (older) cases and the more recent 1982–2001 cases, they were in the opposite direction from what the hypothesis suggested. These "more technical" cases had *less* unanimity and a greater lost potential for an opinion of the court than the average for the 1992–2001 cases generally.

If, in fact, the Law Lords are moving in the direction of an opinion of the court, we should not be surprised. As Chapter 3 explains, Chief Justice Marshall projected the judicial authority of the new U.S. Supreme Court by adhering to the practice of aggregating multiple opinions into an opinion of the court (which was usually unanimous in the early years). A similar effort by the modern House of Lords might be expected as it tries to find a new foundation for judicial lawmaking power in an environment where legislation is the dominant institutional source of law. Although individual judicial opinions, viewed merely as evidence of law, were acceptable when a close-knit bench and bar controlled the law and legal expertise made up for any hint of judicial fallibility, something new is needed when a wider public is skeptical of legal expertise and judges admit to making law. Gathering together the individual judges' disjointed expressions of opinion into a single opinion is one way to project that authority.

E. Comparison of French and English traditions[110]

The distinctive history and evolution of the English style of presenting judicial opinions is underscored by a comparison with the French system as it developed after the French Revolution. It is important to make this comparison because it helps to highlight the ways in which U.S. practices differed from both the English and French—falling in between the older English common law system and the French embrace of an extreme version of legislative sovereignty.

1. French legal culture

The French legal culture differs from the English in the following important ways: (1) the legislature is the sole source of law; there is no common law; and (2) the institutional style of judicial opinion writing consists of (a) an anonymous and unanimous written opinion of the court (rather than signed seriatim opinions), (b) reported officially in a government publication (rather than semi-officially through private publication), and (c) with a compulsory but cryptic statement of reasons in all cases (rather than an extensive but not legally required statement of reasons in most cases of any importance).

The French legal culture is, however, no different from the English in having to serve two potentially incompatible goals: (1) the external goal of projecting judicial authority to the public, and (2) the internal professional goal of adapting the law to change. But the French solve this problem differently from the English. In the English legal system (and, as we will see, in the United States, as well), both tasks must be achieved through the judicial opinion. Consequently, there is a tension in the English institutional style of judicial opinion writing between the need to project legitimate authority to the public and the need within the profession to reach sensible results and adapt to change.

The French legal system experiences no such tension. The French sharply dichotomize how to achieve the external (public) and internal (professional) needs. The job of the French judicial opinion is to project public authority without telling the public too much about how the decision is actually reached. In France, the important professional heavy lifting occurs outside of the written judicial opinion, and is relegated to the internal workings of the judicial system and to academic commentary. This process is well understood by French judges, lawyers, and legal academics, but is concealed from a public that sees only the barebones judicial opinion. Consequently, a French judicial opinion cannot be faulted for the lack of candor that often occurs in the English system, where the judicial opinion is supposed to publicly legitimate judicial authority *and* to serve the internal professional goal of making and explaining difficult legal choices.

The explanation for the French approach lies in its historical origins in the French Revolution. Before the Revolution, judges had immense lawmaking power. They served in decentralized local *parlements,* operating independently from central governmental authority. The judges were nobles who attained judgeships through purchase and longstanding service, and their office often became their private property, capable of sale and inheritance. They operated in complete secrecy and did not reveal the grounds for their decisions. In individual cases, the judges exercised equitable powers roughly analogous to the powers of equitable interpretation adopted by English judges. Bodin wrote (in words reminiscent of Plowden) that "equity . . . [is a power] to declare or correct the law; the judge's equity is to bend or soften the rigor, or stiffen the rigor, where the case has not been foreseen . . . because properly speaking the law without equity is a body without soul. . . ."[111] But French judicial power was even more extensive than in England. Local *parlements* could refuse to register national laws deemed inequitable, thereby preventing them from becoming effective. And the judge could also issue what we would characterize as administrative regulations with the force of law. They were, in other words, powerful lawmakers. As such, they attracted widespread criticism, both from the monarchy whose laws were not implemented and from local residents whose customs might be disregarded in the exercise of equitable judgment. By the time of the Revolution, judicial power had few friends. The Revolution responded radically to these concerns by rejecting judge-made law (along with rejection of the *ancien regime*) and replaced it with a system of legislative supremacy and subservient judges.

2. Source of law: The legislature

Legislative dominance was established in France at the time of the Revolution by vesting the entire power of making law in the legislature. The French Civil Code of 1804 did more than simply implement a notion of legislative supremacy. After all, Parliament was also sovereign in England. French legislative sovereignty meant something more—the completeness of legislation as the source of law. Thereafter, there could be no French common law, in contrast to England, where the common law persisted until replaced by legislation. French law did not mince words about separation of legislative and judicial powers; Article 10, Title II of the 1790 Code stated that ordinary courts were forbidden to exercise legislative power in any way.

French judges were originally required to refer all matters of "interpretation" to the legislature, on the theory that there was no better interpreter than the author. France abandoned this practice in 1828 when referrals to the legislature proved too time-consuming for Parliament, but France never abandoned the theory of judging that led to referrals in the first place. The government continued to monitor what judges did by assigning an agent of the executive branch to the judiciary, a practice that (technically) persists to this day through the office of the Advocate General.

A correlative of exclusive legislative sovereignty is that there is no theory of binding precedent in French law. It is reversible error for a court to state that it is relying on a prior decision. Binding precedent is viewed as an arrogation of judicial power, because French observers of the common law system of judicial precedent stress only its law-creating features, downplaying its potential to constrain what judges do.[112]

3. Who are the judges: Civil servants

There is nothing in the makeup of the French judiciary to overcome the theoretical dominance of legislation as the preeminent source of law. From 1790 to 1800, judges were elected; election of judges gave way to an appointed civil service in 1800, but frequent purges of judges denied them the independence that often goes with an appointed judiciary. Even after the French judiciary achieved independence from the legislature, judicial membership in the civil service deprived them of a sense of lawmaking potential that characterizes English common law judging. French judicial civil servants are not members of an ancient and self-confident profession whose expertise afforded them direct insight into the law. Moreover, a French judge's educational and career path diverges sharply from that of practicing lawyers. After university training, those interested in becoming judges take an exam, sometimes after additional specialized training designed specifically for prospective judges; and practicing lawyers, with rare exceptions, do not become judges. By contrast, in England, members of the bench and bar shared a common educational experience in the Inns of Court, which gave them a common sense of professional expertise and mission; and English judges were chosen by the Lord Chancellor from the ranks of distinguished barristers. Consequently, nothing in the training or experience of French judges allows them to claim a power in reality that they lack institutionally. The French judge's institutional status was (and is) politically subservient, without either the common law to support a more active role in theory or membership in an ancient learned profession to give them lawmaking authority in practice.

4. Institutional style

a. *Institutional presentation*

The French judge's institutional style of opinion writing is suited to a legal culture in which the legislature is sovereign and judges are passive. In contrast to the English style, the court issues a unanimous opinion (there are no dissents or concurrences), without identifying the opinion's author. The French court, therefore, speaks with a single anonymous voice, signifying its lack of lawmaking authority. Anonymity reinforces the image of the faceless, passive judiciary and unanimity reinforces the image of judges who are doing very little in the way of making law.

Of course, anonymity and unanimity do not necessarily imply passive judging in all legal cultures. History explains the function of a particular institution better than *a priori* logic. For example, anonymity and unanimity helped the English Privy Council project a powerful institutional authority to the colonies from which it heard appeals. In the English context, unanimity had this empowering effect because it gathered together the disparate views of individual judges into a unified voice; and anonymity had the effect of projecting judicial power in contrast to the opinions of separately named judges. For the French, anonymity and unanimity had the opposite effect. It canceled out the power of judges, relegating them to institutional insignificance, rather than projecting the authority of a judicial institution.

b. *Writing and reporting opinions*

French judges have been required since the Revolution to write opinions in every case, and what they write is officially reported by the government. But the origins of this practice could not be more different from those in England. In England, the writing and reporting of opinions evolved gradually out of a practice of oral opinions that were unofficially reported through the initiative of expert legal professionals. Eventually, in response to the increasing authority of legislation, the English bar took on the task of publishing most important judicial opinions through semi-official law reports on the theory that, if what English judges said was authoritative, their opinions had to be publicly reported (like legislation). In France, by contrast, the writing and reporting of judicial opinions served the Revolution's goal of making judges publicly accountable to the sovereign legislature. Instead of projecting judicial authority in a form analogous to legislation, publication was a way of reining in judicial power by denying judges the secrecy they enjoyed in the old *parlements*. Consequently, judicial opinions had to be written in all cases to assure public accountability, not just in cases unofficially considered important; and these opinions had to be officially reported by the government, not the private bar.

c. Reasoning

Along with a requirement of writing and officially reporting opinions went an explicit requirement that French judges give reasons for their conclusions. Only in that way (the theory went) could judges be held accountable for their actions. Something that is left to custom and practice in England is, therefore, a legal requirement in France. There is, however, a significant irony in the way the French implement this requirement. French judges give a relatively bare-bones statement of law, facts, and reasoning; opinions are laconic—what John Dawson calls the equivalent of flashing a policeman's badge. They consist of a series of whereas clauses, containing brief statements of facts and legal principle (specifically, the authoritative code provision), followed by the disposition of the case.

The absence of an extensive discussion of facts and law seems especially odd to English and U.S. observers, but it is consistent with the idea of a judiciary engaged in a mechanical task of identifying the governing law and passively applying that law to the facts. The irony about French judicial opinion writing is that minimal reason-giving allows French judges to conceal a bold judicial lawmaking role, perhaps even bolder than in the case of U.S. and English judges because of the lack of any formal notion of precedent.

5. External and internal audience: Accommodating judicial authority

The French institutional style of judicial opinion-writing projects a public image of a passive judiciary by officially publishing anonymous and unanimous written opinions of the court, which contain brief reasons relating the facts to the governing statutory law. Given the judiciary's public posture of "doing little," how do French courts and the legal profession accommodate the need for a more aggressive judicial role without undermining the courts' public authority?

The English judicial opinion-writing style "solves" this problem by requiring the opinion to play both roles—presenting an authoritative public image of the law while still achieving the internal professional goal of making sense of the law. Placing so much pressure on judicial opinions accounts for the continuous criticism of the English opinion's Janus-faced quality, as it attempts to appear authoritative (which, in the modern world of legislative dominance, means "not too creative") and, at the same time, explain how judges make law. The French do not have this problem. The only task for an opinion is to project judicial authority to the public; extensively reasoned judicial opinions are not relied on to convey information about how judges make law. Consequently, French opinions appear incomplete but not duplicitous.

The need for judges to contribute to the law's development cannot, however, be suppressed, and the French judicial system relies on techniques other than the judicial opinion to achieve this goal—specifically, on *rapports* and *conclusions* (both documents internal to the judicial process), and academic commentary.

a. Rapports and conclusions

The adaptability of the French judicial system is achieved, not through the judicial opinion, but through two other institutional practices—*rapports* and *conclusions*. The *rapport* is an internal court document, written by the judge assigned to advise the court about what decision to reach. The *conclusions* are written by the representative of the Advocate General assigned to the court in each case. The Advocate General's role was originally to monitor judges to assure public accountability, but it has been transformed into a vehicle for writing what is in effect an *amicus curiae* brief for the court.

These two documents—the *rapports* and *conclusions*—are totally different in style from the judicial decision itself. For example, the *rapport* often contains multiple proposed opinions, acknowledging the possibilities of disparate results that would have been apparent from multiple seriatim opinions in the English practice. Significantly, the authors of these documents write in the first person and in a chatty, conversational style, much closer to the older style of oral opinions used by English judges and remote from the formal syllogistic style of decisions authored by French courts. The authors of these documents also explore much more than the text of the statute, including social policy and judicial precedent, neither of which easily fits into the French conception equating law with legislation. Although French doctrine formally rejects binding precedent, prior judicial decisions are frequently cited in the *rapports* and *conclusions*.

The *rapports* and *conclusions* are internal to the judicial system and are not readily available to the practicing lawyer. Lasser reports that four to six *conclusions* and one or two *rapports* are published annually and that gaining access to these unpublished documents is very difficult. The *rapports* are considered the authors' property and are taken back by the author once the decision is reached; and some judges believe that the *rapports* are protected by secrecy rules applicable to the internal workings of the judicial system. The *conclusions* are nominally public documents but access depends on negotiating a bureaucratic maze.

b. Academics and the law reports

Although the *rapports* and *conclusions* are internal to the judicial system, the various branches of the French legal profession have ready access to a different source of material that helps them develop the law. In contrast to England, the French legal system relies heavily on academic lawyers. Indeed, the French profession is fractured by training and experience, not only between the bench and bar, but also among academics, bench, and bar. Having completed university training, a potential academic takes an advanced degree and becomes attached to a distinguished professor, in effect learning and apprenticing in an academic environment. This tradition goes back to the early Middle Ages when the European universities became an important locus of legal study, as compared with England where (until recently) the Inns of Court dominated legal education. Immediately after the Revolution, the role of academic lawyers was severely curtailed, but French practice soon returned to historical type. When Napoleon heard that a legal commentary on his Code had been written, he despaired that his Code was lost.

French academics not only exercise their influence through legal treatises but also have a direct impact on the bench and bar through extensive written notes that appear in the law reports, explaining how judicial decisions reflect the evolution of the law. In this respect, they are similar to the older and now defunct English practice of including commentary in published law reports, except that the French material is controlled by academics, not practicing professionals.

The influence of French academics has been so great that it contributed significantly to the shift away from a formal textualist approach to statutory interpretation (the "exegetical" school that dominated for much of the 19th Century) to what the French call "free scientific research." The dominant academic figure was Geny, whose 1899 work "Methode d'Interpretation" ushered in what U.S. observers would recognize as a Legal Realist approach, incorporating social and economic insights into judging. Under Geny's influence, judges set about shifting the law from fault to strict liability, giving legal rights to third-party contract beneficiaries, and developing unjust enrichment law. But they did all this without changing the formal conception of judging as passive or the institutional style of writing unanimous and anonymous opinions with sparse disclosure of the reasoning process.

F. Conclusion

The early English tradition and the post-Revolutionary French tradition mark two extremes in institutional style of presenting judicial opinions, as befits their radically different conceptions of law and judging. When law consists of legal principle expounded by experts to a close-knit group of confident professionals, it makes sense that judges would deliver oral decisions seriatim to inform their fellow professionals about the law, and that these decisions would then be reported unofficially by private members of the bar along with the lawyers' arguments. When law consists solely of legislation, passive judges can be expected to be civil servants, who are required to author and officially publish a written opinion of the court.

However, the pressure of legislation as the dominant source of law places great strain on the English judicial tradition, requiring adjustments so that judges can continue to play a lawmaking role. One such adjustment is a shift away from reliance on an expert bench and bar to access substantive legal principle toward a more secure institutional foundation for judging. On a formal level, very little appears to have happened. Opinions are still seriatim in form and law reports still include lawyers' arguments. But, in one respect, the Law Lords have moved closer in practice to a legislation-like opinion of the court in which the judge's separate opinion is a simple "I concur."

The tension between a legislation-like institutional style for judicial law and the older tradition that the source of law is substantive legal principle outside of a government institution is also apparent in the U.S. experience, which never entirely committed to a sovereign legislature but is suspicious of judges who assume too much lawmaking responsibility. This tension manifests itself in the evolution of the U.S. institutional style of presenting judicial opinions, to which we now turn in Chapters 2 through 4.

2

The United States Founding
Creation of a Judicial Institution

A. *Introduction*

The U.S. institutional style of presenting judicial opinions differs from both the English and the French. Like the English (but unlike the French), judges are not anonymous and they freely express their individual opinions; but, like the French (and unlike the formal English practice), there is an opinion of the court. These differences are the result of history, which contains elements of both (French) revolution and (English) evolution.

One clear inference from early American legal history is that we were not the French—separation of powers meant something very different in the two legal cultures. Separation of powers has three possible meanings. First, it can signify legislative supremacy in the sense that the legislature has not only the first and last word but the only word in making law. That is the French (and Benthamite) understanding of the source of law in which judges have no lawmaking role. But that is obviously not the U.S. approach, in which judges can declare legislation unconstitutional and can create and adapt the common law.

Second, separation of powers can mean that each branch of government is independent of the other so that no one branch can become the handmaiden of the other. For example, in the context of judging, the U.S. Constitution protects the independence of federal judges by prohibiting salary reduction and by limiting their removal to impeachment (a more restrictive standard for removal than had been provided in many pre-1787 state constitutions).[1]

Third, separation of powers can mean that no single branch of government has the entire power of another branch—for example, the legislature cannot reverse a judicial decision.[2] This version of separation of powers still leaves room for government branches to share power (through a system of checks and balances). The federal Constitution adopted the "shared power" approach (along with judicial independence),[3] even though in the context of judging it was uncertain how much power federal judges had. This uncertainty stemmed in part from lack of clarity over the source of judicial power—whether derived from the people (which was the source of power for legislatures and juries)[4] or from the vesting of the judicial power in the courts by Article III of the Constitution.

To achieve this sharing of legislative and judicial power at the federal level, the United States had to depart from the English approach and invent a judicial institution that could hold its own against the legislature. In England, there was no need to locate judges in an institutionally separate branch of government to rival the legislature because an ancient and self-confident legal profession supported English judges in their exercise of authority. It was different in the United States, where the reality of legislative power and suspicion of judges required that the Constitution locate judges in a separate government institution if they were to exercise their lawmaking potential.

The location of the American judiciary in a government institution was accompanied by changes in the institutional style used by judges to present judicial opinions—specifically, a shift from the English tradition of unofficial reporting of oral seriatim opinions to official reporting of written opinions, sometimes delivered as an opinion of the court. This new way of presenting judicial opinions helped courts project a judicial authority that was only precariously established by their status as a government institution. This new institutional style also served two additional rationales that were important in the new republic—the professional need for a fledgling American bar to know how American law reshaped the inherited English common law, and the democratic imperative for judicial accountability to the people.

These developments did not occur in all jurisdictions at the same time because the reasons for providing information about judging differed among jurisdictions. At the federal level, an opinion of the court came first, followed by an official reporting system and, finally, by the routine use of written opinions. In the states, practices varied. State judiciaries were not new inventions; they predated the state constitutions adopted after the Revolution and were, therefore, less vulnerable than the federal judiciary. Moreover, state courts did not have to confront the federalism concerns that dominated disputes over the power of the federal judiciary. Consequently, the rationales for adopting an institutional style of presenting judicial opinions had different weights in different jurisdictions. And, as a result, state rules and practices differed—for example, sometimes written opinions and official reports were simultaneously required; sometimes a requirement of written opinions preceded official reports or vice versa; and there was no uniform practice regarding seriatim opinions or an opinion of the court.

This chapter deals with the evolution and eventual location of the U.S. judicial power in a government institution—beginning with the Montesquieu and Blackstone antecedents, then addressing the uncertainties regarding judicial power in the pre-Founding state constitutions, and ending with the efforts in the U.S. constitutional and ratifying conventions to give the judicial power a government home. Later chapters deal with the evolution in the institutional style of presenting judicial opinions—Chapter 3 (at the federal level) and Chapter 4 (at the state level).

B. Antecedents: Montesquieu and Blackstone: A judicial power

The creation of a significant judicial branch in the various U.S. governments evolved out of early ideas about judicial power in Montesquieu and Blackstone.[5] The idea that government consisted of "powers," including a judicial power, goes back to the mid-17th Century, when one commentator distinguished between the "Power to judge the law, and authority to make new lawes"[6] (that is, judicial and legislative authority). But it was not until Montesquieu in the mid-18th Century that the "power of judging" was clearly understood to be separate from other governmental powers.[7]

Montesquieu insisted on a separate and independent judicial power to secure liberty—there was no "liberty if the power of judging is not separate from legislative power and from executive power"; joining the judicial with either the legislative or executive powers meant "arbitrary" or "oppress[ive]" power over the "the life and liberty of the citizens"; "[a]ll would be lost if the same man or the same body of principal men . . . exercised these three powers. . . ."[8] Blackstone, obviously

relying on Montesquieu, stated that the "distinct and separate existence of the judicial power" was necessary because joining the judicial
power "with the legislative [would mean that the] life, liberty, and property of the subject would be in the hands of arbitrary judges, whose decisions would be then regulated only by their own opinions, and not
by any fundamental principles of law . . . [which] judges are bound to
observe."[9]

However, Blackstone and Montesquieu (although agreeing on the
need for judicial independence) had very different views about whether
judges could exercise significant power, with Montesquieu leaning towards the legislative supremacy model of separation of powers and
Blackstone leaning toward the shared power approach (although as an
18th-Century English lawyer, he was more inclined to favor judging
over legislation). Montesquieu had a very narrow and suspicious view
of judging, probably as a reaction to the significant lawmaking authority of judges in the French *parlements*.[10] Institutionally, he associated
judging with the *temporary* English jury—"The power of judging . . .
should be exercised by persons drawn from the body of the people . . .
to form a tribunal which lasts only as long as necessity requires." He asserted that "[a]mong the three powers of which we have spoken, that of
judging is in some fashion, null."[11] He also described what judges do in
passive terms that would warm the heart of a modern textualist—"But
the judges of the nation are . . . only the mouth that pronounces the
words of the law, inanimate beings who can moderate neither its force
nor its rigor."[12] And: "[J]udgments should be fixed to such a degree that
they are never anything but a precise text of the law. If judgments were
the individual opinion of a judge, one would live in this society without
knowing precisely what engagements one has contracted."[13]

Blackstone's conception of judging is palpably different from Montesquieu's. Where Montesquieu spoke of the power of judging residing
in temporary juries, Blackstone refers to a "judicial power" vested in
permanent courts:[14] "[A]t present . . . our kings have delegated their
whole judicial power to the judges of their several courts. . . ."[15] As for
judicial authority, Blackstone's sense of a robust common law bears no
relation to Montesquieu's image of a minimalist passive judge. Although
the judge's role was "only to declare and pronounce, not to make or
new-model, the law,"[16] Blackstone's judges are still concerned with implementing "fundamental principles of law";[17] and Blackstone's famous

reference to judges as the "living oracles" of the law[18] sounds nothing like Montesquieu's "mouthpiece" image of judging. Finally, Montesquieu's reference to judges unable to moderate the rigor of law is in sharp contrast to the English judges' traditional equitable power of interpretation, described by Blackstone as "the correction of that, wherein the law (by reason of its universality) is deficient."[19]

C. Pre-1787 state constitutions: Uncertain judicial role

The pre-1787 state constitutions addressed the question of judicial power and separation of powers in various ways, but they did not definitively resolve the question of the judicial role.[20] As a result of their experience with England, the post-Revolutionary states accorded significant power to the legislature in fact as well as in theory. The U.S. Revolution began like the French, suspicious of judge-made common law and favoring a strong legislature. Procedurally, judges had been tools of the King, lacking tenure and wielding the power of the monarch in the colonies. Substantively, the common law was viewed as a foreign system of laws suited to European feudal society and unsuited to the newly independent and republican colonies. By contrast, the original state legislatures were potent lawmaking institutions, even to the point of writing state constitutions without popular ratification (except for Massachusetts in 1780 and for New Hampshire's second constitution in 1784, when the constitution was submitted to the people for approval). Clearly, the idea of popular sovereignty in the new states was much more than a theory after the Revolution.[21]

But there was always an ambiguity about the common law and judges in the new American states that prevented anything like the French rejection of judging or an insistence on the legislature as the exclusive lawmaking power. The English common law was the source of rights that Americans demanded from the English government. Denial of these rights was a major complaint in the Declaration of Independence, and at least one state constitution asserted its citizens' right to the common law.[22] On a more practical level, a nation so committed to law and concerned with the practical affairs of government would not jettison the only legal system with which it had become familiar (that is, judge-made common law) without something to replace it. In the end, the states never got rid of the common law even though they incorporated only the English common law that was suitable to U.S. conditions.[23]

Uncertainty about how to fit judging into the government scheme was also obvious in the way the early pre-Founding state constitutions dealt with judicial power and separation of powers. Two states did not consider separation of powers because, as James Madison noted, the adoption of their constitutions occurred before separation-of-powers principles became "an object of political attention"[24]—specifically, the 1662 Connecticut and 1663 Rhode Island Constitutions. And the 1776 Delaware Constitution, for unexplained reasons, makes no reference to legislative, executive, or judicial power; it was not until 1792 that the Delaware Constitution referred to these three governmental powers (undoubtedly influenced by the recently ratified U.S. Constitution).[25]

Five other early post-Revolution state constitutions were implicitly dismissive of judging, failing to mention judicial power while providing explicitly for other government powers. Two of these constitutions might have neglected to mention a separate judicial power because some judging was done by officials from non-judicial branches of government—mixing rather than separating government powers in the same officials. The 1776 New Jersey Constitution, which created a court of appeals including the Governor and Legislative Council, refers only to "executive power" and the "legislative department,"[26] without mentioning a judicial power. The 1777 New York Constitution refers, disapprovingly, to a merger of "legislative, judicial, and executive powers" in an introductory "whereas" clause, but thereafter refers only to a "legislative power" and an "executive power," not to a judicial power; and then goes on to provide for a legislative veto by a Council of Revision that included both judges and senators, and to merge judicial and legislative authority by creating a judicial appellate body that included senators.[27]

Pennsylvania may have omitted a provision for a separate judicial power because of a tilt in the direction of a legislative-supremacy model of separation of powers. The 1776 Pennsylvania Constitution adopted a unicameral legislature[28] while paying little attention to judging. Although it vested legislative and executive powers in specific institutions,[29] it did not make a similar provision for the judicial power until the post-Founding 1790 Pennsylvania Constitution.[30] The Declaration of Rights in the 1776 Pennsylvania Constitution was similarly dismissive of judicial power, stating that "all officers of government, whether legislative or executive, are [the people's] trustees and servants," omitting judges from this description.[31] This constitutional inattention to the judicial link to the people contrasts sharply with the Declaration of Rights in the 1780 Massachusetts Constitution, which stated that "all power residing originally in the people, . . . the several magistrates and officers of government vested with authority, whether legislative, executive, or judicial . . . are at all times accountable to them."[32]

Two other states also paid little attention to a separate judicial power. In South Carolina, the 1776 Constitution mentioned "legislative authority," and the 1778 Constitution mentioned both "legislative authority" and "executive authority,"[33] but it was not until the 1790 Constitution that there was mention of "judicial power."[34] The 1776 New Hampshire Constitution referred to "executive courts," deferring any mention of legislative, executive, and judicial powers until the 1784 Constitution.[35]

Six state constitutions paid explicit attention to the judicial power in separation-of-powers provisions (North Carolina—1776; Maryland—1776; Virginia—1776; Georgia—1777; Massachusetts—1780; New Hampshire's second constitution—1784). All six of these constitutions provided variations on the theme that the legislative, executive, and judicial powers or departments were separate and distinct, the most famous of which was Article XXX of the Declaration of Rights in the 1780 Massachusetts Constitution:[36]

> In the government of this commonwealth, the legislative department shall never exercise the executive and judicial powers, or either of them; the executive shall never exercise the legislative and judicial powers, or either of them; the judicial shall never exercise the legislative and executive powers, or either of them; to the end it may be a government of laws, and not of men.

But these six documents leave us wondering which conception of separation of powers they adopted—legislative supremacy (with judges having no lawmaking role), judicial independence from the legislature, or a prohibition against any one branch having the entire power of another branch (leaving an uncertain space for shared governmental powers).

The easy assumption is that the six state constitutions with separation-of-powers provisions adopted a minimalist view of judging, but that may not be accurate. My best guess is that the dominant principle underlying explicit separation-of-powers provisions was protection against arbitrary lawmaking by the assurance of judicial independence (often by prohibiting judges from holding another office).[37] The existence of "separate and distinct" legislative and judicial powers does not, in other words, prevent sharing powers among these branches of government, as long as there is no threat of arbitrary lawmaking. Strong evidence for this view comes from the placement of four of the "separate and distinct" provisions in the state constitutions' Bill of Rights or Declaration of Rights, rather than in the part of the Constitution dealing with the Form of Government.[38] The Massachusetts Constitution is explicitly focused on prevention of arbitrary interference with individual rights, concluding its separation of powers provision with a purpose statement: "to the end it may be a government of laws, and not of men." It is also worth remembering that Blackstone's reference to "distinct and separate" powers on which the state constitutions were apparently based was explicitly meant to prevent "arbitrary judges."[39]

There were, to be sure, those who objected to any judicial lawmaking discretion after the Revolution, not just arbitrary judging resulting from lack of judicial independence. Gordon Wood quotes one 1777 author as saying that "no axiom is more dangerous than that the spirit of the law ought to be considered, and not the letter."[40] And Morton Horwitz argues that, for the colonists, judicial discretion in statutory interpretation was considered more dangerous than common law adjudication.[41] But that was simply one point of view in the dispute over judicial and legislative power in the post-Revolutionary/pre-Founding period. We should not jump to the conclusion that the intensely contested issue of judicial power was resolved in favor of a legislative-supremacy model of separation of powers by the various state constitutions. Indeed, the 1784 New Hampshire Constitution comes close to self-consciously adopting a judicial-independence and shared-powers conception of separation of powers. The New Hampshire Bill of Rights states that the "three essential powers . . . to wit, the legislative, executive and judicial ought to be kept separate and distinct from and independent of each other, *as the nature of a free government will admit or is consistent with that chain of connection that binds the whole fabric of government in one indissoluble bond of union and unity.*"[42] The italics appear in Madison, Federalist #47, which is the essay containing the argument that the shared powers approach was adopted by the federal Constitution.

It may not be an accident that New Hampshire's provision appears in the last of the pre-Founding constitutions (1784), signifying an evolution towards a shared-powers approach, as the Revolution became more distant.

D. *Federal Constitutional Convention and the ratification debates: A judicial institution*

By the time of the Constitutional Convention in 1787, it was difficult to be sure how judging fit into the government. Judging was clearly understood to be the exercise of a "judicial power," but what that power entailed was unclear. State constitutions varied widely and the import of their provisions was uncertain. In the following pages, I review evidence (especially linguistic evidence) from the Constitutional Convention and ratification debates regarding the judicial role. To facilitate easy reference by the reader, I provide citations in the text to Madison's Notes of Debates in the Federal Convention of 1787 (1966 Norton Paperback edition), with the name of the speaker (where it is not already identified), followed by an M (for Madison) and the page number of the cited edition of the Notes. Thus, a statement by Randolph on page 100 of Madison's Notes would be cited as "Randolph—M,100"). A similar citation method is used for references to the notes of the Constitutional Convention debates by others besides Madison in the various volumes of Max Farrand, The Records of the Federal Convention (1937 Revised Edition). Thus, a statement in the ratification debates on page 100 of Volume I of Farrand would be cited as "F,I,100."

I conclude that there was a conscious effort in the constitutional and ratifying conventions to locate judging in a government institution. This shift provided judicial power with a firmer foundation than it would otherwise have had, creating the potential for the exercise of significant judicial authority that Chief Justice Marshall later exploited. I am not suggesting that the Constitution gave a clear answer regarding the scope of judicial power. Indeed, there is evidence in the observations of Governeur Morris that there remained considerable uncertainty about judging and that this result was purposeful. Morris, who wrote much of the Constitution's text, stated in a December 12, 1814 letter that the judiciary provisions were not clear so as not to "alarm" or "shock" (F,III,

420). Nonetheless, the language used to discuss judging in the debates strongly suggests a shift toward an institutional base for judicial power.

Madison's Notes contain numerous references to judging located in a "Judiciary department" (Franklin—M,54; Dickenson—M,56; Madison —M,337,461; Morris—M,339; Gerry—M,338; Mason—M,346). King even referred to the judiciary as one of "the three *great* departments of government" (M,333), and Madison spoke of the "Judiciary being separate and distinct from the other *great* departments" (emphasis added) (M,80). James Wilson, in the Pennsylvania ratifying convention, also referred to the "three great constituent parts [of the government]—the legislative department, the executive department, and the judicial department."[43]

References to a judicial department also appeared in notes kept by debate participants other than Madison. Paterson's notes attribute to Randolph a reference to a Council of Revision selected out of the "ex. and judy. departments" (F,I,28). George Mason's papers include notes by Randolph about a resolution that would have declared that "these [three] departments shall be distinct, and independent of each other, except in specified cases" (F,II,138). And two letters written by John Jay (outside the Convention) refer to "distribut[ing] the federal sovereignty into its three proper departments of executive, legislative, and judicial"[44] and to "those three great departments of sovereignty [which] should be forever separated, and so distributed as to serve as checks on each other."[45]

In this respect, the Convention was developing a theme that appeared in the pre-Founding Virginia and Massachusetts Constitutions, which referred to "departments" exercising "powers."[46] A departmental location for the exercise of the judicial power also appeared in Madison's failed proposal for a constitutional amendment, which dealt with separation of powers after the ratification of the Constitution.[47]

Another possible institutional reference to judging was the use of the term "judiciary," which recurred constantly in Madison's notes during the debates that led up to the August 6 draft of a constitution proposed by the Committee on Detail. The first article of the Virginia Resolutions proposed by Randolph on May 29 specified that "a National Judiciary be established" (M,32). And, on May 30, after the Convention went into the Committee of the Whole, Randolph proposed considering that the government "ought to be established consisting of a supreme Legislative, Executive, and Judiciary" (M,34). This reference to a "Judiciary" survived into the final report of the Committee of the Whole on June 13 (that a government "ought to be established, consisting of a supreme legislative, executive, and judiciary") (M,115). The Committee of the Whole agreed to this text on June 19 (M,148), as did the Convention on July 26 (M,379). Even the New Jersey plan (which accorded less authority to the national government) specified that a "Judiciary be established" (M,120), although it referred to a "federal" rather than a "national" judiciary. The New Jersey plan also introduced the idea that the "Judiciary of the several states shall be bound" by federal legislation (M,121), a precursor of the "supreme law of the land" provision later found in the U.S. Constitution (introduced on July 17 and adopted on July 26 by the Convention). Other references to "judiciary" include: Wilson — M,61,79,336,343; Dickenson — M,81; Randolph — M,105; and Morris — M,339.

Arguably, we should not make too much of the use of the term "judiciary" as an institutional reference, because the term might have referred to a judicial power, rather than a government institution. The convention debates referred to judging not only as an attribute of a government department but also as the exercise of "judicial power," and the word "judiciary" may have been a synonym for judicial power. For example, the word "judiciary," which had appeared in the resolutions proposed by Randolph, was replaced by "judicial power" when the draft Constitution was presented to the Convention on August 6; Article II stated: "The Government shall consist of supreme legislative, executive; [*sic*] and judicial powers"; and Article XI stated that the "judicial power of the United States shall be vested in one Supreme Court" (M,385,393). Similarly, the word "judiciary" was often used in the phrase "judiciary powers" — as in the Declaration of Independence,[48] in post-Revolutionary pre-Founding state constitutions,[49] and in Randolph's resolutions in the Convention requiring state "judiciary powers" to be bound by oath to support the Constitution (M,33,117,151, 384). This suggests that the use of the word "judiciary" by itself might have been understood to mean "judiciary powers," which may in turn have been a synonym for "judicial power," rather than a reference to a government institution.

Uncertainty about institutional references to judging is consistent with a lack of uniformity in the language used during the debates. Morris referred to the "separation of the departments" and, in the next sentence, to the "three powers" (M,342). In Randolph's resolutions, a federal "judiciary" is created but "judicial powers" take an oath of allegiance to the federal government; and Randolph then changes a reference to "judicial powers" to "judicial officers" in the draft constitution (M,395). Different notetakers also seem to have heard different words: Yates refer to "judicial" (F,I,126—June 5) where Madison refers to "judges" (M,67); Yates refers to "judges" (F,I,207—June 11) where Madison refers to "judiciary" (M,105). This linguistic uncertainty may have simply carried over into the Convention an uncertainty that existed in the provisions of several pre-Founding state constitutions, which referred variously to a judicial department and judicial powers.[50]

Notwithstanding this linguistic uncertainty, there remain convincing indications that the convention participants thought they were creating an important judicial department within the government. As I noted earlier, the phrase "judiciary department" appeared often in the debates. And the word "department" was used unmistakably in various proposals and reports in the Constitutional Convention (M,488,510, 600) and in the Constitution itself as a reference to a government institution—Article I, sec. 8, last clause, which gave Congress the power to make all laws necessary and proper for executing the powers vested in the government or in "any department or officer thereof"; and Article II, sec. 2, cl. 1, which required the opinion in writing of the principal officer of each "executive department." Furthermore, replacing the word "judiciary" with the phrase "judicial power" when the draft Constitution was presented to the Convention on August 6 might not suggest that the institutional reference to a "judiciary" was a synonym for "judicial power." It may simply have been the appropriate "legal" way to refer to what the judicial institution was expected to do—that is, exercise the judicial power—once the Convention's Committee on Detail turned to the task of putting the Constitution into legal language. Several state constitutions had also distinguished between the judicial institution and the powers it exercised—namely, the Georgia 1777 Constitution, the Massachusetts 1780 Constitution, and the Virginia 1776 Constitution all referred to judicial departments exercising powers;[51] and the Massachusetts Constitution referred to a "Judiciary Power" in its "Frame of Government," after insisting on a separate judicial department in its Declaration of Rights, Art. XXX.[52]

The inference that the Convention was shifting toward an institutional conception of judging makes good historical sense. The Founders were well aware that the Articles of Confederation had allowed for only a weak federal judiciary,[53] and they were, by contrast, determined to create a new federal judiciary capable of protecting the federal government from being undermined by the states. This was especially important after the Convention had stripped away most of the other techniques to control state power, such as a national legislative negative (that is, a veto) of state laws, the use of federal military force, mandatory lower federal court jurisdiction, and a Council of Revision with power to negative state laws. Only the state oath to support the federal government survived. This left a significant federal judiciary as the only effective means to assure the supremacy of the federal government, including judicial review of state laws.

A significant judicial institution was also important to provide checks and balances within the federal government. This general theme of shared powers, most famously stated in Federalist #47 by Madison, was advanced in the Convention by Wilson (M,342):

> The separation of the departments does not require that they should have separate objects but that they should act separately though on the same objects. It is necessary that the two branches of the Legislature should be separate and distinct, yet they are both to act precisely on the same object.

The potential power of a new judicial department was certainly apparent to several opponents of the Constitution who refused to sign the draft Constitution. King's notes cite Gerry's objections to the judiciary as "a Star Chamber" (F,II,635), and Mason's notes refer to his concerns about the "Judiciary . . . absorb[ing] and destroy[ing] the judiciaries of the States" (F,II,638). These concerns also carried over into the ratification debates, the best-known example being Brutus's Anti-Federalist attacks on the Constitution. His warnings about the immense power of a supreme judiciary[54] led to Hamilton's response in Federalist ##78–81—that the judiciary was the "least dangerous" branch.[55]

Proponents of the Constitution in the ratification debates also spoke about the judicial branch as a department. Pinckney, for example, was reported to have said the following at the South Carolina ratifying convention:[56]

> The judicial he conceived to be at once the most important and intricate part of the system. It is . . . true that . . . this department might be made

the keystone of the [Constitution's] arch, the means of connecting and binding the whole together. . . .

And the Federalist Papers, which argued for ratification to a New York constituency, often distinguished between judicial powers and the department in which the judiciary was located.[57] Some of Madison's references in Federalist ##47, 48 are clearly to "judicial powers," as when he refers to "[t]he accumulation of all powers, legislative, executive, and judiciary," to "the several classes of powers, as they may in their nature be legislative, executive, or judiciary," and to "powers of government, legislative, executive, and judiciary." But he also refers throughout these two essays to "members of the judiciary department."[58]

Madison's references in Federalist #47 are especially suggestive in indicating a shift toward a departmental government home for judging. His discussions of state constitutions often refer to the "judiciary department," even when that term was nowhere to be found in the state constitutions that he discusses.[59] Even Brutus's Anti-Federalist pamphlets dealing with the judiciary, which argued against positions advanced in the Federalist Papers, seem to acknowledge the location of the judiciary in a government institution. Brutus used the phrase "judicial power,"[60] but he also used language distinguishing the department from the powers it exercises—"powers granted to this department" and "powers vested in the judicial department."[61]

This theme of institution building fits with the Founder's obvious efforts to apply the power of reason to create a new government, apparent both in the constitutional and ratifying conventions. According to Dallas, James Wilson told the Pennsylvania ratifying convention that "America now presents the first instance of a people assembled to weigh deliberately and calmly, and to decide leisurely and peaceably, upon the form of government by which they will bind themselves and their posterity."[62] Drafting the Constitution was often described as an "experiment"—see, for example, Pinckney speaking to the South Carolina legislature in 1788;[63] and Madison, in the Preface to his Convention notes, refers to the "American Experiment" (M,15). The convention debates referred to other countries as examples of what should or should not be done: Madison referred to his "researches into the history of the most distinguished Confederacies, particularly those of antiquity" (M,17); Convention participants often distinguished the United States from

Great Britain (M,46,85,182–187); and, as Abram Chayes noted: "Perhaps more than any other feature of the Constitution, the judicial branch deserves to be called an invention" and as "unique among nations."[64]

In sum, the Constitution failed to completely resolve the uncertainty about judging that was also observable in the pre-1787 state constitutions. But the Founders moved perceptibly toward a robust institutional conception of judging. The Constitution, therefore, created a potential for the exercise of judicial power that was later developed under Chief Justice Marshall's leadership.

E. The Supreme Court's view

It was left to the Supreme Court during its early decades to take the final step of unambiguously affirming the distinction between a judicial department and the powers it exercised. The Justices spoke about "judicial power" to describe what they did—especially the exercise of jurisdiction. This was natural linguistic usage because that is how the Constitution was written—"The judicial power shall extend, etc." As Chief Justice Marshall noted: "The judicial power of the United States, as defined in the constitution, is dependent, 1st. On the nature of the case; and, 2d. On the character of the parties."[65] And Justice Wilson linked "judicial power" with the exercise of jurisdiction in Chisholm v. Georgia to justify lawsuits against a state defendant in federal court.[66]

But the Justices were equally emphatic in their references to a judicial department, stating that "[t]he object of the constitution was to establish three *great* departments of government; the legislative, the executive, and the judicial departments" (emphasis added).[67] The Court also distinguished clearly between the judicial department and the powers it exercised, most famously in Marbury v. Madison:[68]

> It is emphatically the province and duty of the judicial department to say what the law is. Those who apply the rule to particular cases, must of necessity expound and interpret that rule.

The same distinction between the judicial department and its powers recurred in other cases:

> The object of the constitution was to establish three great departments of government; the legislative, the executive, and the judicial departments. The first was to pass laws, the second to approve and execute them, and the third to expound and enforce them.[69]
>
> The judicial power of the United States . . . is to be exercised by Courts. . . .[70]

To be sure, there continued to be some uncertainty in the use of the terms "judicial" and "judiciary," just as there had been in the Constitutional Convention. The following tabulation from pre-1820 cases (including references in lawyers' arguments) summarizes this linguistic confusion: (1) the Judicial Act of 1789 vs. Judiciary Act of 1789 (one case vs. 24 cases); (2) judicial department vs. judiciary department (17 cases vs. three cases); and (3) judicial power vs. judiciary power (33 cases vs. three cases). But this confusion does not contradict the dominant pattern, which contrasts the judicial power (what judges do) with the judicial department (the government institution that exercised that power). The Constitution's success in locating judging in a government institution was nowhere more apparent than in language used by President Andrew Jackson when he included the judiciary in his 1834 reference to the "three great departments" of government,[71] a striking acknowledgment of judicial authority considering that Jackson was asserting the executive's equal right with the judiciary to interpret the Constitution.

F. Conclusion

The Constitution succeeded in institutionalizing the federal judiciary in a government department. But the precise extent of judicial authority was unclear, perhaps purposefully so. The power of federal judges had often been a flashpoint of controversy and too much precision might have threatened the entire enterprise of forming a new nation. Moreover, the goals that judicial authority would advance remained unclear. For Hamilton and, later, Chief Justice Marshall, a strong federal judiciary would help not only to nurture a strong central government but also to advance an economic system that was hospitable to private enterprise. But for Madison (who was from Virginia and had been Hamilton's primary partner in writing the Federalist Papers), a federal judiciary was not meant to advance a capitalist nonagrarian economic agenda, however useful it might be in helping to maintain the federal system. Consequently, the new Constitution left the evolution of judicial authority to the future.

3

Institutional Style in the 19th Century

U.S. Supreme Court

A. Introduction

Institutional status in a government department was insufficient to secure judicial power. Something more was needed and the technique hit upon by the judges was a new institutional style of presenting judicial opinions to replace the inherited English tradition. Instead of oral seriatim opinions published in unofficial reports (as in England), the U.S. courts developed the practice of (1) issuing an opinion of the court rather than seriatim opinions, (2) publishing opinions in official rather than unofficial law reports, and (3) writing their opinions for publication.

This new institutional style was a response to three concerns. First, there was the need for the judicial branch to project public authority. The U.S. Supreme Court felt this need most acutely as a new invention viewed with suspicion by those who feared the aggrandizement of federal power over the states. But state courts, despite their long pre-Revolutionary history and their lack of federalism concerns, also confronted the task of creating law suitable to the American experience in a political environment that grounded the exercise of government power in the people and was suspicious of the legal profession. In this setting, the courts could not rely on the English experience of longstanding confidence in a professional bench and bar to justify their actions, nor was it sufficient to locate judging in a government department. It was also necessary to assimilate what judges did to legislation, which meant official publication of written judicial opinions.

Second, there was a professional need to know the law in a legal environment in which, unlike in England, lawyers did not always cluster in a central jurisdiction and in which courts were making a lot of new law, especially at the state level. For legislation, this need would be satisfied through the revision and consolidation of statutes (stopping short of codification of the common law).[1] For judging, this need was satisfied by a reliable system of law reports, at least for important cases, which often meant replacing error-prone and dilatory unofficial reports with an official reporting system, and (sometimes) by a legal requirement that judges write opinions to assure reliable reporting.

Third, there was a democratic imperative for judges to account to the public for their actions. This need could be satisfied by a requirement that opinions be in writing to facilitate public scrutiny, backed up by reliable reports to disseminate the information. Published reports might also limit judicial power by supplying precedent for the judge to follow. As Hamilton noted in Federalist #78: "To avoid an arbitrary discretion in the courts, it is indispensable that they should be bound down by strict rules and precedent. . . ."

These three concerns were not entirely unrelated. For example, projecting judicial power would benefit from public accountability in a republic that traced power to the people. And there was a reciprocal relationship between judicial power and the profession's need to know the law—the profession's knowledge of the law helped judges make law, and judicial power was a prerequisite to making the law that the profession needed to know. But there were differences in the way these needs played out in different jurisdictions at different times, depending on which concern seemed most important.

The remainder of this chapter explains the evolution of an institutional style of presenting judicial opinions in the U.S. Supreme Court. The dominant picture is one of a determined effort to shore up federal power over the states (in part to help establish a new capitalist economic order),[2] although there are a few hints that the profession's need to know the law and the importance of public accountability may have played some role in the initial development of an unofficial reporting system.[3] Chapter 4 will discuss the development of state law and practice during the 19th Century, when the evolution of an institutional style of presenting judicial opinions was more complex than at the federal level.

B. Opinion of the court

As the head of the "least dangerous" branch of government, without purse or will,[4] the U.S. Supreme Court had to secure a place in a republic that located significant power in the people and the states. The first step in projecting federal judicial power was the replacement of seriatim opinions with an opinion of the court, projecting an image of the Court as a significant government department rather than simply an aggregation of individual judges. The common view is that this step was associated with the Marshall Court, but that account is oversimplified. As John Kelsh notes in a 1999 article,[5] the pre-Marshall Court often employed a nascent form of an opinion of the court, rather than seriatim opinions. Marshall, therefore, built on a practice that had already begun to recognize the Court as something more than an aggregation of judges. In addition, the legal environment in at least some states before 1800 favored something like an opinion of the court, and that may have helped pave the way for Marshall.

1. Pre-Marshall Court: Tentative beginnings

There is evidence of a nascent "opinion of the court" practice in the pre-Marshall Court decisions (from 1791 to 1800). By my count, there are 63 pre-Marshall Court decisions (omitting seven decisions that were not on the merits, and treating two cases as containing four decisions because each case dealt with two issues).[6]

These opinions break down into three categories. The first category consisted of 14 seriatim decisions (three of which were not labeled as such by Dallas).[7] These are obviously not nascent opinions of the court.

The second category included 18 cases in which there was a section labeled by the reporter as "By the Court" unaccompanied by additional material outside of the "By the Court" section. Many of these 18 cases were similar to an opinion of the court. At first, this conclusion might seem too obvious to belabor—what else would a statement "By the Court" be if not an opinion of the court? But that fails to take account of the fact that "By the Court" is an English translation of the Latin "*per curiam*" and is often used to state what the court has done—that is, to designate the court's judgment or disposition of the case, rather than to provide the reasoning that we now associate with an opinion of the court. Indeed, 10 of the 14 seriatim opinions concluded with a statement "By the Court."

A close examination of the narrative in these 18 "By the Court" cases reveals that many of them were examples of a nascent opinion of the court practice, containing reasoning to support the Court's decision. My own breakdown of these 18 cases identifies 12 of them as examples of an opinion of the court and six, as judgment-dispositions (lacking enough reasoning to be called an opinion of the court). The difficulty in categorizing these decisions is that the "By the Court" material often included relatively short statements, much shorter than the opinions of the court in the Marshall era.

A third category of opinions in Dallas's pre-Marshall cases—which I labeled "other"—contained neither seriatim opinions nor a "By the Court" statement unaccompanied by additional material explaining the outcome. In these cases—which numbered almost one-half of the total (31 cases)—Dallas told the reader what the Justices did, often with sufficient judicial reasoning to be considered a nascent opinion of the court. My breakdown of these cases concluded that 23 were like an opinion of the court, and eight were like a judgment-disposition.

A list of these decisions broken down by category appears in the following Table 3.1. The table includes three types of decisions: (1) seriatim opinions (14 total); (2) an opinion with a "By the Court" section unaccompanied by any other material besides what appeared in the "By the Court" section of the report (18 total—referred to as "B/C-UNACC"); and (3) "other" (which includes the remaining decisions—31 total). I identified which of the "BC-UNACC" and "other" decisions were more like an opinion of the court (OP/CT) or more like a judgment (JGT) that does no more than peremptorily state what the court did.

The language used in Dallas's Reports to explain the Court's action often conveys the idea of a court issuing an opinion as an institutional body. In the 18 "By the Court" cases, Dallas tells us that the opinion was unanimous in four cases, while taking care to mention that there was only a majority opinion in one case.[8] Dallas even anticipates Marshall's practice of speaking for the Court as the Chief Justice; he identifies the Chief Justice as the source of an unaccompanied "By the Court" decision in five of these cases.[9]

In the 31 "other" cases, Dallas also describes the Court's action in ways that are suggestive of an opinion of the court, with an increasing

TABLE 3.1
Pre-Marshall Court Cases with "Opinion of the Court" (OP/CT)

Citation	Seriatim	BC-UNACC	Other
1. 2 U.S. 401 (1st case) (1791)	—	—	JGT
2. 2 U.S. 401 (2d case) (1791)	—	JGT	—
3. 2 U.S. 402 (1st case) (1792)	—	—	JGT
4. 2 U.S. 402 (2d case) (1792)	YES	—	—
5. 2 U.S. 415 (1st case) (1793)	—	JGT	—
6. 2 U.S. 415 (2d case) (1793)	—	—	OP/CT
7. 2 U.S. 419 (1793)	YES	—	—
8. 3 U.S. 1 (1794)	—	—	OP/CT
9. 3 U.S. 6 (1794)	—	OP/CT	—
10. 3 U.S. 17 (1795)	—	—	OP/CT
11. 3 U.S. 19 (1795)	YES	—	—
12. 3 U.S. 42 (1795)	—	OP/CT	—
13. 3 U.S. 54 (1795)	YES	—	—
14. 3 U.S. 121 (1795)	—	OP/CT	—
15. 3 U.S. 133 (1795)	YES	—	—
16. 3 U.S. 171 (1796)	YES	—	—
17. 3 U.S. 184 (1796)	—	—	OP/CT
18. 3 U.S. 188 (1796)	—	OP/CT	—
19. 3 U.S. 199 (1796)	YES	—	—
20. 3 U.S. 285 (1796)	—	—	JGT
21. 3 U.S. 297 (1796)	—	OP/CT	—
22. 3 U.S. 302 (1796)	—	—	OP/CT
23. 3 U.S. 305 (1796)	—	OP/CT	—
24. 3 U.S. 306 (1796)	—	OP/CT	—
25. 3 U.S. 307 (1796)	—	—	JGT
26. 3 U.S. 308 (1796)	—	OP/CT	JGT
(2 issues in case)			
27. 3 U.S. 309 (1796)	—	—	OP/CT
28. 3 U.S. 320 (1796)	—	OP/CT	—
29. 3 U.S. 321 (1796)	—	—	OP/CT
30. 3 U.S. 331 (1796)	—	—	OP/CT
31. 3 U.S. 333 (1796)	—	—	OP/CT
32. 3 U.S. 336 (1797)	—	—	OP/CT
33. 3 U.S. 339 (1797)	—	—	OP/CT
34. 3 U.S. 342 (1797)	—	JGT	—
35. 3 U.S. 344 (1797)	—	OP/CT	—
36. 3 U.S. 357 (1797)	YES	—	—
37. 3 U.S. 365 (1797)	—	—	OP/CT
38. 3 U.S. 371 (1797)	—	—	OP/CT
39. 3 U.S. 378 (1798)	—	—	OP/CT
40. 3 U.S. 382 (1798)	—	—	OP/CT
41. 3 U.S. 384 (1798)	—	—	OP/CT
42. 3 U.S. 386 (1798)	YES	—	—
43. 3 U.S. 401 (1798)	—	—	OP/CT
44. 3 U.S. 409 (1799)	—	—	JGT
45. 3 U.S. 411 (1799)	YES	—	—
46. 3 U.S. 415 (1799)	YES	—	OP/CT
(2 issues in case)			
47. 3 U.S. 425 (1799)	—	—	OP/CT
48. 4 U.S. 1 (1799)	—	—	OP/CT
49. 4 U.S. 3 (1799)	—	—	OP/CT
50. 4 U.S. 7 (1799)	—	JGT	—

TABLE 3.1 (*continued*)
Pre-Marshall Court Cases with "Opinion of the Court" (OP/CT)

Citation	Seriatim	BC-UNACC	Other
51. 4 U.S. 8 (1799)	—	—	OP/CT
52. 4 U.S. 12 (1800)	—	OP/CT	—
53. 4 U.S. 14 (1800)	YES	—	—
54. 4 U.S. 19 (1800)	—	JGT	—
55. 4 U.S. 21 (1st case) (1800)	—	OP/CT	—
56. 4 U.S. 21 (2d case) (1800)	—	—	JGT
57. 4 U.S. 22 (1st case) (1800)	—	—	JGT
58. 4 U.S. 22 (2d case) (1800)	—	JGT	—
59. 4 U.S. 28 (1800)	YES	—	—
60. 4 U.S. 33 (1800)	—	—	OP/CT
61. 4 U.S. 35 (1800)	YES	—	—

emphasis on the role of the Chief Justice. The Chief Justice is described as delivering the "opinion of the court" in ten of these 31 cases—six of which explicitly name Chief Justice Ellsworth as the author, and four of which refer simply to the Chief Justice.[10] In another two cases, the reports identify the author as Ellsworth, C.J., without labeling what he said as an "opinion of the court."[11] Ellsworth's prominence as the author of the Court's opinions is probably no accident. He was Marshall's immediate predecessor and, like Marshall, was an ardent Federalist—a member of the Committee on Detail to draft the Federal Constitution, an advocate of the Supreme Court acting (along with the President) as a Council of Revision to review legislation, and one of the authors of the Judiciary Act of 1789.[12] He may also have been encouraged to write an opinion of the court by his experience as a Connecticut state court judge from 1784 to 1789, when something like an opinion of the court was a common practice.[13]

A potential qualification to these conclusions is that we cannot be sure how much of the description in the reports is an artifact of how the reporter presented what the judges did, rather than an accurate description of the Court's behavior. The text in some of the reported cases sounds as though Dallas was giving an abbreviated version of the judge's decision without all the details: for example, in 3 U.S. 333, Dallas wrote that the Court delivered opinions on several issues at different times, but he provided only a one-sentence summary of the conclusions on each of four points; in 3 U.S. 336, he wrote that the Court concurred in a brief one-sentence statement of the opinion of a particular Justice; and, in 4 U.S. 28, Dallas wrote that brief seriatim opinions concurred in a result set forth in a "By the Court" statement, but he does not give the seriatim opinions. In an era when the reporter was busy with other professional obligations, when written judicial opinions were sketchy at best and were not routinely available, and when it was important to reduce the cost of publishing reports for a less-than-enthusiastic market, the reporter may have presented the essence of the individual judge's reasoning as "By the Court" or as an opinion of the court (especially in less important cases), even though the judges might have followed a seriatim practice. Because Dallas apparently failed to report about 2/3rds of the decisions,[14] it is plausible to assume that he also omitted some of the details of the reported decisions and might have characterized multiple judicial opinions as a single opinion of the court.

The internal evidence about whether Dallas actually omitted seriatim opinions is conflicting and inconclusive. Dallas's statement that brief, unreported seriatim opinions concurred in the Court's opinion contained in a "By the Court" statement (4 U.S. 28) might imply that there were *no* unreported seriatim opinions in other cases. But, in another case, Dallas explicitly reported that the Court's decision was *not* accompanied by reasons (3 U.S. 285), which might imply that reasons accompanied other decisions even though they were not reported. There is, however, some evidence that seriatim opinions were not uniformly rendered and that Dallas may, therefore, have been accurate in not reporting them. According to Thomas Jefferson (in a letter to Justice William Johnson), Attorney General Randolph made a legislative proposal during the 1790s (which was eventually dropped) that seriatim opinions be required, implying that the practice was in decline.[15] (I am unable to verify Jefferson's claim from any independent source.) And Justice Chase in 1800 stated that there was no need for him to prepare a "formal argument" (that is, a separate seriatim opinion) because the Court was unanimous.[16]

But even if the reporter omitted some seriatim opinions and gathered multiple judicial views into summary form so that the Court appeared to speak with a single voice, that style of presentation would be significant as an indication of an evolving conception of judges acting as an institution. The English reporting tradition inherited by the United States assigned the reporter an important role in developing judicial law along with the bench and bar, quite different from the contemporary practice, which sharply distinguishes among the roles played by judges, lawyers, and reporters. U.S. reporters continued the English tradition, by writing headnotes, marginal notes, and essays for inclusion in the reports, and by exercising discretion about how much of the lawyers' arguments to include along with the judicial opinion.[17] The reporter's significant role in deciding what material to present to the public explains one commentator's observation that early American reporters were often considered more important than judges.[18] Indeed, as late as 1860, a state court relied on a marginal note to understand the holding of an earlier case, "whether the note was made by Judge Whipple, who delivered the opinion of the court, or by Judge Douglass, the reporter."[19] Consequently, if Dallas decided to report judicial opinions as "By the Court" or as opinions of the court, whatever the judges did, that is an indication that the idea of the Court as an institution rather than as a mere aggregation of individual judges was gaining some currency.

I do not want to overstate the extent to which the pre-Marshall Court had a well-defined conception of how it should present opinions. As Kelsh notes, the practice of the pre-Marshall Court had "no set form" and was "unsettled."[20] The reports of several cases did not follow any particular pattern—for example, in one case Chief Justice Jay spoke for all of the Court except for two dissenters, but the dissenters' opinions are presented first;[21] in another case the report concludes with the Court's concurrence in an opinion by a named justice;[22] and in a third case Chief Justice Ellsworth delivered the "opinion of the court," followed by a dissent and a concurrence in the judgment, and then by a further explanation from the Chief Justice.[23] Moreover, although Chief Justice Ellsworth was often named as the author of an opinion of the court, Dallas portrays him in a less-than-exalted position by reporting his seriatim opinion as next to last in 3 U.S. 357 and last in 3 U.S. 415. (Similarly, Chief Justice Jay's seriatim opinions had been reported last in 2 U.S. 402 [2d case] and 2 U.S. 419, as was Chief Justice Rutledge's opinion in 3 U.S. 133.) There even appears to have been uncertainty in the pre-Marshall Court about whether "By the Court" statements should be characterized as judgments or opinions of the court. For example, Dallas reported an 1801 Marshall decision in a case postponed from 1800 as a "judgment of the court," but Cranch (Dallas's successor as reporter) describes the same decision as an "opinion of the court."[24]

The proper inference to draw from reports of pre-Marshall Court opinions is that the Supreme Court was becoming comfortable with, but not committed to, an "opinion of the court" approach in which the Chief Justice sometimes spoke for the Court. To use the language of the constitutional convention debates, the pre-Marshall Court showed signs of expressing itself as a government department, but it was up to Marshall to develop the opinion of the court in order to project judicial power as located in one of the three *great* departments of government.

2. The legal environment: State law practice

I am not arguing that Marshall consciously relied on prior Supreme Court practice, only that it was part of the developing legal environment that made an opinion of the court an acceptable vehicle for expressing the Court's opinion. This developing legal environment can also be observed in several state courts during the pre-Marshall period. Although early state court opinion-writing practices were just as "unsettled" and the reporters' role just as unclear as for the pre-Marshall Court, the reports of state cases before 1800 suggest that judges sometimes viewed themselves or were viewed by the reporters as speaking for a judicial institution.

Connecticut. Kirby's Reports[25] were the earliest of the state reports, appearing in 1789.[26] He used the designation "By the Court" or "By the Whole Court" in the majority of cases, the former designation sometimes occurring when there was a dissent or when a judge recused himself.[27] Occasionally, a decision is reported as coming from a group of named judges—not from each judge seriatim and not from the court.[28] These practices occurred despite a statutory requirement of seriatim opinions.[29] After Kirby, Root's "Reports of Cases Adjudged in the Superior Court and Supreme Court of Errors (1789–1798)" frequently used a "By the Court" heading, though less often than Kirby.

New Jersey. Coxe's unofficial New Jersey Reports (Vol. I), which appeared in 1816, covered decisions from 1790 to 1795. The dominant form of introduction for a case was either "Kinsey, C. J." or "*per curiam*," with some additional cases beginning with "Kinsey, C.J., delivered the opinion of the court."[30] Some of the *per curiam* opinions contain significant reasoning, and the cases that begin with "Kinsey, C.J." suggest the important role played by the Chief Justice. However, Kinsey's opinions use both the "I" and "we" pronouns—sometimes both in the same opinion[31]—undercutting the idea that the Chief Justice was speaking for an institution.

New York. Volume I of Johnson's unofficial New York Reports for

1799 to 1800 contain many seriatim decisions as well as many decisions introduced by the statement—"Lansing, C.J. delivered the opinion of the court,"[32] or, occasionally, "[another judge] delivered the opinion of the court."[33] There are also many *per curiam* decisions, some of which contain significant reasoning. In several cases, Lansing, C.J. or another judge gives the opinion, but the "opinion of the court" label is not used, often when another judge concurred on separate grounds.[34] An "opinion of the court" may, therefore, refer to a unanimous decision, but I cannot be completely sure whether this label is an artifact of reporting or a description of a court issuing a single opinion.

Pennsylvania. Dallas's Reports (Volumes 1–4 of the U.S. Reports) includes cases from the Pennsylvania Supreme Court from 1788 to 1800. Sometimes Dallas reports that "the Judges delivered their opinions separately" and concludes with a "By the Court" statement of the judgment (as he did with U.S. Supreme Court cases).[35] But there were also many opinions introduced by the broad statement "The Chief Justice delivered the opinion of the court," followed by "McKean, Chief Justice" as author of the court's opinion[36]—which sounds like a single opinion of the court.

South Carolina. An early South Carolina volume (Book 1, Vol. I, of Bay's Reports, for the years 1783 to 1795) states in the preface (at p. vii) that the reporter gave "the opinions of the judges seriatim as they were delivered" when "there has been occasionally any difference of sentiments on the bench, or where the novelty and importance of the points decided, made it proper." In three cases reported in Volume II of Book 1 where the court was unanimous,[37] Bay states that a named justice "delivered the opinion of the judges," "delivered the opinion of the court which was substantially as follows," or "the opinion of the court was delivered by," which sounds like a single opinion of the court. This suggests that an "opinion of the court" might have been reserved, as Bay's preface suggests, for cases where the judges did not feel strongly enough to write separately and the judgment was unanimous.

Vermont. In Vermont, N. Chipman stated in his 1792 preface to his unofficial reports: "It was not practiced for the Judges to give their opinions seriatim on those points, in which they were agreed. I conceived it necessary to mention this, lest I should be thought to have omitted the arguments of my brethren on the bench."[38] And numerous cases begin with the statement: "The Chief Justice delivered the unanimous opinion of the court."[39] This strongly suggests that the Chief

Justice was speaking for the court as an institution. The contrary impression is created, however, by a case in which the reporter introduces the court's opinion with "Chief Justice,"and the opinion then uses the pronoun "I."[40]

Virginia. Numerous decisions of the Virginia Court of Appeals before 1801—appearing in the Virginia Reports, Volumes 1–2 of Bushrod Washington and Volumes 1–2 of Daniel Call—were reported with an introduction: "The President delivered the opinion of the court" (the President was the equivalent of the Chief Justice); or, in Call's phraseology, "The President delivered the resolution of the court."[41] Sometimes the report of a case begins with a reference to "The President," without any suggestion of additional opinions.[42] All this occurred during Edmund Pendleton's tenure as President of the Virginia Court of Appeals (which lasted from 1789 to 1803). Other judges besides Pendleton also delivered an "opinion of the court" (for example, Lyons).[43]

The most interesting point about Pendleton's practice of speaking for the Virginia court is its likely influence on Marshall, who had extensive experience practicing before Pendleton's court prior to becoming Chief Justice.[44] Marshall was politically close to Pendleton and was chosen by the Federalists to argue at the Virginia ratifying convention in favor of Article III of the U.S. Constitution, so as to relieve Pendleton of the burdens of debate because of his ill health.[45] Indeed, Jefferson, in his later 1822 correspondence with Justice Johnson, speculated that Pendleton, as well as Mansfield, had influenced Marshall's suppression of seriatim opinions.[46] The "opinion of the court" practice in Virginia seems to be more than an artifact of the reporter's style, whatever may have occurred in other states.

3. The Marshall Court

a. Opinion of the court: Creation of modern practice

Before Marshall became Chief Justice, an opinion of the court practice was (at most) nascent in the U.S. Supreme Court and was probably used in some states some of the time. But there is no mistaking the fact that Marshall created the modern institutional style in which the Court routinely spoke through an extensively reasoned opinion of the court. Two well-documented aspects of the Court's practice during the first decade of Marshall's tenure illustrate how he used the Court's opinions to project federal judicial power,[47] which suggested to one commentator an effort to make the Court appear to speak through its chief officer in the same way that the President speaks for the executive branch.[48] First, as Chief Justice, he rigorously followed the practice of delivering an opinion of the court. His first opinion began "Chief Justice Marshall delivered the opinion of the court."[49] Marshall's name was dropped for a few years—the reporter says only that "the Chief Justice delivered the opinion of the Court" or some similar phrasing[50]—perhaps to emphasize that the Court itself and not any particular judge was the source of the opinion. However, the initial practice of naming the judge who delivered the Court's opinion was revived in 1804,[51] producing that combination of individual and institutional judging that characterizes U.S. practice. From 1801 to 1806, Marshall spoke for the Court in all but seven of 67 non–*per curiam* opinions and, in two of those seven cases, the senior-most Justice delivered the Court's opinion. In the other five cases, the Court reverted to seriatim opinions, almost certainly because Marshall was absent or had recused himself.[52]

Second, Marshall succeeded in forcing the appearance of unanimity on the Court, suppressing the expression of dissents and concurrences. Marshall sometimes failed to circulate opinions for comment so that the opinions were issued in his own voice without influence or contribution from colleagues.[53] And he sometimes spoke for the entire Court whether or not he agreed with the result.[54]

Marshall's more or less complete dominance of the Court did not last. Although separate opinions were not unknown in the early years of his tenure (there was one concurrence in the first four years),[55] they became more common beginning in 1808; moreover, at about the same time, the practice of having the Chief Justice or senior Justice routinely deliver the Court's opinion was breached.[56] An occasional opinion explicitly stated that a Justice was instructed to deliver the opinion of the court,[57] which suggests that the Justice whose name usually appeared as the Court's spokesman was speaking in his own voice.

But it was a reflection of Marshall's success in getting the Court to speak with a single voice that separate opinions never became common until the 1940s. Despite some fluctuations in the tendency of the Justices to write separately, decisions with separate opinions hovered around 20% or less until the 1930s, after which there was a gradual rise and then a dramatic increase in 1941. Marshall's success in discouraging, if not suppressing, separate opinions was especially apparent in their decline from 1818 to 1827, during which time Justice Johnson was almost alone in writing separately (he wrote 17 of the 23 separate opinions).[58] It was this decline, especially in the important constitutional cases from 1819 to 1822,[59] that led Jefferson to write Justice Johnson (who had been a Jefferson appointee to the Court) to object to the abandonment of the seriatim practice. Jefferson was concerned that, without seriatim opinions, judges could not be held accountable to the public. He considered impeachment of judges to be a "scarecrow," so that judges could be kept in line only by their concern with public reputation, which would only work as a check if judges wrote publicly available, individual opinions.[60] Jefferson also hoped that separate opinions would reduce the value of a decision as precedent,[61] as did Madison, who argued that seriatim opinions were better because they "might either, by the harmony of their reasoning, have produced a greater conviction in the public mind; or by its discordance, have impaired the force of the precedent, now ostensibly supported by a unanimous and perfect concurrence in every argument and dictum in the judgment pronounced."[62]

Of course, Marshall had no intention of allowing public accountability to interfere with his agenda of projecting judicial authority. Even if Marshall was unable to impose unanimity on the Court or to speak for the Court in all cases, he succeeded in virtually eliminating seriatim opinions,[63] and in rendering dissents and concurrences sufficiently suspect that judges who wrote separately felt the need to apologize or explain their action (recounted in Chapter 5).

b. A plural judicial institution: Evidence of survival

One might conclude from this discussion that Marshall succeeded completely in shifting the view of the Court from a group of individual judges to an institution of government. But the evidence is more mixed than might at first appear. The grammar of the Court's opinions sometimes revealed an understanding of the Court as consisting of plural membership.

Marshall usually referred to the Court in the singular, which is consistent with his sense of the Court as the head of a great department of government, instead of a mere aggregation of judges. Citations to Marshall's references to a singular Court are too numerous to record, but his very first opinion states that "the Court *is* therefore of opinion" (italics added),[64] and he continued to use that style throughout most of his tenure. Marshall also referred to a singular institution when speaking about what the Court did—the Court "has," "does," "understands," and "considers."[65] Without explanation, however, Marshall departed from this pattern of referring to the Court in the singular toward the latter part of his tenure, around 1828.[66] This grammatical shift may have resulted from Marshall's growing despair at a loss of collegiality, possibly brought on by the fact (explicitly lamented by Marshall) that the Justices no longer shared lodgings in a common location,[67] or perhaps because there was an infusion of new blood on the Court—from Story's appointment in 1811 to Thompson's in 1823, the Court's membership had not changed. Evidence of an increasingly fractured Court is also apparent in Marshall's 1834 decision that constitutional judgments would be issued only when four of the seven Justices agreed.[68]

Opinions by other Justices during Marshall's tenure as Chief Justice reveal a mixed grammatical pattern. Once again, the cases are too numerous for a complete tabulation, but my impression is that Story—a fellow nationalist with Marshall but a political Republican—more often referred to the Court in the plural than the singular. (In one case, Story sent mixed signals. He used the singular "I" as the author of the opinion, but was careful to refer to the Court "in whose name I speak.")[69] Washington, the first President's nephew (and, like Marshall, a Federalist), almost always referred to the Court in the singular. Johnson, somewhat surprisingly in light of his Jeffersonian roots and his greater willingness to write separately, often used the singular as well as the plural.

Arguably, we cannot make too much of these grammatical practices. The word "court" (like "government," "jury," "Congress," and "United States") is what is known as a "noun of multitude" and can take either the singular or plural verb. Modern observers suggest that plural or singular usage is associated with the author's emphasis on the action of the individual members or the collective body,[70] which would suggest that a judge's inclination to use the singular or plural is politically meaningful. However, grammatical practices in the late 18th and early 19th Century may have been too casual for us to draw inferences about the author's conception of the institution to which he referred. During this period, there were efforts to standardize usage about the agreement between noun and verb generally, not just for nouns of multitude, but there was nothing approaching complete agreement.[71]

Indeed, to this day, English usage is less likely to require the singular with nouns of multitude than American usage.[72] Nonetheless, Marshall's obvious adoption of the singular when he became Chief Justice and his shift to the plural toward the end of his tenure seems too clear to be merely a sign of casual grammar. And, surely, the fact that the "United States" is now routinely used with the singular "is," in contrast with an earlier time when a plural reference was common,[73] tells us something about our history.

Moreover, as Figure 3.1 indicates, there has been a steady shift in grammatical practices over time in federal, state, and English cases. The data are based on a Westlaw search identifying cases using the singular phrase "court is (was) of opinion" and cases using the plural phrase "court are (were) of opinion"; an endnote gives a more precise description of the search technique, which was necessary to avoid missing some cases and to avoid some false positives (as in "majority of the court were of opinion").[74]

I divided the U.S. Supreme Court into the following periods: pre-Marshall (before 1801); 1801–1829 (after which the Justices stopped living together in the same boarding house); 1830–1865 (through the Civil War period); 1866–1900 (when the Justices' views were probably still shaped by pre–Civil War training); and after 1900. The periods for

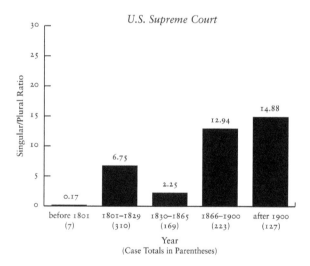

Fig. 3.1 (*above and opposite*). Ratio of references to court as singular to court as plural.

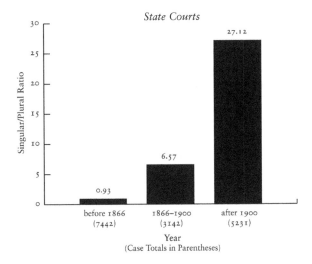

State Courts

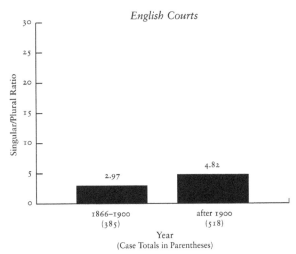

English Courts

researching state courts were: before 1866; 1866–1900; and after 1900. English cases were researched from 1866 to 1900 (the Westlaw database began after 1865); and after 1900. "After 1900" refers to a search conducted on July 31, 2003.

Figure 3.1 presents the ratio of singular to plural references during the specified time periods. (For example, the 6.75 ratio for the U.S. Supreme Court from 1801 to 1829 means that there were almost seven times as many singular as plural references.) The data show a linear shift over time toward a singular reference in the United States—both the U.S. Supreme Court and state courts—with an interesting exception. The exception is the period from 1801 to 1829, when Marshall still dominated the Court and was able to impose a reference to the Court as a singular institution, a pattern that declined thereafter until the post–Civil War period. For England, the overall singular-plural ratio is lower than in the United States, perhaps reflecting the greater propensity in England to use the plural for nouns of multitude, but the ratio of singular to plural references still increases after 1900.

C. Reporting decisions[75]

1. Legislating an "official" reporter

An opinion of the court presented the U.S. Supreme Court as a unified institution, but the impact would have been muted if a wider audience (professional or public) could not read what the Court had done. Consequently, by the mid-1810s, Congress was persuaded to provide a financial subsidy for official reports of the Court's opinions.[76]

The reporting of U.S. Supreme Court decisions began in the same haphazard way that characterized its English predecessors. The Judiciary Act of 1789[77] creating the federal judiciary said nothing about official reports, and the first two reporters (Dallas, 1791–1800, and Cranch, 1801–1815) had no official status. They took on the task of reporting Supreme Court decisions out of a desire for profit and professional reputation, but they continued parallel professional lives. Dallas was a Philadelphia lawyer who also held state and federal government jobs. His reports contained Pennsylvania and Delaware state cases as well as Supreme Court decisions when the Court sat in Philadelphia. When Dallas did not accompany the Court in its move from Philadelphia to Washington in 1800, Cranch became the reporter in 1801 even though he was a federal judge.

Wheaton succeeded Cranch, reporting cases from 1816 to 1827. He began his tenure as reporter without official status, but with the promise of access to the Justices' written opinions and notes. Nonetheless, Wheaton (like Cranch before him) was disappointed in the financial return, perhaps because the admiralty cases that made up a significant portion of the Court's business were not the meat and potatoes of legal practice. (Dallas's first volume—Volume 1 of the U.S. Reports—contained only Pennsylvania cases and sold better than the next three volumes, which included U.S. Supreme Court cases.) There were no published reviews of Wheaton's reports until his third volume,[78] and Wheaton was forced to sell the copyright in his first volume to arrange for its printing. Wheaton, therefore, lobbied for a federal subsidy and, in 1817, Congress passed a law providing the reporter with $1,000 annual compensation to supplement any profits from sale, on condition that publication occur within six months after the decisions were made and that the reporter supply the Secretary of State with a specified number of copies.[79] Consequently, Wheaton became the first "official" reporter of U.S. Supreme Court cases, but "official" is in quotes because he did not become a government employee and the government did not take over responsibility for publication. (In this early period, even the Attorney General was paid a retainer for what one author called a "consultative role," in the expectation that he would retain private clients to supplement his compensation.)[80]

Support for an official U.S. Supreme Court reporter arose from the same motivation that led to replacing seriatim opinions with an opinion of the court—the need to project the institutional authority of the federal judiciary—except that Story rather than Marshall was the prime mover. Story understood the importance of reporters in enhancing judicial power and believed that an effective reporting system would establish national policy, especially through the exercise of admiralty jurisdiction.

To implement these goals at the federal level, Story authored a bill to establish a U.S. Supreme Court reporter as early as 1814, citing state precedent for official reports—specifically, Massachusetts (1804), New York (1804), New Jersey (1806), and Kentucky (1804). Passage was repeatedly delayed, however, and Marshall's assistance was sought in the form of a letter dated Feb. 7, 1817 to a Senator supporting passage of the bill. The law passed the Senate two days later, the House on March 1, and was signed by the President on March 3, 1817.[81]

Story had seen a special opportunity to achieve his goal of enhancing federal judicial authority through appointment as the reporter of his friend Wheaton, with whom he shared a strong scholarly interest, as well as lodging in a boarding house after Wheaton's appointment. Substantively, Story's nationalist views of admiralty law had much in common with Wheaton's published writings. And, on a more general level, Wheaton's view of law as a science was in tune with the views of judges like Story and Kent,[82] whose commentaries and treatises advanced the judge-friendly English conception of law as a legal science, but with a distinctly American content.

The Story/Wheaton connection and its importance in establishing federal judicial authority was also evident in the way Wheaton did his job. Their relationship was so close that Story gave Wheaton a draft opinion in an admiralty case that he had withheld from publication out of "delicacy" for Marshall's feelings. (The opinion had concurred with Marshall's result but on different grounds, and Wheaton was expected to use the draft opinion to justify support for the Court's enhanced admiralty jurisdiction.) Story also contributed some anonymous admiralty law essays to be published in Wheaton's reports. Moreover, the Story/Wheaton relationship was reciprocal; in one instance, Wheaton supplied Story with case authorities for use in preparing an opinion.

A growing perception that judicial opinions were similar to legislation may also have influenced passage of the official reporting law (just as it would later influence the development of the semi-official English law reporting system, discussed in Chapter 1). Two pieces of indirect evidence support this inference. First, opponents of a congressional subsidy for a U.S. Supreme Court reporter explicitly rejected the analogy of judicial opinions to legislation; one speaker noted (in a losing cause) that decisions of the Supreme Court were not entitled to the status of laws binding on their successors. Second, a lawyer arguing successfully against a copyright for judicial opinions in the 1834 case of Wheaton v. Peters stressed the similarity between statutes and judicial opinions:

> The matter which [the reports] disseminate is . . . the law of the land. Not indeed the actual productions of the legislature. Those are the rules which govern the action of the citizen. But they are constantly in want of interpretation, and that is afforded by the judge. He is the "lex loquens." His explanations of what is written are often more important that the mere naked written law itself.[83]

It would be a mistake to conclude, however, that creation of an official U.S. reporter displaced the older tradition of collaboration among the bench, bar, and reporter to access the substantive source of judicial law with the more modern view that the judicial opinion is the institutional source of judicial law. Quite the contrary. The designation of an official reporter reflected his importance in helping to shape judicial law through such techniques as deciding what additional material to include along with selected cases, such as essays, marginal notes, headnotes, and lawyers' arguments. Although inclusion of lawyers' arguments raised costs significantly and some published reports were financially successful without them,[84] the reporter had to decide how much of these arguments were necessary for the reader to understand the Court's decision, especially when many opinions were brief and/or delivered orally. (The reporters may also have been concerned that omission of lawyers' arguments would antagonize prominent members of the profession whose support was needed to sell the volumes.)

The reporter's continued independence was clearly apparent in the determined efforts throughout the first half of the 19th Century to improve the way the reporter did his job—by eliminating delay, omissions, and inaccuracy. Delay was the first problem to be successfully addressed. Volume 2 of Dallas's reports (the first to include U.S. Supreme Court cases) was published five years after the last decision included in the volume, and Volume 4 was seven years tardy, appearing after the first three of Cranch's volumes had been published. Cranch was also tardy; when Marshall received prepublication copies of Volumes 7 and 8 of Cranch's Reports two years after Wheaton's appointment, he mistakenly wrote Wheaton a letter of thanks. Even Wheaton had trouble getting out his first volume covering the 1816 term but managed to do so before the beginning of the next term. Thereafter, he published reports no later than the October following the close of the term for which cases were reported (and usually earlier, during the summer), probably because his compensation was conditioned on timely publication.

Omissions were also a concern. The most recent guess is that Dallas omitted about 2/3rds of the decisions. Cranch and Wheaton also omitted some cases, but Peters (who succeeded Wheaton in 1827) claimed to report nearly every decision. However, Davis's Appendix to Volume 131 of the U.S. Reports (at pp. lxiv–ccxix) records the omission of 351 cases from 1839 to 1881, noting that 221 of these cases contained only very short opinions (often not more than two or three lines) and did not involve significant legal issues.

Finally, there were frequent complaints about inaccurate reporting. A recent study of manuscript opinions indicates that Dallas did not always

report accurately. Story complained of Cranch's errors. Wheaton reduced inaccuracies to a minimum, although he had a major dispute
with Justice Johnson regarding alleged errors in reporting a lawyer's argument.[85] And Peters's discharge in 1843 was allegedly based on reporting inaccuracies.

I do not mean that complaints about omissions and inaccuracy were
necessarily justified. Omissions may have kept unimportant decisions
from cluttering up the reports; Wheaton, for example, was explicit
about not reporting cases that he considered unimportant or primarily
factual. As for inaccuracy, the evidence is somewhat sketchy. My reading of the evidence suggests that Dallas's alleged errors might not have
significantly altered the substantive views that the Justices presented.[86]
As for Peters, his disputes with several Justices were probably a more
important factor in his dismissal than inaccuracies in his reports. Criticism of reporting errors must also take account of the fact that, at least
during the early decades, the reporter had to transcribe orally delivered
opinions whenever a written opinion was unavailable and that manuscripts received from judges in their own hand were not always easy to
read.[87]

The fundamental point, however, is not whether the reporter's delay,
omissions, or inaccuracies were serious or excusable, but that concerns
about these problems were a symptom of the reporter's continued significant role in accessing a substantive source of judicial law and presenting that law to the public. If the reporter had been a passive government employee charged with publishing all judicial opinions, any delay
or inaccuracy would have been a minor technical problem calling for
personnel changes or improvements in administrative efficiency, and
omissions would not have occurred. It was the reporter's independent,
entrepreneurial, and discretionary role that gave rise to persistent efforts
to improve the "official" reporting system in the first half of the 19th
Century.

2. The transition to the modern reporter

The transition to the modern system of a publicly anonymous reporter who only arranges for the publication of the judges' text took a
much longer time to develop than the institution of a reliable official
reporter. An initial small step in that direction was the elevation of the

Supreme Court clerk to the keeper of judicial opinions, downgrading the role of the reporter. When someone sought a copy of an opinion in 1830, Marshall referred the person to the reporter rather than the clerk, because "opinions were delivered to [the reporter] after they were read, and not to the clerk. . . ."[88] Then, in 1834, the Court ordered the reporter to provide the clerk of the Court with the opinions once publication had occurred.[89] The Court's order may have been a response to arguments in the Wheaton v. Peters case that the reporter might destroy opinions (the order came down on March, 14, 1834, and oral argument in the case occurred on March 11–14, 1834). By 1835, the clerk's role as keeper of the Court's opinions was paramount, as evidenced by an order requiring opinions to be given first to the clerk and then to the reporter.[90]

Another important step in changing the reporter's status from that of a participant in making law to that of a more or less passive civil servant occurred in 1874, beginning with Volume 91 of the U.S. Reports, when the government appropriated $25,000 to finance their publication. (This appears to be one of several attempts at this time to improve public dissemination of information about the government, including the government's taking over publication of the Congressional Record in 1873 and the codification of federal legislation in the Revised Statutes of 1874.) Despite the federal government's financial subsidy for reporting cases, however, the reports were still privately published and the reporter's name still appeared on both the title page and the spine of the reports in Volumes 91–107 (for example, specifying "1 to 17 Otto" as well as U.S. Reports 91–107). It was only after Volume 107 in 1882, when Davis became the reporter, that the reporter's name appeared only on the title page.

In 1922, the method of publication was completely revised, further diminishing the reporter's role. The Government Printing Office took over the job of publication, and the Superintendent of Documents took over sale. In addition, the reporter was divested of all financial interest arising from the sale of the volumes (beginning with Volume 257).[91] But, even then, the reporter continued to exercise discretion in presenting lawyers' arguments until 1941, although their quantity had tapered off before then.[92] It is unclear why lawyers' arguments were dropped from the reports after 1941, but I would guess that this was done not only because judicial opinions contained thorough consideration of the arguments (which long predated 1941) but also because the size of the volumes might have dramatically increased with the significant rise in separate opinions at that time (discussed in Chapter 5). In sum, the modern U.S. Supreme Court reporter operates very differently from the early 19th-Century reporters. He or she no longer has any discretion in shaping judicial law, but only edits opinions for accuracy of cites, quotes, typos, misspellings, grammar, and compliance with style rules, and all changes must be approved by the Justices.[93] Although the syllabus is still the reporter's responsibility, the Justices can suggest changes, which are routinely accepted.[94]

The modern reporter's loss of discretion is not simply the result of a desire for greater efficiency in reporting cases. It also reflects a shift in the legal culture—the fact that the contemporary U.S. Supreme Court has now become the sole institutional voice of judicial law without the reporter acting as an important intermediary in accessing a substantive source of law. At the beginning of the 19th Century, proponents of a strong federal judiciary used the reporter's historically significant role in shaping judicial law to help project the Supreme Court's judicial power by giving him "official" status. But once the Court's authority was secure, the reporter evolved into a passive government employee.[95]

D. *Writing opinions*

Writing judicial opinions, like official reporting, was not part of the English judicial tradition inherited by U.S. courts; and determining when the Supreme Court adopted that practice proves surprisingly difficult. It is clear that some of the opinions reported by Dallas, Cranch, and Wheaton were delivered orally and transcribed by the reporter (or someone on whom the reporter relied), although their number probably declined over time. But it also appears that manuscripts were sometimes provided to the reporters as useful supplements to whatever the reporter wrote down. Davis says that Dallas probably got written opinions in cases involving important and novel constitutional law cases, although a recent study suggests that the Justices "generally" spoke from notes at this time and "in a few instances" provided texts to the reporter.[96] Davis also refers to Cranch's statement that the Justices had adopted a practice "of reducing their opinion to writing in all cases of difficulty and importance,"[97] although one commentator suggests that Cranch may have referred only to the Justice's notes.[98] Wheaton said that several opinions in every volume were delivered orally and written down by him, noting also that no law or custom required Justices to write opinions.[99] Peters, who took over as reporter in 1827, proposed to print opinions that he had shown to the Justices for their approval,[100] but it is not clear whether Peters provided the Justices with his own record of their opinions or gave them proofs of written opinions he had received from the Justices.

The Court's 1834 order that the reporter deliver opinions of the Court to the clerk for safekeeping is sometimes understood as a requirement that Justices write opinions. But the order does not have that broad implication; it only required the reporter to turn over the opinions that were in his possession after publication had occurred. These opinions might have been the reporter's record of the Justice's views rather than something the Justices had written; and, in any event, the requirement does not specify that there should be a written opinion in every case, only that the reporter turn over whatever opinions he possessed. At most, the 1834 order reflects a growing practice of written opinions, not their requirement.

My best guess about what happened is that the practice of writing judicial opinions, at least in important cases, began as a way for the judge to deliver oral opinions efficiently (by reading from a manuscript) and as a response to concerns about reportorial accuracy. The reporters were obviously very worried about accuracy and obtaining written opinions from the Justices would have seemed the most efficient (if not the only) way of achieving that goal. It is, therefore, unlikely that writing judicial opinions was either a direct way for the U.S. Supreme Court to project its power or an effort to equate judging with legislation; if it turned out that efficient reporting also had that effect, so much the better. Certainly, the Marshall Court was not focused on achieving another possible reason for writing opinions—the Jeffersonian goal of assuring public accountability for what judges did.

Writing judicial opinions may also have reflected a general shift toward writing down legal argument, which was evident in the gradual increase in written briefs submitted by lawyers. The Court's rules required something in writing from counsel in the nature of what Corzine calls "coming attractions" beginning in 1795, and in 1833 the Court's rules granted lawyers an option to proceed solely on the basis of written argument.[101] But Corzine's data show that there was a growing practice of presenting written briefs even before adoption of explicit rules on the subject. Some date the routine practice of providing written briefs to the first time oral argument was limited (to two hours) in 1849; and, in 1854, the clerk began to keep written briefs on a regular basis, implying that the practice had grown common by that time.

In any event, writing opinions for official publication eventually became the norm in the U.S. Supreme Court, even though there is still no law or court rule that explicitly requires written judicial opinions except by inference from Rule 41 (which requires the Clerk of the Court to "release" opinions immediately after their announcement and to cause them to be issued in "slip form.")[102] The same evolution seems to have occurred in the lower federal courts; the 1880 preface to Volume 1 of West's unofficial Federal Reporter series states that it

> publishes both oral and written opinions. . . . The copies of the written opinions are in most instances supplied by the clerks, and the stenographic reports of the oral opinions prepared by the authorized stenographers, of the respective courts. In some districts, however, all the opinions, both oral and written, are regularly reported by qualified attorneys, employed specially for that purpose.

The only federal court for which there is a written-opinion requirement (of which I am aware) is the Court of Appeals for the District of Columbia, mandated by an 1893 law.[103] But this court served the District in the same manner as the state appellate courts in the states and should not be confused with the federal Court of Appeals for the D.C. Circuit. (As the next chapter explains, some state laws mandated written judicial opinions, and the 1893 federal law extended that treatment to local appellate court decisions in the District of Columbia.)

E. Conclusion

The Supreme Court successfully lifted itself by its own bootstraps in the early decades of the 19th Century through its adoption of an institutional style of presenting judicial opinions—first by issuing an opinion of the court rather than seriatim opinions, then through legislation providing for an official reporter, and, later, by routinely issuing written opinions. This process lacked the clarity associated with the Constitution's creation of a federal judicial institution, but the result was no less dramatic. The Constitutional Convention and subsequent ratification gave the Court an institutional home in the new government that enabled it to stand on its own alongside the legislative and executive branches and gave it the potential to project federal power over the states. However, an officially reported written opinion of the court helped to establish the Court as one of the three great departments of government. Like the legislature, the Court now spoke "officially" to the public with a unified, written voice. In this process, the reporter initially played an important role in deciding how to transmit judicial opinions to the public. But, eventually, the traditional lawyer-reporter-judge collaboration in making judicial law dissolved, and the Court became the sole voice of judicial law.

4

Institutional Style in the 19th Century
States

A. *Introduction*

The institutional style of presenting judicial opinions evolved in a more unstructured way in the states than in the U.S. Supreme Court because of differences in the weights attached to three institutional concerns: the need to project judicial authority, the professional concern with developing judicial law, and public accountability for what judges did.[1] The U.S. Supreme Court focused on the first of these concerns—projecting the judicial power of a court—because the Court was an entirely new political invention,[2] faced with the need to establish federal power over the states. States, however, followed a more varied pattern.

This chapter describes that pattern, with primary emphasis on what happened before the Civil War, followed by some concluding comments about the transition to modern practice. I focused on the 13 original states plus Vermont and Kentucky; Vermont is included because it claimed independence from New York in 1777 and was admitted to the United States on March 4, 1791;[3] Kentucky is included because it was one of the first states to attempt official reports (in 1804).[4] The information is based on an examination of statutes passed in the individual states and on introductory material in the published law reports, as well as secondary sources. I may have overlooked some statutes, in part because provisions about law reporting sometimes appeared in appropriations or other legislation whose titles provided no clue as to their specific content.

Chapter 4B addresses the way institutional concerns influenced the states' judicial style of presenting judicial opinions before the Civil War.

There are two major issues: (1) which of the three institutional concerns dominated (if any); and (2) how the states began to shift the role of the official reporter from individual entrepreneur to government civil servant. The discussion draws on the detailed presentation in Appendix 1 of the laws and practices about the reporting and writing of judicial opinions in the 15 states.

Chapter 4C then recounts the post–Civil War completion of the transition in the reporter's role from an entrepreneurial private reporter, who had both the opportunity for financial gain and loss and discretion about what cases and lawyers' arguments to report, to a reporter who is an employee of the government or a private publisher, who has no financial stake in the reports and who does little more than report the written opinions provided by the judge. The chapter concludes with an explanation of the change in the legal culture that accompanied this change in the reporter's role. Instead of judicial law being the result of an effort by the bench, bar, and reporter to collaborate in identifying and applying a substantive source of law, judicial law was reconceptualized as a written text issued through an opinion of the court by one of the three great departments of government.

B. State institutional styles of presenting judicial opinions

1. Three institutional concerns

a. Project judicial authority; and professional development of U.S. law

Because state courts (unlike federal courts) were not new inventions, had an inherited institutional base, and did not confront federalism concerns, projecting judicial authority was less imperative than at the federal level.

Nonetheless, state judges could not neglect efforts to enhance their judicial role. Many members of the legal profession were Tories who left the country during the Revolution or were discredited by their royalist leanings; and, more importantly, the Revolution had replaced the old institutional order with constitutions created by the "people," and statutes rather than judges were expected to modernize the obsolete English common law.[5] The state bench and bar had to find ways to overcome anti-judicial sentiment and successfully project their authority if they were to participate with legislatures in developing U.S. common law.[6] Indeed, it is difficult to disentangle the dual concerns about judges enhancing their authority and the legal profession developing U.S. law in the pre–Civil War period. Anything that enhanced the profession's ability to develop judicial law would not only help them secure their place as an American "natural aristocracy" (in Alexis de Tocqueville's famous description)[7] and buttress their own sense of professionalism,[8] but would also help them advance whatever goals were served by the exercise of judicial authority (including the development of an indigenous judicial law that would encourage private economic enterprise— justifying one author's description of lawyers as "the shock troops of capitalism").[9]

The symbiotic relationship between professional and judicial concerns was apparent in the evolution of state law reporting systems.[10] The U.S. bench and bar were both determined to collaborate with state legislatures to develop U.S. law to suit American traditions, in part because English precedents were often inappropriate for the United States and because there were prohibitions in several states on citing post-Independence English decisions in U.S. courts.[11] To help U.S. judges develop U.S. common law, the profession needed knowledge of judicial law; and, for this purpose, reliable published reports of judicial opinions were essential, especially given the geographical dispersion of the American legal profession, which (unlike in England) did not cluster around a central location (similar to London).[12]

Several reporters noted explicitly that published reports were necessary because the legal profession's memory was inadequate to the task of identifying prior law, and reliance on memory alone led to legal contradiction and legal uncertainty (Connecticut, Georgia, Kentucky, Maryland, New York, South Carolina, and Vermont). The reviewer of an 1805 volume of Massachusetts cases made a similar point;[13] and an 1808 Preface to the official Massachusetts law reports emphasized education of younger members of the bar as a rationale for their publication (reminiscent of the old English Yearbooks). A number of reporters argued that law reports were needed to enable states to replace English law (Connecticut, New York, South Carolina, and Vermont), and it is probably no accident that two of the states with the earliest official law reports (New York and Massachusetts in 1804) were in the forefront of creating U.S. common law in the first decade of the 19th Century.[14] An

1828 article emphasized that reliable reports were a mechanism for improving the common law.[15] And one observer concluded that by 1839 "the decisions and opinions of the judicial tribunals [in the United States] have received more of a legislative sanction" than in other countries; and "[i]n almost all the United States, the decisions of the higher courts are required by law to be reported, either by judges or some of them, or by a reporter officially appointed and paid in part at least by the government; they are distributed at public expense, in the same manner as the statute laws, besides being sold by the reporter on his own account."[16] Later commentators also concluded that early 19th-Century legislation about official law reports "was evidence of the desire of the states to form their own common law."[17] The issuance of law reports covering judicial opinions of a much earlier period than the report's publication date was further evidence of the profession's desire to help judges develop state judicial law—see, for example, the material in Appendix 1 on Delaware, New Hampshire, and New Jersey.[18]

Law reports were also probably useful in helping state judges enhance their power over juries. The gradual loss of lawmaking power by juries during the 19th Century has been well documented.[19] And law reports would have been a critical tool in facilitating that process, by informing judges about the law that they instructed the juries to apply and educating lawyers about the judicial law that they presented to the court.

To achieve these professional and judicial goals, law reports made an early appearance in many states. Unofficial reports appeared in five states before 1800 (Connecticut, North Carolina, Pennsylvania, Vermont, and Virginia); and in four states from 1800 to 1810 (Kentucky, Maryland, New York, and South Carolina). In two other states (Massachusetts and New Jersey), the first reports were official and appeared in 1804 and 1806, respectively. There is no clear pattern regarding how quickly states adopted official reports after unofficial reports began, some waiting less than five years (Kentucky and New York) and some over twenty years (Connecticut, North Carolina, Pennsylvania, Vermont, and Virginia). Two states that began their reports with an official reporter did so several decades into the 19th Century (Delaware in the 1830s and Rhode Island in the 1840s); perhaps as small states they did not feel the need for widespread dissemination of judicial opinions.

Several other features in the development of state law reports demonstrate a dual concern for professional development of judicial law and projection of judicial authority. One example is the linkage of judicial opinions and legislation as similar forms of law to justify publication of law reports. Virtually every state officially published state statutes at the beginning of the 19th Century,[20] and promulgated "revised" legislative codes before the Civil War.[21] What better way to secure judicial authority than to present judicial opinions in statute-like fashion—that is, in official law reports that gathered the opinions in one convenient place? The Preface to the Kentucky reports in 1815 stated that the "decisions of the courts are not less operative than the acts of the legislature" and "ought, therefore, to be as public as the acts of the legislature"; the Preface to the first volume of the New Hampshire reports in 1819 stated that "[i]f . . . the law should be known, the decisions of the judges should be as carefully promulgated as the acts of the Legislature"; an 1806 New Jersey law said that law reports should be "distributed in the same manner" as legislation; and an 1838 Preface to the Georgia reports said that, just as legislation is known, so should cases interpreting statutes be known. One commentator stated that almost all jurisdictions required official law reports as of 1839 in the same manner as statutes, which gave opinions a sanction and authority they lacked in England,[22] although the lag time between requiring official publication of statutes and official publication of judicial decisions suggests some reluctance to analogize the two sources of law.[23]

State legislation also paid close attention to the details of law reporting to assure both quality and timely publication, which directly helped the legal profession develop U.S. law and indirectly enhanced judicial authority by providing reliable law reports. Many state laws set quality standards for the law reports—for example, the type, paper, binding (Kentucky, Maryland, New Jersey, New York, North Carolina, Pennsylvania, and Virginia).[24] And some states controlled the price at which reports could be sold (four states fixed a dollar ceiling—Maryland, New Hampshire, New York, and Pennsylvania).

Similarly, timely publication was a constant concern and complaints about delay were common. Virginia's adoption of official reports was the result of a petition from judges objecting to delays in publishing unofficial reports. Legislation addressed the problem of delay in various ways. A number of states required publication annually, by a certain date, or "as soon as practicable" (for example, Kentucky, Maryland, New York, and Rhode Island), without backing up this requirement with sanctions. But some states put teeth into the requirement of timely publication by conditioning payment of compensation on delivery of the reports by a certain date (Kentucky, New Jersey, North Carolina) or forfeiting some part of compensation for late delivery (Georgia). In at least one state (Connecticut), laws about when judges had to file their opinions were periodically adjusted, suggesting that delay was sometimes the fault of the judges rather than the reporter. Some states found specific publication dates too rigorous and relaxed the requirement— for example, Kentucky repealed a requirement that copies be received by the Secretary of State within 60 days of the close of the term (unless the reporter could not obtain paper or for some other reason beyond his control) and specified only that the reporter act with "practicable dispatch"; New York switched the publication date from three months after the decision to as soon as "practicable"; North Carolina shifted the publication date from nine to three and then to five months after the decision; and Virginia replaced an annual publication requirement with a publication-when-ready rule.

Apart from law reporting, one other aspect of the institutional style of presenting judicial opinions deserves mention—the use of an opinion of the court. Although the bench and bar in the various states were concerned with developing a robust judicial law, there was not the same urgency that was apparent at the federal level. Consequently, there was not the same single-minded determination to adopt an opinion of the court practice. Although there was frequent use of introductory language specifying that an "opinion of the court was delivered by [a named judge]" (or some variation thereof), there was no uniform pattern. Many states made at least some use of seriatim opinions prior to the Civil War—for example: Connecticut, Georgia, Maryland, Massachusetts, Michigan, New Jersey, North Carolina, Pennsylvania, South Carolina, Virginia, and Wisconsin[25]—before they adopted a style similar to that introduced by Marshall in which a named justice delivered an opinion for the court, speaking in the plural "we" and usually concluding with a sentence listing concurring justices.

b. Public accountability

Another institutional concern at the state level was assuring public accountability for judging. The most extreme manifestation of this concern (favored by Jefferson) was to expose judging to political scrutiny by requiring seriatim opinions. But states clearly had doubts on this score. According to one commentator, Connecticut disregarded its first law imposing a seriatim requirement[26] and later Connecticut legislation went back and forth on this issue.[27] Georgia passed a law requiring seriatim opinions (unless the judges were unanimous) and then repealed the statute. South Carolina's legal requirement of seriatim opinions was later replaced by a statute explicitly dispensing with seriatim opinions. A Vermont reporter, in order to assure readers that he had not omitted opinions from his reports, stated that the court did not follow the practice of issuing seriatim opinions. And, as noted by Patton and Heath in their 1856 Preface, the Virginia Special Court shifted to issuing a single opinion in 1856, after the first session of the court. Two states imposed a requirement less demanding than seriatim opinions—Connecticut and Kentucky required the opinion's author to sign his name and South Carolina required that concurring judges sign their names.

Publishing law reports might also have assured public accountability for judging.[28] In some states, the reporter stressed the professional need for law reports—for example, a New Jersey reporter addressed his reports to the "learned profession" and a number of states required the reporter to be "learned in the law" (Massachusetts, New Hampshire, and Vermont), although Vermont later deleted this requirement. But many state reporters also wrote about the importance of law reports providing information to the "people," "citizens," or "all classes of men" (Connecticut, Delaware, Georgia, Maryland, New Jersey, and South Carolina), which may suggest a concern about public awareness of judicial opinions. (Or perhaps these comments were little more than empty verbal gestures about the importance of the public knowing the law.)

Assuring public accountability for judicial law through published law reports at the state level carries with it some of the same ambiguity that we encountered in trying to untangle the interaction between professional concern for developing U.S. law and enhancing judicial authority. Although public accountability is usually associated with the impulses of Jeffersonian and Jacksonian democracy, it might also have secured the legal profession and judicial law from too much interference by appearing to accede to democratic pressures. In a similar vein, one author has even argued that the widespread adoption of an elective judiciary, after New York adopted this approach in 1846, was as much attributable to the profession's concern with securing independent judicial authority as to any democratic political impulses.[29]

c. Written opinions: Rules and practices

The uncertainty about why states adopted any particular institutional style of presenting judicial opinions before the Civil War also extends to the rules and practices about writing judicial opinions. Several commentators refer to a widespread use of written judicial opinions before the Civil War: specifically, to the "requirement of written opinions in some states," to the "voluntary adoption of the practice by the courts of other states," to the judicial practice of "universally . . . writ[ing] their opinions at length," to the fact that "the opinions of the judges are for the most part drawn up in writing," and to the practice of "the court . . . prepar[ing] written opinions, although not required to do so."[30] My own tally finds a statutory requirement of written opinions for at least some cases at some time in 13 out of the 15 states in the study (the dates for the first statutory requirement appear in parentheses)—Connecticut (1784), Georgia (1841), Kentucky (1792), Maryland (1851), Massachusetts (1826), New Hampshire (1850), New Jersey (1806), New York (1847), North Carolina (1836), Pennsylvania (1806), Rhode Island (1844), South Carolina (1816), and Vermont (1827). And several state reporters mentioned the existence of written opinions without regard to a statutory requirement (Georgia, Maryland, New Hampshire, Massachusetts, New York, and Virginia). (Some reporters also mentioned the availability of judges' notes. Although notes might have been similar to opinions, I did not make that assumption.)

The more significant point is not the total tally of states in which judges wrote opinions, but that writing opinions was a developing trend. For example: a Maryland 1824 resolution said that "the court of appeals have *of late years* reduced their opinions to writing" (emphasis added); a Georgia reporter stated that "the practice in our circuit, (particularly of *late years*,) has been, to give written opinion in all matters, to which deliberate investigation has been bestowed" (emphasis added); and Massachusetts went from issuing written opinions in selected cases in 1826 to doing so in almost all cases in 1859.

It is true that some states retreated from a requirement of written opinions in *all* cases. In 1823, Kentucky rewrote its written-opinion requirement so that it applied only to cases establishing new principles, and Connecticut shifted from a mandatory written-opinion rule to one that gave judges a choice between written and oral opinions. But these changes may have simply reflected the fact that a comprehensive writing requirement was unrealistic in a period before typewriters and word processors. A Vermont reporter said that judges did not comply with a 1797 law requiring written opinions and a Connecticut reporter said that the 1784 law requiring written opinions was ineffective because some opinions were mislaid. The salient point is that written opinions became common when it mattered—in important cases.

Some of the legislation requiring written opinions was undoubtedly intended to help the bench and bar develop U.S. judicial law. This was Kirby's understanding of the rationale for the 1784 Connecticut law requiring written opinions, and it probably explains the writing requirement in five midwestern states—Indiana (1816); Illinois (1819); Iowa (1840); Wisconsin (1836); Minnesota (1849)[31]—all of which were "frontier" jurisdictions where law might otherwise have been a scarce commodity.[32] Some laws linked the writing of judicial opinions to the reporter's need for information—for example, an 1826 Massachusetts law required an opinion to be in writing if the opinion was not given at the court's term, probably to make it easier for the reporter to obtain the information; an 1847 New York law explicitly stated that a written opinion was required if the opinion was not delivered orally in open court so that the reporter would be able to do his job; an 1844 Rhode Island law required written opinions if the reporter asked for it; and an 1806 Pennsylvania law required written opinions if the parties or their lawyers requested them.

But it is also possible that some of the statutes requiring written judicial opinions were meant to encourage public accountability, responding to democratic pressures associated with the Jeffersonian and Jacksonian political movements. After New York shifted to popular election of judges in 1846, this formal democratic link between judging and the people spread rapidly throughout the country. Previously, Mississippi had been the only state to require election of all judges (since 1832), but after 1846, 15 of the 29 states existing at that time provided by constitutional amendment for elected judges, and all states entering the union after that date did so.[33] It is, therefore, reasonable to assume that these democratic pressures might have led in some instances to adoption or retention of a legal requirement of written judicial opinions. This assumption is consistent with the inference that the proliferation of laws requiring judges to write opinions *after* the Civil War[34] had a populist tinge. At least one commentator thought that post–Civil War written-opinion requirements arose from "distrust" of the judges;[35] and this distrust was reciprocal—some courts balked at a legislatively imposed writing requirement for *all* cases, holding them to be directory and not mandatory,[36] and three courts held that the requirement was unconstitutional.[37] (There is one curious counter-example of a judge in North Dakota who ran for office on a platform that included a promise *not* to write opinions).[38]

But it is unlikely that a public accountability rationale explains the early laws requiring written opinions—for example, Connecticut (1784), New Jersey (1806), and Pennsylvania (1806). And, as I previously noted, some of the later laws seem intended to help the reporter do his job (for example, New York [1847] and Rhode Island [1844]). Nor were written-opinion requirements closely correlated with a shift to popular election of judges in many states: Kentucky required written opinions in 1792 but did not provide for popular election of judges until 1850; Maryland provided that some opinions had to be written in 1833, but did not adopt a broader writing requirement until 1851, when it also adopted popular election of judges; North Carolina required written judicial opinions in 1847 but did not provide for elected judges until 1868; Pennsylvania had a written-opinion requirement in 1806 but provided for elected judges in 1850.[39]

As I suggested in Chapter 3D in connection with the U.S. Supreme Court, the practice of writing judicial opinions probably began as a way to help judges read oral opinions in court, rather than as a conscious effort to satisfy a professional need, project judicial authority, or provide public accountability. But, eventually, it must have become obvious that written opinions would help reporters do their job, which would (indirectly) help to secure the authority of judicial law. One clear bit of evidence associating a written judicial opinion with projecting judicial authority was New York Chancellor Kent's use of written chancery court opinions without a legislative mandate. Moreover, as one author has argued,[40] the American legal culture was especially apt to consider law as a text, and associating judicial law with a written text probably reflected the growing acceptance of judging into the institutional mainstream of American lawmaking, whatever the origin of written-opinion rules and practices.

2. The evolving role of the reporter

The evolution in the institutional style of presenting judicial opinions is apparent not only in the publication of unofficial and official reports and in the development of a practice of writing opinions but also in the changing role of the law reporter. There was an observable shift in many states before the Civil War away from the traditional, independent entrepreneurial reporter with discretion about what to report toward the more modern arrangement whereby the reporter's income was dependent on the state and his decision about what to report was limited. This shift manifested itself in various ways in different states and was a harbinger of the eventual transition to the modern law reporter who is a passive, salaried employee at both the federal and state levels. The variations in state patterns and the gradual shift in the reporter's role are discussed in the remainder of Chapter 4B, based on the detailed material on individual states in Appendix 1.

a. Reporter's loss of financial risk and opportunity

On paper, most states continued some version of the traditional, entrepreneurial model before the Civil War—the reporter was an independent individual (often a distinguished member of the bar) who was appointed either by a court, the Governor, or the legislature, or some combination thereof, rather than holding government office (such as a court clerk).[41] Nonetheless, the compensation arrangements often modified the traditional model to reduce or even eliminate the reporter's financial risk and opportunity, thereby more closely approximating the modern reporter as a salaried civil servant.

In a few instances, the state paid the reporter compensation and did nothing else either to subsidize the reporter or to reduce his opportunity for profit (Connecticut [1814], Delaware [1837], Kentucky [1808], and New Hampshire [1815]). But state legislatures often modified the traditional private entrepreneurial model to reduce the reporter's financial risk—not only by paying compensation but also by guaranteeing the purchase of some number of volumes (Delaware [1842], Maryland [1852], New Jersey [1857], and Rhode Island [1844]), by covering all or part of the publication expenses (Delaware [1830, 1831], New Jersey [1806 and subsequent years], North Carolina [1822], and Vermont [1847, 1858]), or by providing an advance for expenses against compensation (Kentucky [1824], and Virginia [1821]). Three states agreed (at one time or another) to purchase copies, without providing compensation (Kentucky [1804], Maryland [1824], and New Hampshire [1835, 1851]).

A statutory subsidy for the salaried official reporter did not, technically, convert him into the equivalent of the modern government employee without financial risk or opportunity. The reporter usually retained, at least on paper, the risk of not recouping publication expenses and usually retained the opportunity for profit. But the reporter with a compensation/subsidy arrangement may have been the equivalent of the modern government employee if the subsidy was substantial and the opportunity for financial profit unrealistic. Although many state laws explicitly allowed reporters the profits from sale (Massachusetts [1804], Rhode Island [1844], Vermont [1823], and Virginia [1820]), or the copyright (Georgia [1845], Kentucky [1810, 1815], Maryland [1852], North Carolina [1822, 1836], and Pennsylvania [1845]), the value of this assurance was reduced after the decision in Wheaton v. Peters,[42] which held that the reporter could not obtain a copyright in the judicial opinions (although he could still copyright the material that he prepared).[43]

The frequency with which official reporters complained about inadequate financial rewards supports the inference that his opportunity to profit from publishing law reports was precarious.[44] For example, the New Hampshire and South Carolina reporters explicitly complained about compensation and an introduction to the Rhode Island reports noted that the compensation arrangement was the worst imaginable. And perhaps it was the inadequacy of reporter compensation that led North Carolina to provide that the clerk would perform the reporter's duties if the reporter's job could not be filled; that led the Virginia legislature to advance $1,000 to the reporter to cover publication costs; and that led to Georgia's 1847 repeal of an 1845 prohibition on the reporter's appearance as counsel before the court.

The reporter's concerns about inadequate profits were well founded. Legislation in several states reduced their opportunity for gain (and thereby more closely approximated the modern salaried government employee) by requiring the reporter to supply the state with a specified number of copies in exchange for the compensation (Georgia [1845], Kentucky [1810, 1815, 1822, 1825, 1833, 1851], New York [1804], North Carolina [1818, 1822], South Carolina [1823], Vermont [1837], and Virginia [1820]). (The same provision had appeared in the 1817 congressional legislation.) A few states even explicitly denied the reporter the copyright (New York [1847, 1848, 1850] and Virginia [1829]) or the right to profits (New Hampshire [1850, 1855] and New York [1847, 1848, 1850]).

Some states completely abandoned the traditional model by giving the responsibility to arrange for law reports to a preexisting government official other than a judge, such as a court clerk or the Secretary of State (Georgia [1841], Kentucky [1804], New York [1847, 1848, 1850], South Carolina [1816], Vermont [1827], and Virginia [1842]). Although four of these states reverted to some version of the traditional entrepreneurial model in a later pre–Civil War year, New York and Virginia stuck to their "modern" approach. Both these states retained a reporter to perform some editorial tasks, but took the additional step of denying him the copyright or right to profits.

In sum, whatever the formal legal arrangement for state reporters before the Civil War, the combination of state financial subsidy (often more than compensation) and the lack of a profit opportunity (whether because of legal arrangements or financial reality) often reduced the reporter to something like the modern salaried employee, rather than the traditional private entrepreneur.

b. Reporter's loss of discretion to report cases and lawyers' arguments

The transition from the traditional to the modern approach to law reporting was reflected not only in changes in financial risk and opportunity but also in the reduction of reportorial discretion about what to include in the reports. The traditional approach called for the reporter to exercise discretion in deciding what cases to report, but before the Civil War many states passed laws modifying that approach. Table 4.1 indicates which states, at one time or another, passed legislation dealing with the reporter's discretion to report cases, with the year of the legislation in parentheses—"[D]" means there was a law allowing discretion; "[NO D]" means there was a law denying discretion.

The data show that 11 of the 15 states had laws denying the reporter discretion about which cases to report, two of which combined mandatory reporting for some cases (as the court required) and discretion for

TABLE 4.1

State	[D]iscretion or [NO D]iscretion to Report Cases (Year of Law)
Connecticut	NO LAW
Delaware	[D] (1837)
Georgia	[NO D] (1845)
Kentucky	[NO D] (1851)
Maryland	[NO D] (1851)
Massachusetts	[D] (1826)
New Hampshire	[NO D] (1850)
New Jersey	[D] (1806)
New York	[both D and NO D] (1847)
North Carolina	[NO D] (1818)
Pennsylvania	[both D and NO D] (1845)
Rhode Island	[NO D] (1844)
South Carolina	[NO D] (1816)
Vermont	[D] (1823); [NO D] (1837)
Virginia	[NO D] (1820 and 1842)

other cases, and one of which switched from discretion to no discretion in 1837.

The inherited tradition also gave reporters discretion to include lawyers' arguments, but this tradition was often modified for pre–Civil War law reports. A few states passed laws limiting the reporting of lawyers' arguments: for example, Georgia (1850—no more than a "simple statement" of authorities cited and "points made"); Kentucky (1815— "omitting the arguments of counsel in all cases"; 1860—include only names of counsel and authorities on which they rely).[45] And South Carolina permitted the reporting of "such arguments . . . as shall be necessary to a correct understanding" of the decisions. But more important than legislation about lawyers' arguments were the concerns expressed by many reporters over whether and how much of the lawyers' arguments to include regardless of what the law required. According to one commentator, reporters at the end of the 18th Century were primarily interested in lawyers' arguments;[46] but, as the 19th Century progressed, reporters became less and less enthusiastic about including this material.

The reporters were worried about increasing cost (if they included too much) and about offending their professional consumers (if they included too little). Many prefaces are filled with apologies for not doing justice to the lawyers' arguments. Here are some paraphrases of reporters' comments on the inclusion of lawyers' arguments:

—Connecticut (presentation is concise);
—Georgia (they are valuable even though some say inclusion is a "useless expense"; apology for not including them because they were not found in the judge's records);
—Massachusetts (include only a "sketch");
—New Jersey (presentation is concise; noting the expense of inclusion, and stating that lawyers will not suffer from this practice because "their professional character is built upon foundations too solid");
—New York (there were numerous comments by different reporters: one commented that lawyers' arguments were omitted; another that they were included if important; and another that, despite suggestions for their omission, they were needed to provide a link between the case and the decision);
—Pennsylvania (comment on omission with apology);
—Virginia (include them sometimes, but apologize that the reports give no idea of lawyers' ability).

Reporters were probably emboldened to reduce the presentation of lawyers' arguments because of the more thorough coverage of the issues and reasoning in the judges' written opinions. Several reporters mentioned the need for lawyers' arguments to enable the reader to understand what was going on in the case—which made sense when the report of an oral opinion was laconic or the written opinion incomplete.[47] But as judges began to write opinions with a more thorough canvassing of issues, the need to include lawyers' arguments in the reports declined —a point explicitly made by Johnson (writing as the New York chancery reporter), and by the first official Connecticut reporter in 1817.[48]

C. The post–Civil War transition to modern practice

Pre–Civil War rules and practices about state law reporting began the transition from the traditional, private entrepreneurial approach to the modern approach, in which the reporter (if there is one) exercises little discretion about what to report and has neither financial risk nor opportunity. A major influence in effecting this transition after the Civil

War was the intrusion, beginning in the 1880s, of the privately published West National Reporter system into the law reporting business.
This section traces these developments, first for the unofficial West reporter system and then for official state reports.

1. Law reporting

a. Unofficial reports: West National Reporter system

The most striking change in law reporting after the Civil War was the
success of the privately published unofficial West National Reporter system. Although many states continued to insist on citation to the official
reports, the West Reporters were financially successful. As West noted
proudly, by the late 1880s the profession looked to private enterprise
without government aid and without bar association sponsorship (as in
England) for its law reports.[49]

The National Reporter system did away with the traditional, independent, creative law reporter. West relied on faceless employees in a
large organization, which published the entire text of all judicial opinions—everything without editing. They had reliable access to written
opinions, usually furnished by the court clerk;[50] and accuracy was guar-
anteed by arranging for judicial revision of the opinions before publication.[51] Efforts to prevent clerks from delivering opinions other than to
publishers of the official reports were unsuccessful,[52] when the U.S. Supreme Court affirmed in 1888 that states could not restrict access to judicial opinions through control of the copyright; under U.S. law, copyright is based solely on federal legislation and neither the judge, the reporter, nor the state could obtain a copyright in the judicial opinion.[53]
West's reports also omitted summaries of lawyers' arguments, on the
theory that lawyers did not need them.[54] As one observer noted, West
shifted from the "old school" of "instructive" reports to a "democratiz-
ing" public access approach to reporting judicial opinions.[55]

The innovation in West's reports that assured its success was the key
number system, in which every opinion was preceded by standardized,
numbered headnotes briefly summarizing the legal issues in the opinion,
with none of the variation in writing style and content found among the
pre-West official and unofficial reporters. As a result, West's National
Reporter system provided a comprehensive and easily comparable view

of judicial law from every jurisdiction. Although one commentator has called this "a sterile court reporting system,"[56] this was what the profession wanted, and the more selective law reports could not compete.[57]

The commercial success of the National Reporter system was also attributable to overcoming the problem of delay (official reports were often several years behind). Until the advent of the Northwestern Reporter in 1879, which was the first of the West regional reporters to appear,[58] "the prompt publication of opinions was practically unknown. . . . In each State lawyers were compelled to wait in the first instance, on the convenience of their State reporter, whose official duties were more or less subject to the exigencies of his private practice; and in the second place, upon the delays incident to the conflicting business demands of the local publisher."[59] Consequently, lawyers felt that they had to buy the unofficial reports before publication of the official reports.[60]

b. Changes in official reports

Official law reports did not disappear after the Civil War. Indeed, two American Bar Association committee reports (in 1895[61] and 1916)[62] indicated that the profession continued to be concerned with improving the official reports despite the popularity of the West National Reporter system. The 1895 ABA Report even claimed that the profession still preferred the official reports to anything done by private enterprise, stating that "the work of the official reporter, if honestly done, *should* be much superior to any report owing its existence to private capital." But this favorable comment on official reports may have reflected a legal requirement that they be cited in the jurisdiction; the ABA Report notes that "not the least" of the reasons for professional preference for the official version is that a "majority of citations are to these volumes." Another commentator asserted that "virtually all the reporters in the many jurisdictions in this country say that lawyers . . . have a decided preference for the official reports."[63] But this commentator was a Deputy Supreme Court Reporter in New York and it is possible that his observations about the official reports were colored by his position, just as West may have exaggerated the status of his unofficial reports.

Whatever the profession wanted, it is clear that the role of the official state law reporter changed after the Civil War—completing the transition from being a collaborator with the bench and bar in developing judicial law to becoming a faceless government employee with little discretion. As Berring noted of the early reporters:[64]

> There was an enormous amount of subjective, intellectual input involved in the production of even the best reporters. It was the individual case reporter who structured and perhaps significantly rewrote the text of the report. . . . Indeed, these early nominative court reporters were reviewed in the fashion of contemporary book reviews, and one can comb the literature to find attacks on, and praise of, certain nominative reports.

But, Berring continued: "[Although] the evolution followed different patterns in different jurisdictions, in general the early sparks of [reporter] creativity died out." Another author writing in a 1927–28 publication made a similar observation—that "[m]odern day methods of reporting afford little scope for the employment of the individualistic talents of the reporter. . . ."[65] In this respect, reporters may have been following the 1916 American Bar Association Report, which urged that all decisions of the highest state court should be published, without selection by either the court or the reporter, and that lawyers' arguments should not be included, stating that "there is no useful purpose served by printing an abstract of the briefs of counsel."[66]

I did not track the state-by-state details of the change in the official reporter's role after the Civil War, but there is ample evidence from responses to a questionnaire published in the 1916 ABA Report to support these generalizations about the loss of creative reportorial discretion. Although these responses did not follow a uniform pattern and it is hard in every instance to be sure exactly what the responses meant, respondents in nearly every state who addressed the issue indicated that either all decisions had to be published or the court (not the reporter) made the choice.[67] Responses from only two states indicated that the reporter had some choice about what to publish—in Illinois, whenever the court failed to designate a case for publication and there were not already too many volumes; and in New York, where the court made some publication decisions and the reporter could decide on additional cases to report.[68] By 1974, those few reporters who still had some discretion about what cases to report did so only with the formal or informal approval of one or more judges.[69]

Reporters were also moving away from providing information about lawyers' arguments after the Civil War. An 1861 Georgia law stated that the "volumes of reports must not contain any argument or brief of counsel, beyond a statement of the points and authorities."[70] And a commentator on Kentucky practice noted that an 1860 law had limited the reporter to "stating only the names of the counsel and the authorities upon which they relied," but that not even this information was published after 1910.[71] The 1895 ABA Report noted that "sixteen reporters either summarize or print in full the briefs and citations of counsel, while twenty give no attention to this feature."[72] The 1916 ABA Report noted that only two states explicitly allowed lawyers' arguments to be published—Arizona ("briefs of counsel, if necessary"); and Kansas (briefs of counsel with no restriction).[73] This Report also stated that Alabama law prohibited publication of counsel's briefs; that Ohio law allowed publication of points and authorities cited by counsel, but not briefs unless ordered to do so by the court; and that Georgia and Minnesota allowed publication of only points and authorities cited by counsel.[74]

A telling marker of the change in the reporter's status was the elimination of the nominative reports (that is, the citation of the reports by the reporter's name). The first state to use "state reports" rather than the nominative designation was Connecticut (1814). Many other states made this change in the middle of the 19th Century or began their official reports with state reports.[75] Some states also renumbered earlier nominative reports as "state reports"—for example, North Carolina, South Carolina, and Virginia.[76] By 1874, one commentator could state that nominative reports are an "evil" and "inconvenient," and that every series of reports should be titled by the state to which they belong.[77] This trend was undoubtedly encouraged by the fact that the reporters no longer came from a highly distinguished professional or political background.[78] The 1916 ABA Report notes that "reporters are practically publication agents and not men learned in the law."[79]

Whatever may have been the details in the evolution of the law reporter's role in each state, it is clear that the modern law reporting system (after World War II) makes little use of the traditional approach. Twenty-six states have simply given up on the traditional law reporter and rely on West—either by adopting the West National Reporter system as their only official reports or by reprinting copies of the West reports as their official state reports.[80] (These 26 states should not be confused with other states that arrange for West or another company to publish their official law reports.)

Moreover, these data do not capture the extent to which the role of the traditional reporter has been superseded. Of the 24 states that do not rely on West, three do not even designate someone as a "reporter" (New Jersey, Oregon, and Wisconsin). And, among the 21 states that do not rely on West and that still designate someone as a reporter, five use West to author and copyright the editorial material, such as the syllabus/synopsis, headnotes, and/or key numbers (Maryland, Nevada, Ohio, Pennsylvania, and South Carolina) and, in two other states, Lexis/Nexis owns the copyright (California and Montana).[81] In the remaining 14 states, an individual reporter cannot benefit financially, either because the copyright is obtained for or by the state[82] or the reporter is denied a pecuniary interest in the reports,[83] or there is no copyright in the reports.[84] (The lack of a copyright in the reporter is not a foregone conclusion following from the reporter's contemporary status as a government employee. Although by the end of the 19th Century the work-product of people receiving a salary generally belonged to the person providing the compensation,[85] the Supreme Court held in 1888 that a salaried reporter could still retain the copyright interest in his own work-product, though not the judge's opinion.)[86]

Another indication that the reporter's traditional role is now obsolete is the lack of authority to contract for publication of the law reports. Either the reporter plays no role in choosing a publisher,[87] is one of a panel that arranges for publication,[88] must have his decision regarding publication approved,[89] or the state printer does the job;[90] in only six states does the reporter retain the authority to contract with the publisher.[91]

In sum, by the beginning of the 21st Century we had come a long way from the individual/entrepreneurial reporter who contributed to making judicial law through selective reporting of both judicial opinions and lawyers' arguments and who had financial risks and opportunities arising from the publication of judicial opinions.[92] The modern official reporter, when there is one, no longer has an important professional life independent of his reporter's role but has become a salaried civil servant who assists in the editorial preparation of written opinions for publication, with little choice about what to present, except (in some instances) to provide an index, table of cases, headnotes, and/or syllabus.

2. Institutional style and the changing legal culture

But there is more to this story than simply a change in the reporter's role. The institutional style of presenting judicial opinions, of which the reporter's role is one feature, tells us something about the legal culture. The reporter's modern role was associated with a fundamental shift in the conception of judicial law—away from being the product of a collaborative effort of the bench, bar, and reporter to identify and apply a substantive source of law and toward the modern view that judicial law is a written text issued as an opinion of the court by one of the three great departments of government. This change in the legal culture enabled judicial law to appear like legislation and, therefore, provided a firmer foundation for judge-made law when statutes had displaced judging as the primary source of law.

Equating law with a written legal text—whether legislation or judicial law—fit well with the emerging 19th-Century formalist conception of law as embodied in clear rules. This formalist vision had several other manifestations—legal education was conceptualized by Dean Langdell at Harvard Law School in the 1870s as a science with rules inferred from the cases in the same way that scientific principles were inferred from data; the headnotes in West's National Reporter system were uniform statements of legal rules that crowded out the disparate marginal notes in the decentralized reporter systems of the various state jurisdictions; and the codification of U.S. legislation in the Revised Code of 1874 and the federal financing of the Congressional Record in 1873 made federal legislative texts and their history more readily available. Somewhat later, the Restatements of Law promulgated by the American Law Institute (founded in 1923) presented the common law as black letter rules.

Whether a formalist conception of judicial law as a written text emanating from a government institution is robust enough to completely replace the older idea that there is a substantive source of judicial law remains to be seen. The late-19th-Century approach to judicial law neatly combined the idea that the judicial opinion was a text originating from an institutional source with its own version of substantive judicial law —specifically, that there was a set of stable apolitical legal principles accessible to those with legal training that protected private economic enterprise. In this view, judicial law was radically different from legislative law, which was the realm of politics and which often sought to regulate the economic marketplace. Some might argue that the demise of this apolitical substantive conception of judicial law means the final passing of the idea that judicial law can have a substantive source, citing Holmes's famous affirmation in 1917 that the "common law is not a brooding omnipresence in the sky, but the articulate voice of some sovereign or quasi sovereign that can be identified."[93] But I do not believe that we can do without a substantive source of judicial law, which exists alongside the notion of judicial law as a text emanating from a government institution. The following chapters will explain why both substantive and institutional sources of judicial law are essential, and explore the implications of a persisting conception of judicial law as substantive principle for the institutional and individual style of presenting judicial opinions.

5

Contemporary United States Practice

Institutional Style

A. *Introduction: Institutional and substantive sources of judicial law*

In the 19th Century, U.S. courts successfully located the source of judicial law in a text emanating from a government institution, enabling courts to hold their own against legislation. But the question remained whether judicial law also had a substantive source outside of the government institution from which the text emerged.

Uncertainty regarding the substantive and institutional sources of law has English roots. The traditional source of law underlying judicial power was substantive—legal principle embodied in the ancient common law.[1] And this substantive law was accessible to the legal profession (bench, bar, and reporter) through what Coke called artificial reason and would today be called legal training. But there were also efforts to establish an institutional foundation for judicial law in England—inevitably so, once Parliament acquired sovereignty. Blackstone asserted that "the jurisdiction exercised in [the courts] is derived from the crown of England, and not from any . . . intrinsic authority of their own. . . ."[2] And there has always been a vague sense that substantive judicial law was linked to the "people" on the theory that the common law was based on popular usage and custom. But English attempts to locate judicial law firmly in an institutional base—whether the King or the people—had such a strong fictional element that it could never completely persuade. There were simply too many judicial bodies in England (for example, King's Bench, Chancery, Admiralty, and Law Lords) to base judging securely on an institutional source, and the "people" remained too much of an institutional abstraction. This lack of a clear institutional foundation for judicial law contributed to Bentham's denial that what courts said was law at all.[3] H.L.A. Hart's more recent attempt to ground legitimate government authority in a "rule of recognition"[4] encounters the same ambiguity—does the rule identify a substantive source of law or a judicial institution that interprets and applies that law?[5]

U.S. judging has suffered from a similar uncertainty. An institutional link between judging and the people was established in the newly independent United States after the American Revolution. The people were the legitimizing source of both legislation and the state and federal constitutions, but they also provided a foundation for judging as a result of state legislative appointment of judges for limited terms (with or without the participation of other political officials) and, less clearly at the federal level, through life-tenure appointment by the President with Senate approval. Democratic movements in many states later added other institutional techniques to link judging to the people—through the popular election of judges (which spread rapidly after the mid-19th Century) and with the popular recall of judges as part of the Progressive/Populist movement in the early 20th Century.

But U.S. judging has never embraced a direct institutional link to the people as a legitimizing source of law because the intrusion of partisan politics and/or volatile popular passions into judicial law would have threatened to undermine judicial independence. Instead, as earlier chapters explained, the judicial power gained institutional authority primarily from being one of the three departments of government established by the federal and state constitutions and from making judicial opinions appear like legislation through the publication of official reports of written opinions of the court.

However, this institutional base for judging was never completely secure in a democracy that traced government power to the people. During the 19th Century, courts could overcome this insecurity by suggesting that immigrant masses untutored in our political ways or special-interest groups controlled explicitly democratic institutions (such as the legislature). But the successes of legislative politics in the first half of the 20th Century seriously undermined this view (especially after the New Deal),[6] and recent efforts to justify a selective exercise of judicial power as a corrective to shortcomings in the legislative process have been met with justified skepticism.[7] Consequently, judicial authority cannot rely alone on an institutional base but must also claim access to a substantive source of law.

Judges rely on a substantive source of law not only in the common law, where they must obviously seek out substantive principle to decide cases, but also in statutory and constitutional interpretation. In statutory interpretation, judges rely on the substantive legal landscape (sometimes referred to as background considerations).[8] One way to link the legal landscape to statutory interpretation is to claim that it is embodied in the legislative text or in the historical legislative intent or purpose, which judges can identify and apply as faithful agents of the legislature.[9] But critics of such efforts are right when they observe that the concepts of text, legislative intent, and legislative purpose are too uncertain to block out judicial consideration of the legal landscape in which the legislation is embedded. This is especially obvious when the modern textualist engages in "holistic" interpretation or when the purposivist judge decides how enthusiastically and sympathetically to elaborate a legislative purpose.

Constitutional interpretation also requires judicial reliance on a substantive source of law, even more so than with legislation. First, many constitutional phrases are open-ended, requiring the judge to consider substantive background considerations. Second, equitable (purposive) interpretation, which requires the judge to take account of the text's purpose and the legal landscape, has been a feature of constitutional interpretation from the beginning—noted by both the Constitution's opponents (the Anti-Federalists) and its supporters (Chief Justice Marshall), even if there was doubt about using this approach for statutory interpretation.[10]

Third, the fact that the U.S. Constitution is hard to amend requires a more aggressive judicial role to fit the document into the contemporary legal landscape. That is what Marshall's phrase "it is a constitution we are expounding"[11] has come to mean,[12] although Marshall probably meant only that legislative power had to be adaptable to meet contemporary needs.[13] The argument that the Constitution embraces evolving modern values has attracted many judges, including some who are often considered "conservative." For example: Justice O'Connor argued in a case involving the death penalty for minors that the Constitution incorporates "the maturing values of civilized society" (including consideration of "clear agreement" by the "international community"), rather than a "static command";[14] and Justice Harlan expressed a similar idea when he affirmed that the constitutional tradition on which judges rely is "a living thing."[15]

The persistent reliance by judges on a substantive as well as an institutional source of judicial law has both strengths and weaknesses. Its strength lies in an appeal to a value system that underlies what judges say. Its weakness lies in the difficulty of achieving agreement on what those values are or should be and the association of this approach with the discredited 19th-Century view of law as consisting of clear and stable substantive rules. Modern Legal Realists have successfully highlighted these shortcomings by emphasizing that law and politics are inexorably intertwined and that judges can no longer justify what they do by relying on expert access to traditional substantive sources of law, such as custom or legal principle. Even the U.S. Supreme Court has recognized the reality of "political" judging in two cases, one of which interpreted the statutory term "representatives" to include elected judges,[16] and one of which struck down as a violation of free speech a state's prohibition of comments by judicial electoral candidates on issues that might arise in litigation.[17] But, whatever the theoretical difficulties, modern courts cannot do without either a substantive or institutional base for judging, sometimes emphasizing one or the other.

This varying emphasis on substantive and institutional sources of judicial power is apparent in recent opinions by U.S. Supreme Court Justices, some of which rely on the Court's institutional foundation and others on an appeal to a substantive source of law. The Court's December 12, 2000 decision in Bush v. Gore illustrates the Court's confidence in speaking from a firm institutional base, overriding reliance on state and congressional institutions to settle a dispute over the disposition of Florida's electoral votes for President.[18] It did this despite the majority's usual deference to the states and in opposition to the historical understanding that Congress would resolve conflicts in presidential elections ever since passage of the 1887 Electoral Count Act[19] following the deadlock in the Hayes-Tilden 1876 election. The Court instead boldly asserted its own authority to determine Florida law—specifically, that Florida wanted its vote count settled by December 12, 2000, even though the Florida Supreme Court's statements on this issue were far from clear.[20] Anyone who lived through that period could not help but conclude that the U.S. Supreme Court took it upon itself to be the final institutional arbiter of a partisan political dispute. This view was most apparent in Justice Scalia's opinion supporting a December 9, 2000 stay of the Florida Supreme Court's order to recount votes in which he argued that "[c]ount first, and rule upon legality afterwards, is not a recipe for producing election results that have the public acceptance democratic stability requires."[21] Scalia's opinion clearly asserted the Court's role as institutional arbiter of how our democracy should operate.

Similarly, the Court's meandering application of the Chevron doctrine[22]—which requires courts to decide whether or not to rely on agency rulemaking rather than leave an issue for judicial or legislative resolution—is a technique by which judges allocate power among various government institutions. Recent examples involve disputes over (1) the level of deference owed to agency rulemaking that has not gone through public notice and comment procedures;[23] (2) the appropriate standard to use in deciding whether the statute is unclear, thereby authorizing deference to reasonable agency rules;[24] and (3) deciding whether an issue is too politically controversial to leave to agency regulation rather than explicit legislation.[25]

By contrast, the Court's reliance on a substantive source of law is apparent in Kennedy's majority opinions in Lawrence v. Texas and Roper v. Simmons, holding (respectively) that criminal prosecution of private intimate sexual conduct by homosexuals violates the Due Process Clause and that the death penalty for juveniles is cruel and unusual punishment.[26] These decisions explicitly rely on values located in the contemporary U.S. legal landscape, the "wider civilization," and the views of "other nations."[27] And, while Kennedy appealed to *contemporary* values, other judges have placed emphasis on *traditional* substantive values—to insist on state sovereign immunity as part of the "fundamental jurisprudence of all civilized nations" (Justice Rehnquist) and to invoke the "wisdom of the ages" to prevent retroactive legislation (Justice Scalia).[28]

Those who are familiar with critical commentaries on modern judging will object that my description of judges relying on a substantive source of law does not justify what judges do. Critics argue that this practice makes for arbitrary judging, as judges flit from one substantive source to the other. Thus, judges have relied on natural law, custom, legal science, and more recently on nonlegal sources, such as Cardozo's somewhat unstructured emphasis on sociology in the early 20th Century[29] and, even more recently, on an analytically more rigorous reliance on law and economics.[30] The content of the substantive law emphasized by judges has also varied—namely, common law property and contract rights during the Lochner period and, lately, civil rights. And there has always been a debate over whether the relevant substantive source of law is tradition or the contemporary legal landscape—for example, Coke's reliance on tradition vs. Matthew Hale's reliance on the adaptation of law to contemporary values.[31] Rather than illustrate judicial whimsy, however, persistent judicial resort to various substantive sources of law reveals something intrinsic and inevitable about the need to trace judicial authority to a substantive as well as an institutional foundation, which derives from the inevitable process of thinking about how rules apply to facts to decide cases.

The only debate is over how pervasively courts should exercise power based on access to a substantive source of law. There is no gainsaying the difficulty modern judges have in sustaining this stance in a democratic society after legislatures achieved institutional dominance in the 20th Century, and after the Legal Realists discredited judicial reliance on a substantive source of law in the form of clear and stable legal principles accessible to legal experts. But the Legal Realists' insistence that judicial law is a mixture of law and politics did nothing to reject the idea that judicial law had a substantive source. Indeed, by broadening the range of judicially accessible values to include a messy, fluid, and changing mix of substantive concerns, Legal Realism made it clear that judges could not avoid thinking about the influence of the substantive legal landscape on the law. Those who remain deeply troubled by legitimacy concerns regarding this exercise of judicial power would narrow its application as much as possible; those who accept judicial authority based on access to a substantive source of law see the issue primarily as one of judicial competence, which leaves certain decisions to other institutions (such as agencies or legislatures) whenever technical or political concerns so indicate. The competence perspective on the exercise of judicial power can be at least as restrained as the legitimacy perspective— perhaps even more so because no decision is ever automatically open to legitimate judicial resolution when competence is at issue. About all we can be sure of is that, as I explain elsewhere, ordinary judging requires judges to think about how law fits into the substantive legal landscape when they try to apply rules and principles in the context of historical and contemporary facts.[32] That is simply what judging entails and no amount of angst over the lack of democratic foundations for judging can suppress that fact.

But if judicial reliance on substantive sources of law is inevitable, judges had better consider how to communicate with their public and professional audiences to shore up their authority, just as they did in the first half of the 19th Century. And this in turn means that judges must pay attention to institutional and individual styles of presenting judicial opinions, because the way in which modern judges communicate to their audience(s) will determine how they fit into contemporary government.

The remainder of this chapter deals with institutional style.[33] Chapter 5B explains how the older practice of seriatim opinions has, in effect, enjoyed a revival in the form of much greater use of separate opinions (dissents and concurrences) in the U.S. Supreme Court. This reflects the greater uncertainty about the substantive source of judicial law and the emboldening of judges to state their individual opinions as a result of the perceived interaction of law and politics associated with Legal Realism. Chapter 5C recounts the similar but much less dramatic increase in separate opinions in state supreme courts.

Chapter 6 considers individual judicial style in the United States— what voice and tone is appropriate to the modern judicial opinion. Although the issue of individual style has received limited attention, I believe it is a question of considerable importance today, raising questions about how modern judges can participate as one of the three branches of modern government.

B. United States: From Marshall's opinion of the court to modern "seriatim" opinions

The modern U.S. Supreme Court's institutional style is characterized by what one commentator describes as a return to seriatim practice[34]— meaning a dramatic increase in separate opinions (dissents and concurrences). Before 1940, separate opinions appeared annually in about 20% of the cases, but since then, the number of such cases has risen to about 60–80%.[35] How did the Court get to the point where consensus norms disintegrated? What caused this to happen in the early 1940s? And is the current practice a good idea?

1. Historical antecedents: A gradual evolution

Changes in opinion-writing practices evolved gradually. As Kelsh explains, separate opinions were rare when Marshall was Chief Justice until 1808 (with roughly one per year from 1804 to 1807), increasing slightly from 1808 to 1812 (with Justice Johnson, a Jefferson appointee, contributing six in 1809), and further from 1812 to 1816 (with all but one Justice delivering at least two separate opinions). Kelsh notes that the Justices "occasionally gave their reasons for choosing to write separately, but more frequently did not."[36] From 1818 to 1827, Johnson was virtually alone in writing separately (17 opinions, compared to a total of six from all other Justices), but there followed an increase in separate opinions during the last years of Marshall's tenure (which ended in 1835). Justices also increasingly gave reasons for writing separately, usually when cases involved constitutional issues or matters of great importance.

Kelsh notes a greater propensity to write separately after Taney became Chief Justice at the beginning of the 1837 term—with the nonunanimity rate increasing from 11% to 20%. Moreover, by 1841, the Justices began to give a new reason to justify separate opinions—primarily to "maintain personal consistency." Kelsh suggests that this new attitude toward dissent was "part of a larger shift in the Justices' conception of the Court," in which they "began to think of the Court less as a cohesive whole and more as a collection of individuals." Other evidence of this new perspective during Taney's tenure as Chief Justice (which lasted until 1864) was an increase in dissents and concurrences without opinion and a decline in the civility that had characterized individual opinions in the Marshall and early Taney courts.

Kelsh's data for 1864–1940 show a further centripetal trend evidenced by an increase in the types of issues attracting separate opinions and a tendency for the Justices to expand their justification for speaking individually to include the "serious consequences" of the decision, a departure from principles of prior cases, and (even more broadly) disagreement with the majority (which is no reason at all). In addition, Justices increased their citation of separate opinions and, in the 1930s, almost completely stopped explaining why they wrote separately. In 1928, Chief Justice Hughes could speak favorably of separate opinions—stating that dissents were an appeal to "the brooding spirit of the law" and that "[d]issenting opinions enable a judge to express his individuality."[37] And Justice Frankfurter expressed regret in 1939 that the "healthy practice" of seriatim opinions had been abandoned because of the volume of court business (an historically inaccurate but Anglophile take on legal history).[38]

These changes in judicial attitude toward separate opinions produced only a modest increase in the nonunanimity rate, to about 30% in the 1930s. But there was a dramatic increase in 1941 (more than double the prior rate), reaching 86% in 1947, one year before the Harvard Law Review began to provide annual data.[39] Figure 5.1 summarizing the Harvard data shows that the nonunanimity rate never fell below 50% during the 1948–2001 U.S. Supreme Court terms and clustered around 60–70% most of the time. It lends credibility to Justice Jackson's statement in 1955 that "the Court functions less as one deliberative body than as nine, each judge working largely in isolation, except as he chooses to work with others. These working methods tend to cultivate a highly individualistic rather than group viewpoint."[40]

2. Why the dramatic change in the 1940s?

If I am correct that the institutional style of judicial opinion writing provides a window on how law fits into the legal culture, we need to explain why this tilt toward separate opinions occurred in the 1940s. The best explanation is a shift away from viewing judicial law as formal, static legal principle and toward an age of Legal Realism in which judicial law draws meaning from an evolving and complex political, social, and economic context. This shift in legal culture encouraged separate judicial opinions in three ways. First, the fiction that law consisted of static legal principle had encouraged the idea that judicial legal experts could agree on the law. Without that prop, one rationale for unanimity evaporated. Second, to the extent that law had political, social, and economic content, legal expertise was unavailing. Each person's views were legitimate and could lead to disagreement—among judges as well as anyone else—as they tried to make law rather than simply declare and apply timeless legal principle. Third, the pluralistic politics experienced during the 20th Century, when Legal Realism came of age, encouraged the idea that there were in fact multiple perspectives that had a legitimate claim to be included in judicial law. To understand these developments, we need to take a closer look at Legal Realism.

Fig. 5.1. Percentage (%) of total U.S. Supreme Court decisions that were not unanimous. *Note:* The vertical dotted lines mark a break between periods of initially lower, then higher, and (under Justice Rehnquist's influence) again lower caseloads. The average caseload during these three periods was: 1948–1970 (107.65); 1971–1992 (145.14); 1993–2001 (83.56); the caseload in the years straddling the breaks are: 1970 (122)/1971 (151); 1992 (114)/1993 (87). *Source:* The data are from the Harvard Law Review (Volumes 63–116). The Harvard data may understate the lack of unanimity because they record a case as unanimous if there is only a concurrence with the majority opinion, as long as it is not a concurrence in the judgment. See 84 Harv. L. Rev. at p. 253, fn. h to Table III; 70 Harv. L. Rev. at pp. 102–03, fns. k–l to Table IV. Beginning with Vol. 91, 1976 Term, the data distinguish between a concurrence and dissent; I added these together to record cases that were not unanimous.

As Morton Horwitz observes, Legal Realism was neither a coherent nor a consistent movement, but more of an "intellectual mood,"[41] which contained wide differences of focus (concerned with judicial law, legal education, legislation, and administrative law) and strong divergences of opinion, especially about judicial law and legal education. Indeed, there is considerable dispute over who should be counted as a Legal Realist. The primary dividing line is between (1) progressive legal thinkers who rejected the formalist, static view of the law as embodying clear rules and who argued that political, social, and economic factors influenced the evolution of legal principle; and (2) those who embraced the more radical view that such factors more or less determined judicial decisions.[42]

The origin of the Legal Realist movement can be traced to Holmes's famous aphorism in his 1881 book "The Common Law" that the life of the law is experience, not logic.[43] An unmistakable sign of this shifting image of law occurred some five years later when an American Bar Association president took note of "a long favorite fiction that the judges did not make, but only declared law," and then observed that "it is no longer anywhere denied, nor can it be, that the judges . . . are actually, though indirectly, engaged in *legislating.* . . ."[44] By the early 20th

Century, Roscoe Pound's sociological jurisprudence[45] and Cardozo's emphasis on the sociological aspects of judicial law in his 1921 book "The Nature of the Judicial Process" were major intellectual contributions to the demise of the formalist conception of law as abstract legal principle and the rise of a Legal Realist view of law. Thereafter, in the 1920s and 1930s, Legal Realists built on this new conception of law to press for a revision of legal education that would emphasize its political, social, and economic components.[46]

There were, however, significant differences among those who shared a Legal Realist vision. Rhetorical battle lines were drawn over whether and when the judge could be considered a legislator and whether the judge exercised will rather than judgment. At its extreme, Jerome Frank advanced a version of Legal Realism that emphasized a psychologically determined image of judging, unconstrained by legal principle and nestled firmly in the variety of fact situations confronting the judge in each separate case. Similar differences played out in legal education.[47] Columbia and then Yale Law Schools made efforts in the 1920s and 1930s to introduce Legal Realism material into the curriculum and into the casebooks used to teach law, but (as with the conception of judicial law) there was considerable dispute over how far such material should be integrated into legal education. But despite differences of emphasis, the Legal Realists shared a new conception of judicial law as an evolving enterprise that was imbued (even riddled) with contemporary political, social, and economic considerations, rather than the embodiment of timeless legal principle. And it was this Legal Realist conception of judicial law that contributed to the dramatic rise in separate opinions in the 1940s.

There are rival explanations for the change in the Court's institutional style but none of them undermine the Legal Realist explanation. First, 1925 legislation gave the Court greater discretion over what cases to hear through use of the writ of certiorari.[48] This docket control would almost certainly have increased the difficulty of cases reaching the Court, thereby increasing the likelihood of divergent judicial opinions. But this explanation does not take account of the much-later dramatic rise in separate opinions in the 1940s.[49] And, in any event, as Figure 5.1 shows, the Supreme Court's more careful selection of cases for review since 1993 has been accompanied by a *reduction* rather than an increase in the nonunanimity rate.

Second, changes in the caseload volume might have influenced the Justices' tendency to write separate opinions, but that influence could be in either direction—a greater workload might reduce the time to hammer out compromise or might reduce the time available to write separately. One study found no impact on the use of separate opinions from increasing workloads,[50] and my discussion of state court opinions in Chapter 5C reaches the same conclusion.

Two further explanations—based on what happened during Harlan Fiske Stone's tenure as Chief Justice of the U.S. Supreme Court (from 1941 to 1946)—might seem to call into question the Legal Realist explanation. Indeed, one study goes so far as to attribute the dramatic increase in separate opinions to the way Stone ran the Court.[51] First, as Stone's biographer explained, he conducted case conferences like a university seminar in which multiple points of view were encouraged (he had, after all, been a professor and dean at Columbia Law School from 1910 to 1923 prior to his appointment as Associate Justice of the Supreme Court in 1925), and he was critical of his predecessor's failure to use these conferences to exchange ideas.[52] Justice Douglas attested to the fact that the conferences had "never assumed more importance" than under Stone because of his "tolerance of full and free discussion,"[53] and one author has suggested that he had a New Englander's faith in town meeting debate.[54] More importantly, Stone was exceedingly respectful of colleagues who wanted to write separately as well as indulging in that practice himself (in one term, his dissent total of 29 was second only to Justice Roberts's total of 53).[55]

Second, the Justices in the early 1940s were an especially unruly lot —Stone referred to them as "wild horses."[56] (Their unruliness erupted on January 3, 1944, when only 3 of 14 decisions handed down were unanimous, and there were 28 different opinions.)[57] The Justices' tendency to reject traditional consensus norms made sense in light of their prior experience. Eight Justices who served while Stone was Chief Justice were appointed by Roosevelt, and they came from institutions that bred and even thrived on contention. Three had been university professors—Frankfurter, appointed in 1939; Douglas, appointed in 1939; and Rutledge, appointed in 1943. (Frankfurter had explicitly rejected Stone's suggestion that judges should be more restrained than teachers.)[58] Two came directly from the Senate—Black, appointed in 1937; and Byrnes, appointed in 1941. And three had been high-ranking lawyers in the Department of Justice—Reed, appointed in 1938, Solicitor General; Murphy, appointed in 1940, Attorney General; Jackson, appointed in 1941, Attorney General.

The "Justice Stone" explanation has some traction. It is hard to discount completely his influence on the way the Court behaved. His emphasis on deliberation heightened a tendency toward judicial disagreement,[59] and dissents clearly increased sharply during his tenure—1941 (158); 1942 (165); 1943 (186); 1944 (231).[60] But a lack of consensus norms among both Stone as leader of the Court and the Associate Justices during Stone's tenure does not dispel the idea that a shift in legal culture was the critical factor. First, focusing on what happened during Stone's tenure as Chief Justice does not begin to account for what happened before and after. As Chapter 5B1 explained, centripetal forces within the Court had been building up long before then, and the dramatic rise in separate opinions in the early 1940s was simply the whistling of the pot previously brought to a boil. Moreover, it is hard to attribute the current persistence of nonconsensus norms to the predisposition of Justices in the early 1940s.[61] Something more permanent must have been brewing in the legal culture, even if external forces in the form of Court leadership and unruly Justices tipped the balance toward a more "seriatim-like" institutional style of presenting opinions.[62]

Second, describing the behavior of the Justices in the early 1940s simply invites the question why they carried the nonconsensual norms nurtured in other institutions into their judicial role when the historical practice among judges had been so different. The best answer to that question is the legal culture explanation—that a Legal Realist approach to law influenced the judges to embrace a change in institutional style toward separate opinions.

Stone himself had a cautious view of Legal Realism. His tenure as Columbia Law School dean ended in 1923, in part because he was less than enthusiastic about importing sociology and economics into the law school curriculum, based on his suspicion that it was too faddish and would be superficially taught, crowding out the need to train professionals.[63] And, as a member of the original committee that organized the American Law Institute in 1923, he was willing to associate himself with those who were committed to a more formalist conception of law (such as Beale and Williston) in an effort to develop black-letter restatements of the law.[64] However, Stone's views evolved substantially after 1923 in the direction of integrating sociology and economics into the law,[65] although he leaned more toward the view that their insights should be incorporated into legal principle than toward a radical version of Legal Realism.

If Stone's Legal Realism was substantively modest, his procedural Legal Realism was robust—in his conviction that judicial law evolves, that judges cannot fall back on formulas, and that open deliberation and judicial candor were essential to an evolutionary and nonformulaic judicial process.[66] He shared with Frankfurter the view that judging should be democratic in the sense of opening up the judges' views to public scrutiny, as with any other government institution; he believed that public airing of the Court's decisions was useful as long as there was no loss of prestige; and he thought that the public perception of judicial independence and dissent better served the interest of long-term public confidence in judging than a false illusion of unanimity and harmony.[67] He also went out of his way while serving as Chief Justice to write a defense of dissenting opinions in 1942,[68] perhaps as a result of his efforts to find his own dissenting voice during the Taft Court in the 1920s and his experience with earlier dissents becoming the majority opinion of the Court in the late 1930s.[69] One author in 1945 even described Stone as a "legal realist."[70]

There is one apparent puzzle about the impact of Legal Realism on the Court's practice of presenting judicial opinions that needs explaining. A major feature of the Legal Realist critique of judging in the 1930s had been that judges associated with a static, formalist view of law had in fact been reading into the Constitution their own political points of view to strike down progressive federal and state legislation. With the reversal of the Justices' position in the late 1930s toward accepting such legislation against constitutional attack, we might have expected judicial law to take a less political path, eschewing the politicized judging that had been the target of criticism.

But the opposite occurred. Now that legislatures had free rein to reshape public law, the Court was confronted with a variety of contentious statutory and administrative issues that might never have arisen if the laws had been unconstitutional. Once the Court deferred to legislation, it had to figure out what the statutes meant (relying on the uncertain criterion of legislative purpose)[71] and how to draw the boundaries of administrative lawmaking. For example, judges who said that they favored judicial restraint were exceedingly bold in their approach to interpreting legislation—for example, Frankfurter in labor law,[72] and

Learned Hand in tax law.[73] In addition, there was the beginning of a new judicial commitment in constitutional law to civil rights, supported by Stone's famous footnote 4 in Carolene Products, which suggested that those who were disadvantaged in a political forum deserved judicial protection.[74]

In sum, although it is hard to tease out a legal-culture explanation for what happened in the early 1940s from the empirical data,[75] Legal Realism is still the best explanation for the tilt toward separate opinions. As one political science study concluded—"At the end of the day, perhaps what our study suggests is that . . . what is most important for anticipating the behavior of Supreme Court Justices is information about their policy preferences, since consensus in and of itself is not viewed by the Justices, except on the rarest occasions . . . as something for which to strive."[76]

3. Are separate opinions a good idea?

The proliferation of separate judicial opinions has always evoked concern that it would have a negative impact on judicial authority. With the backing of a committee chaired by Chief Justice Taft, the American Bar Association promulgated Canon 19 of its Canons of Judicial Ethics in 1924, which stated:

> It is of higher importance that judges constituting a court of last resort should use effort and self-restraint to promote solidarity of conclusion and the consequent influence of judicial decision. A judge should not yield to pride of opinion or value more highly his individual reputation than that of the court to which he should be loyal. Except in cases of conscientious difference of opinion on fundamental principle, dissenting opinions should be discouraged in courts of last resort.[77]

Observers of the Stone Court were also concerned about the uncertainty and potential loss of respect for judging arising from the increase in concurring opinions as well as dissents.[78] And some later commentators suggested that separate opinions might have a deleterious effect on judicial authority.[79]

But the Court's authority is no longer so fragile that suppression of separate opinions is necessary to preserve a capital of goodwill for the judiciary, which may explain why Canon 19 was dropped in 1972.[80] There has been no attack on judicial authority that can compare to what occurred in the early 19th Century when Marshall nurtured the Court during its infancy, or in the mid-19th Century after Dred Scott undermined the prestige of the Court in a nation on the verge of civil war. Even the contemporary invocation of substantive due process to protect civil rights (associated with the political Left) and the renewed enthusiasm for federalism principles through a narrow interpretation of the Commerce Clause and section 5 of the Fourteenth Amendment (associated with the political Right) evokes none of the antagonism toward judging that occurred in the first third of the 20th Century when the Court repeatedly struck down progressive state and federal regulatory and welfare legislation. Instead, the preferred reaction to political judging is now political scrutiny of new judicial appointments (backed up by a filibuster threat in the Senate).[81]

Evaluation of concerns about the public reaction to judging must take account of a distinction between two types of public support— "diffuse support," which refers to the capital of goodwill on which courts draw to sustain confidence in and obedience to its decisions; and specific support for particular decisions.[82] If we focus on diffuse support, it seems very unlikely that the modern Court is vulnerable. One observer writing in 1999 noted the remarkably steady confidence in the Supreme Court throughout the last twenty-five years.[83] Moreover, reaction to the recent Bush v. Gore decision, resolving the dispute over the 2000 presidential election, suggests that diffuse support is not fragile. The specifics of that decision attracted the usual complaints about whether the judges followed the law or were influenced by political considerations, with the public's reaction being based primarily on their political persuasion (Republicans viewing the decision as law-based and Democrats seeing a political decision).[84] One study found a decline in confidence in the Court from December 2000 to February 2001, followed by a rebound to August 2000 levels;[85] and another post–Bush v. Gore study concluded that the Court still enjoyed a great deal of confidence, uninfluenced by decisions in specific cases.[86] Justice Breyer offered a dire prediction in his Bush v. Gore dissent that "the appearance of a split decision runs the risk of undermining the public's confidence in the Court itself," which "is a vitally necessary ingredient of any successful effort to protect basic liberty and, indeed, the rule of law itself."[87] But it is unlikely that the decision impaired the Court's reservoir of political capital and, if the Court's authority can emerge unscathed from Bush v. Gore (which posed a risk of appearing partisan and not just political), the issuance of separate opinions can hardly be expected to undermine the modern U.S. judiciary.

It is possible that studies of diffuse support are too focused on aggregate and national data and do not adequately account for reactions to decisions that are of interest in a particular community. A recent study suggests that reactions within an affected community might have some effect on public confidence in the Supreme Court, although the impact is likely to be incremental, rather than immediate.[88] This incremental perspective has the advantage over many other studies of being more sensitive to the way individuals critically respond to the behavior of political institutions—which is to experience a gradual corrosive effect from what are perceived as a series of objectionable events. Nonetheless, it is still a stretch to conclude that public confidence in the Court will be negatively affected by the existence of separate opinions (rather than substantive outcomes), except perhaps if it takes the form of increased nastiness among judges.

Concern about separate opinions seems more focused on the public reaction to specific decisions than on diffuse support. The Court has occasionally worked hard to obtain unanimity in the unusual situation where disobedience was a real possibility, especially in the field of civil rights. It has relied on three techniques—the unanimous opinion of the court written by the Chief Justice; the opinion of the court signed by all the Justices; and the *per curiam* opinion (which is an anonymous opinion by the court). Brown v. Board of Education is the most famous example of a case in which all Justices joined a unanimous opinion by the Chief Justice.[89] In Cooper v. Aaron, involving desegregation of Arkansas schools, the Court spoke in an opinion signed by all of the Justices, which emphasized that all agreed on a single opinion and implicitly acknowledged that, in the usual case, a Justice speaks to some extent as an individual even when writing for the Court.[90] And, in numerous post-Brown desegregation cases, the Court issued unanimous *per curiam* opinions to put the full weight of the Court behind their decision.[91] The reliance on unanimous opinions is effective, however, precisely because it stands in sharp contrast to the current image of a fractured bench. Except in the unusual case (such as President Nixon's statement that he would honor only a "definitive" decision of the Supreme Court to hand over potentially incriminating tapes subpoenaed by a special prosecutor),[92] separate opinions are not likely to undermine obedience to a specific judicial decision.

I am not arguing that separate opinions will have no effect at all. Concurrences and dissents will affect the future evolution of the law by increasing the likelihood that a decision will be judicially revisited and either limited or overturned in the future, as litigants test its outer boundaries and staying power. But this "threat" from separate opinions does not undermine public compliance with a controversial decision; it is simply how judicial law evolves through the normal judicial process.[93] Objections to separate opinions are, I suspect, often driven by a commitment to the result in a particular case and to its future potential for growth rather than any serious concern about undermining judicial authority. Indeed, the now-defunct Canon 19 of Judicial Ethics, which discouraged dissent, was probably intended (especially by its major sponsor, Chief Justice Taft) to maintain the momentum behind the Court's substantive due process jurisprudence rather than to obtain compliance with the Court's judgments. Certainly, on today's Court, the dissenters from the U.S. Supreme Court's "federalism" decisions persist in their dissent precisely because they hope the Court's decisions will be "fleeting";[94] and Justice Scalia's refusal to go along with the Court's references to legislative history is meant to lay the groundwork for new judicial law.[95] None of these dissents is likely to encourage noncompliance with judicial decisions.

Perhaps I am focusing too much on the potential for disobeying a judicial decision. There are ways for the legislature to show displeasure with what judges do—such as limiting the courts' jurisdiction (a possibility noted in Chief Justice Rehnquist's 2004 Year-End Report on the Federal Judiciary),[96] recalling or not reelecting judges, not providing salary increases, or adopting resolutions objecting to what the Court has done.[97] And perhaps legislative threats to take such actions might undermine judicial independence. But these threats are unlikely to materialize at the federal level where salary concerns are more likely to result in declining a judicial appointment rather than influencing an opinion and where popular recall and election are impossible. Even the sporadic threats that Congress might limit the courts' jurisdiction seem unlikely to affect the way a judge decides a particular case. In any event, it is (again) a significant stretch of the imagination to go from a concern about legislative threats to judicial independence to the idea that judicial unanimity will deflect those threats.

A final consideration to weigh in the balance when thinking about the impact of separate opinions is their potential advantages. Rather than have a negative effect, separate opinions might contribute to a positive public image of judging. I put to one side the technical arguments in favor of separate opinions—that they force other judges to think and write more carefully and that they produce clearer decisions because of a reduced need to accommodate disparate views in a single opinion. I rely instead on the more fundamental point that judicial style responds to the demands of the legal culture and that separate opinions fit well with the modern Legal Realist conception of judicial law, thereby maintaining a close link between judging and the legal culture on which judicial authority depends. The modern reliance on separate opinions is not simply an unfortunate result of the intersection of law and politics. If judicial law has lost the certainty associated with the myth of static, apolitical legal principle, then litigants, the legal profession, and (perhaps) the public will be more reconciled to what courts do if they perceive a process in which judges openly appear to debate the results. When people know that the law is uncertain, a facade of certainty is an affront to the audience's intelligence and sense of fair play. This affront is even more likely today, when diversity among judges and respect for diverse perspectives in the law has become the norm. Multiple judicial opinions that grapple with legal issues are the judicial analogue to a deliberative democratic legislative process, which might not only help judges reach a sound result but also project an image of accountable judging and participation by interested audiences.[98]

This conclusion should hardly be surprising, given the historical role of seriatim opinions in England. In the English tradition, each judge spoke his mind because the opinion was only evidence of the law (as Blackstone said). Judges would, in effect, converse with their professional audience about what the right substantive answer might be through the institutional technique of seriatim opinions. Modern judging is even more uncertain, now that political choices obviously intrude into the traditional realm of legal principle. But, in this contemporary political environment, it is just as natural that judges explore the meaning of law by writing separately and by conversing with the wider legal and political audience. Their failure to carry on this conversation is more likely to undermine than to preserve judicial authority.

C. The 50 States

Do state high court judges display the same tendency toward writing separate opinions as modern U.S. Supreme Court Justices? To answer that question, I looked at state high court decisions for six years (1950, 1960, 1970, 1980, 1990, and 2000). My data show an increase since 1950 in the tendency of judges in the highest state court to write separate opinions, which I refer to as nonunanimity rates—measured by the percentage of cases in which there was at least one dissenting or concurring opinion. The state nonunanimity rate was, however, significantly lower than in the U.S. Supreme Court and there was significant variation among states. Finding an explanation for the state court data is difficult. In addition to the Legal Realist explanation, there were several operational factors that might have encouraged writing separate opinions that were not applicable to the U.S. Supreme Court, such as the introduction of an intermediate court of appeals and an increase in the number of judges during the study period.

Chapter 5C provides information about nonunanimity rates and operational factors at the state level and suggests several explanations for why separate opinions increased and the overall nonunanimity rate was lower than for the U.S. Supreme Court. The data are summarized in the text and in Table 5.1 (below), in Figure 5.2 at the end of this chapter (which provides a graph for every state), and in Appendices 2, 3A, and 3B. Appendix 2 also includes an explanation of my research design.

1. Summary of data: Explanation of inferences

a. Increase in nonunanimity rates

State high court judges are clearly less prone to writing separately than Justices on the current U.S. Supreme Court. According to my data (summarized in Table 5.1), the average nonunanimity rate in state high courts for the six years in the study had the following ranges, clustering around the 10–30% range and rarely coming close to 60%.[99] By comparison, the Harvard Law Review data presented in Figure 5.1 for 1948–2001 show that the U.S. Supreme Court's nonunanimity rate fell below 60% in only seven of the 54 terms for which the Review compiled information and mostly clustered in the 60–80% range.

TABLE 5.1
Number of Highest State Courts in Which
Percentage of Decisions Not Unanimous

Not Unanimous	Number of Courts*
0–10%	7
> 10%–20%	16
> 20%–30%	16
> 30%–40%	8
> 40%–50%	4
> 50%–60%	1
Total Courts	52

* Texas and Oklahoma had two high courts—one each for civil and criminal appeals.

Although the state court nonunanimity rates are lower than for the U.S. Supreme Court, there is still an unmistakable increase in the use of separate opinions. In Appendix 2, I provide two ways to measure an increase in the nonunanimity rate in state courts for the six years in the study—indicated by a "Yes" in columns 3 or 4. First, column 3 identifies whether the nonunanimity rates for the last three years (1980, 1990, and 2000) were all above the nonunanimity rates for the first three years (1950, 1960, and 1970). (For example, a pattern of 1, 2, 3, 8, 9, 10 or 1, 2, 3, 4, 9, 10 would fit that description.) Second, column 4 identifies states in which the *average* nonunanimity rate for the last three years was higher than the average for the first three years, even though the latter three years were not all above the earlier three years (for example, 1, 4, 10, 8, 11, 15). Every state in column 3 would also fit the description in column 4, but the pattern in column 4 is less dramatic —that is, the latter three years are less sharply distinguished from the earlier three years.

The number of states in which high court judges increased their use of separate opinions was 46 out of a total of 52—there were 29 states in column 3 and 17 states in column 4.[100] The most comprehensive study of state court opinions of which I am aware is consistent with mine, although it deals with dissents and not the broader category of separate opinions.[101]

The best explanation for this increase in nonunanimity rates, subject to some caveats regarding operational factors below, is the same as for the U.S. Supreme Court—the pervasive influence of Legal Realism on judicial attitudes. This influence is apparent in the increased politicization of the selection and retention of state judges regardless of how judges are chosen—whether partisan or nonpartisan elections, election by the legislature, or gubernatorial appointment, as well as the possibility of recall.[102] As for the lower *overall* rate of separate opinions in state high courts (in contrast to their *increasing* nonunanimity rate over time), I would guess that this also has something to do with the politicized process of selecting and retaining judges. If it is true that judges view a united front as one way to head off public dissatisfaction with judicial performance—whether or not the perception is accurate—an ethic of discouraging separate opinions might be internalized as a norm of judicial behavior. In other words, the politicization of judging has a double effect: lowering the overall nonunanimity rates in state high courts by creating concern over public reaction to a fractured bench; and, within the boundaries of these lower rates, shifting toward a greater propensity to write separate opinions by making the expression of multiple political points of view a more accepted judicial practice.

b. Operational rules

There are a number of operational rules that might encourage or discourage judges from writing separately and that might provide alternative explanations to rival or supplement the Legal Realist explanation. First, rules regarding the court's jurisdiction can affect the difficulty of cases that reach the highest court, and the more difficult the case the more likely there will be separate opinions. The variable that is most likely to have this effect is the presence of an intermediate appellate court, which will usually reduce the high court's mandatory jurisdiction and, consequently, the percentage of easier cases reaching the high court.[103] (Some mandatory jurisdiction rules—such as those involving the death penalty—might be more rather than less likely to increase the number of cases that attract a dissent,[104] but I did not make a systematic attempt to gather this information.)

Second, operational rules might subject judges to a sanction for writing separately. The sanction might arise from something as mundane as the chief judge's practice in assigning opinion-writing responsibility to different judges,[105] or the size of the panels (either a small court or smaller panels of a larger court) on the theory that the smaller the panel the less likely the judge will want to aggravate colleagues.[106] Or the sanction might be political, resulting from the process by which judges are retained in office—such as elections or legislative/gubernatorial re-appointment review.[107] Other forms of political review include possible overriding of specific decisions by the legislature or the people, especially when constitutional amendment is easier at the state than at the federal level, and legislative consideration of the judicial budget (especially given the fact that judicial salaries and judicial administration budgets are so much lower at the state than at the federal level). Some commentators suggest that judicial unanimity is perceived by many state judges as a way of preventing negative review of the judges' work-product, even though the evidence may not support that conclusion.[108]

Third, a large workload (which might also correlate with mandatory jurisdiction) might discourage judges from taking the time to write separate decisions, although a willingness to state a concurrence or dissent without opinion could compensate for this effect. However, the opposite might be true—a high workload might reduce the time in which to hammer out consensus, producing more rather than fewer separate opinions. There is some support in the data for U.S. Supreme Court cases since the 1993 term (when Chief Justice Rehnquist succeeded in reducing the Court's workload) for the inference that a smaller workload results in *more* consensus—that is, a lower nonunanimity rate. As Figure 5.1 shows, the lower U.S. Supreme Court workload beginning in 1993 was associated with an average nonunanimity rate for 1993–2001 of 65.21%, a reduction from the average for 1971–1992 of 76.74% (although the reduced rate was virtually a return to the 1948–1970 average of 66.9%).

I gathered information about the following operational rules—intermediate courts of appeals, workload, and the number of judges. To the extent that the operational rules remain constant over the entire period for which I obtained data, their impact is on the overall tendency of the judges to write separately for the entire period, not on shifts in the nonunanimity rate within the study period. But if an operational rule changed during the study period, that might provide an explanation for changes in nonunanimity rates other than or in addition to the impact of judicial attitudes associated with Legal Realism.

The data are summarized here and presented in tabular form in Appendices 3A and 3B. They suggest that the adoption of an intermediate court of appeals might contribute to an overall increase in nonunanimity rates and that a larger number of judges on the highest state court might have the same impact.[109] Nonetheless, the tendency for separate opinions to increase during the period of the study persists independent of operational rules, which suggests that attitudes associated with Legal Realism continue to have an impact.[110]

i. Intermediate appellate court (IAC)

(A) NO CHANGE DURING STUDY PERIOD

The most significant data indicating that an increase in the nonunanimity rate occurred independently of operational rules come from the 23 states in which there was no change in the presence or absence of an IAC during the study period (see Appendix 3A)—13 states in which there was an IAC beginning with the first year of the study (1950),[111] and ten states that lacked an intermediate court of appeals during all years in the study.[112] If nonunanimity rates increased in these states, the Legal Realist explanation is not undermined by this operational factor.[113]

In 18 of these 23 states, there was an increase in nonunanimity rates by at least one of the two measures (set forth in Appendix 2).

—Each of last three years greater than each of first three years (ten states): Alabama, California, Georgia, Illinois, Louisiana, Missouri, Nevada, Ohio, South Dakota, Texas (criminal)
—Average of last three years greater than average of first three years, but not listed above (eight states): Indiana, Maine, New Jersey, Tennessee, Texas (civil), Vermont, West Virginia, Wyoming

I also looked at data for the "no change" states to see whether the presence or absence of an IAC helped to explain *overall* nonunanimity rates, perhaps by increasing or decreasing the percentage of difficult cases reaching the highest state court. An IAC appears to correlate well with higher overall nonunanimity rates. For those states with an IAC in every year of the study, the average nonunanimity rate was 28.8%; for those states with no IAC during the entire study period, the average nonunanimity rate was about half that figure—only 14.24%. (Appendix 3B, column 2, gives the average nonunanimity rates during the study period for each state.)

(B) INTRODUCTION OF IAC DURING STUDY PERIOD

The introduction of an IAC during the study period correlated, as expected, with increasing nonunanimity rates. (This is indicated with a "Yes" in Appendix 3A, columns 3 and 4.) There were 29 states in which an IAC was introduced during the study period. In 16 of these states, the nonunanimity rate in *every* year after introduction of an IAC was greater than in every year before introduction of an IAC (Arkansas, Connecticut, Kentucky, Massachusetts, Michigan, Minnesota, Mississippi, North Carolina, North Dakota,[114] Oklahoma [criminal], Oregon, Pennsylvania, South Carolina, Virginia, Washington, and Wisconsin). In another nine states the *average* nonunanimity rate after introduction of an IAC was greater than the average before an IAC (Arizona, Florida, Hawaii, Idaho, Kansas, Maryland, New Mexico, Oklahoma [civil], and Utah). In only four states did the nonunanimity rate not increase by either of these two measures (Alaska, Colorado, Iowa, and Nebraska).

The introduction of an IAC might have an impact on judges writing separate opinions simply by lowering the high court's workload, on the assumption that judges with more time will write more opinions. However, there did not appear to be a correlation between increases in nonunanimity rates and workload changes. Appendix 3A, column 5, provides information about workload changes for states that introduced an IAC during the study period. A workload change was determined by comparing the *average* case workload for years after introduction of an IAC with the workload in the study year immediately prior to introduction of an IAC. Thus, assume year and workload figures as follows, with workload in parentheses: 1950 (100), 1960 (100), 1970 (200), 1980 (150), 1990 (160), 2000 (170), with introduction of an IAC as of 1980. The post-IAC average workload is 160, which is down from the workload in 1970 (200). (Relating workload changes to changes in operational rules is subject to a caveat that I could not measure. A new operational rule might not have an immediate impact because cases might be working their way through the judicial pipeline unaffected by the introduction of an IAC. Thus, introduction of an IAC as of 1980 might not reduce 1980 cases significantly if lower court decisions before 1980 still reached the highest state court under a pre-1980 mandatory jurisdiction law.)

Among the 25 states with rising nonunanimity rates after introduction of an IAC as determined by at least one of two measures noted above, workload did in fact decline after introduction of an IAC (down in 17 states, stayed about the same in six states, and rose in two states). But it was also true that, in the four states where nonunanimity rates did not increase after introduction of an intermediate court of appeals by either of the two measures, workload still went down in three states and stayed about the same in one state. In sum, although there were only a small number of states where nonunanimity rates did *not* increase after introduction of an IAC, post-IAC workload declines did not seem to be an independent factor leading to an increase in separate opinions. Recall that there is good reason to expect this result, on the theory that judges with fewer cases to decide are just as likely to have more time to hammer out consensus opinions as to write separately.

ii. Number of judges

(A) NO CHANGE DURING STUDY PERIOD

The number of judges on the highest state court might have an impact on the judges' *overall* tendency to write separately, on the theory that peer pressure is less effective when there are more judges. Appendix 3B, columns 2 and 3, which give the average nonunanimity rate and the number of judges, supports that hypothesis. Among the states that had a constant number of judges during the entire study period, the larger the number of judges the higher the nonunanimity rate—namely, nine judges in four states (31.85%); seven judges in 19 states (24.41%); five judges in 13 states (17.15%).

(B) CHANGE DURING STUDY PERIOD

If we look at average nonunanimity rates for years before and after a significant change in the number of judges, we see a pattern of rising nonunanimity rates associated with more judges on the bench. I defined a "significant change" as an increase (or, occasionally, a decrease) of at least two judges (the number of judges on the highest state court was usually three, five, seven, or nine). The data about the impact of this change appear in Appendix 3B, column 4; the pre-change average is before the slash; the post-change average is after the slash. Thus, if there was a change in 1980, 10/25 means that the average nonunanimity rates rose from 10% before 1980 to a 25% average for 1980, 1990, and 2000. (Caveat: A change in the number of judges might take time to have an impact; for example, the operation of a court that increased its numbers from five to seven judges as of 1970 might still operate as though it were a smaller bench in 1970, as judges appointed before the change were still socialized to a consensus style.)

The data show 14 states with a change in the number of judges of at least two—for example, from three to five, but not from three to four;

three states are counted twice in the total because they each made two changes in the size of the bench of at least two judges. The data indicate that an increase in the number of judges correlated with an increase in nonunanimity rates in 11 states and a decrease in number of judges correlated with a decrease in nonunanimity rates in one state (Delaware)—which is consistent with the theory that peer pressure for consensus declines with more judges. Two states varied from this pattern—Minnesota, with a decline in judges, increased its nonunanimity rate (from 11.9% to 27.7%); and Montana, with an increase in judges, lowered its rate (though only from 27.6% to 23.3%).

An increase in the number of judges might not only encourage separate opinions as a matter of small-group dynamics but may also be consistent with the Legal Realist hypothesis. More judges allow for increasingly diverse political/legal perspectives, perhaps in response to specific efforts to obtain racial, ethnic, and/or gender diversity on the bench. The larger numbers of judges may, therefore, be a symptom of the Legal Realist view of the law—that judges should reflect varying political perspectives—which would in turn encourage an inclination to write separately.

c. Summary of conclusions

It is difficult to find a direct measure of the influence of Legal Realism on the tendency of high court judges to write separate opinions, whether at the state or federal level, but that still seems the most likely explanation for the increase in nonunanimity rates in the past decades. The most plausible rival explanation is the existence of an intermediate appellate court, which filters out the easier cases, leaving the more difficult cases to attract separate opinions in the highest court of the state. But the increase in separate opinions in the many states with no change in the presence or absence of an IAC supports the Legal Realist explanation. There was also an increase in separate opinions after an increase in the number of judges, which might result from a reduction in small-group pressure for consensus, but which might also bear a Legal Realist explanation as more judges are appointed to represent diverse and previously excluded political points of view.

The following graphs provide information about the nonunanimity rates in the highest state court and relevant operational factors for 1950, 1960, 1970, 1980, 1990, and 2000—specifically:

—the percentage of cases in the highest court of the state in which at least one separate opinion was filed;

—the total number of cases (appearing below the year);

—the first year in the study for which there is an intermediate appellate court (if any): "IAC" appears after the "Number of Cases" line, if there was an IAC during the entire study period; "IAC" appears between the specified number of cases for two years during the study period, if an IAC was adopted between those two years during the study period; "No IAC" appears after the "Number of Cases" line, if there was no IAC during the entire study period;

—the average rate of separate opinions for the six years in the study (AVG);

—the number of judges in 1950, followed by a change in number (if any) as of the indicated year; for example, 5; 7(1980) means five judges in 1950, and then seven judges in 1980 and thereafter.

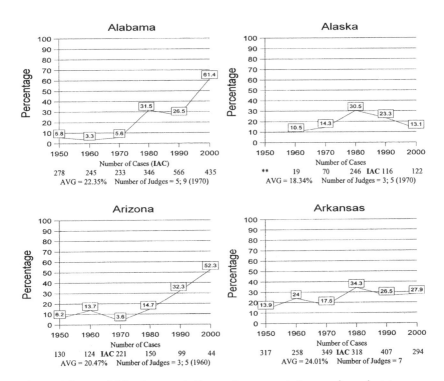

Fig. 5.2 (*above and following pages*). Changes in nonunanimity rates for each state.

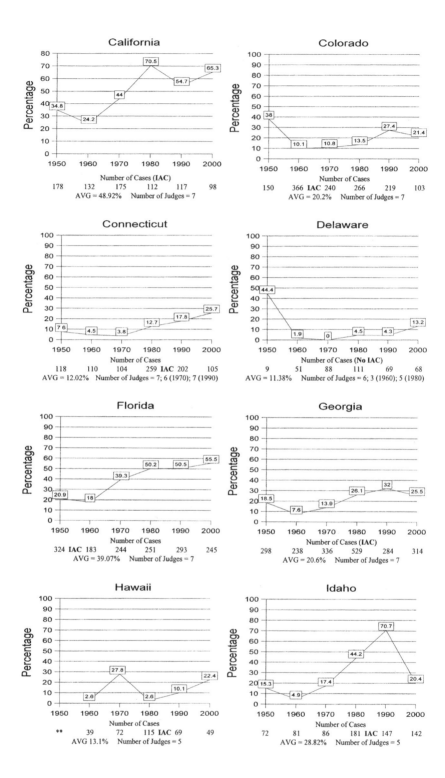

California

Number of Cases (IAC)

| 178 | 132 | 175 | 112 | 117 | 98 |

AVG = 48.92%   Number of Judges = 7

Colorado

Number of Cases

| 150 | 366 IAC 240 | 266 | 219 | 103 |

AVG = 20.2%   Number of Judges = 7

Connecticut

Number of Cases

| 118 | 110 | 104 | 259 IAC 202 | 105 |

AVG = 12.02%   Number of Judges = 7; 6 (1970); 7 (1990)

Delaware

Number of Cases (No IAC)

| 9 | 51 | 88 | 111 | 69 | 68 |

AVG = 11.38%   Number of Judges = 6; 3 (1960); 5 (1980)

Florida

Number of Cases

| 324 IAC 183 | 244 | 251 | 293 | 245 |

AVG = 39.07%   Number of Judges = 7

Georgia

Number of Cases (IAC)

| 298 | 238 | 336 | 529 | 284 | 314 |

AVG = 20.6%   Number of Judges = 7

Hawaii

Number of Cases

| ** | 39 | 72 | 115 IAC 69 | 49 |

AVG 13.1%   Number of Judges = 5

Idaho

Number of Cases

| 72 | 81 | 86 | 181 IAC 147 | 142 |

AVG = 28.82%   Number of Judges = 5

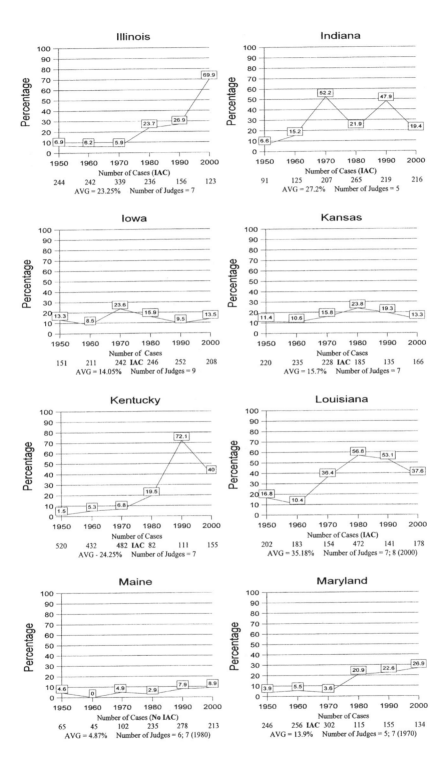

Illinois

| | 1950 | 1960 | 1970 | 1980 | 1990 | 2000 |
| Number of Cases (IAC) | 244 | 242 | 339 | 236 | 156 | 123 |

AVG = 23.25%   Number of Judges = 7

Indiana

| | 1950 | 1960 | 1970 | 1980 | 1990 | 2000 |
| Number of Cases (IAC) | 91 | 125 | 207 | 265 | 219 | 216 |

AVG = 27.2%   Number of Judges = 5

Iowa

| | 1950 | 1960 | 1970 | 1980 | 1990 | 2000 |
| Number of Cases | 151 | 211 | 242 IAC 246 | | 252 | 208 |

AVG = 14.05%   Number of Judges = 9

Kansas

| | 1950 | 1960 | 1970 | 1980 | 1990 | 2000 |
| Number of Cases | 220 | 235 | 228 IAC 185 | | 135 | 166 |

AVG = 15.7%   Number of Judges = 7

Kentucky

| | 1950 | 1960 | 1970 | 1980 | 1990 | 2000 |
| Number of Cases | 520 | 432 | 482 IAC 82 | | 111 | 155 |

AVG - 24.25%   Number of Judges = 7

Louisiana

| | 1950 | 1960 | 1970 | 1980 | 1990 | 2000 |
| Number of Cases (IAC) | 202 | 183 | 154 | 472 | 141 | 178 |

AVG = 35.18%   Number of Judges = 7; 8 (2000)

Maine

| | 1950 | 1960 | 1970 | 1980 | 1990 | 2000 |
| Number of Cases (No IAC) | 65 | 45 | 102 | 235 | 278 | 213 |

AVG = 4.87%   Number of Judges = 6; 7 (1980)

Maryland

| | 1950 | 1960 | 1970 | 1980 | 1990 | 2000 |
| Number of Cases | 246 | 256 IAC 302 | | 115 | 155 | 134 |

AVG = 13.9%   Number of Judges = 5; 7 (1970)

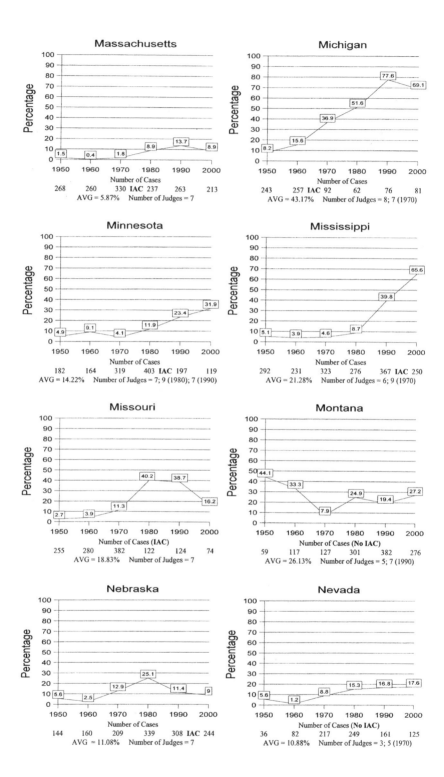

Massachusetts

Number of Cases
| 268 | 260 | 330 IAC 237 | 263 | 213 |

AVG = 5.87%   Number of Judges = 7

Michigan

Number of Cases
| 243 | 257 IAC 92 | 62 | 76 | 81 |

AVG = 43.17%   Number of Judges = 8; 7 (1970)

Minnesota

Number of Cases
| 182 | 164 | 319 | 403 IAC 197 | 119 |

AVG = 14.22%   Number of Judges = 7; 9 (1980); 7 (1990)

Mississippi

Number of Cases
| 292 | 231 | 323 | 276 | 367 IAC 250 |

AVG = 21.28%   Number of Judges = 6; 9 (1970)

Missouri

Number of Cases (IAC)
| 255 | 280 | 382 | 122 | 124 | 74 |

AVG = 18.83%   Number of Judges = 7

Montana

Number of Cases (No IAC)
| 59 | 117 | 127 | 301 | 382 | 276 |

AVG = 26.13%   Number of Judges = 5; 7 (1990)

Nebraska

Number of Cases
| 144 | 160 | 209 | 339 | 308 IAC 244 |

AVG = 11.08%   Number of Judges = 7

Nevada

Number of Cases (No IAC)
| 36 | 82 | 217 | 249 | 161 | 125 |

AVG = 10.88%   Number of Judges = 3; 5 (1970)

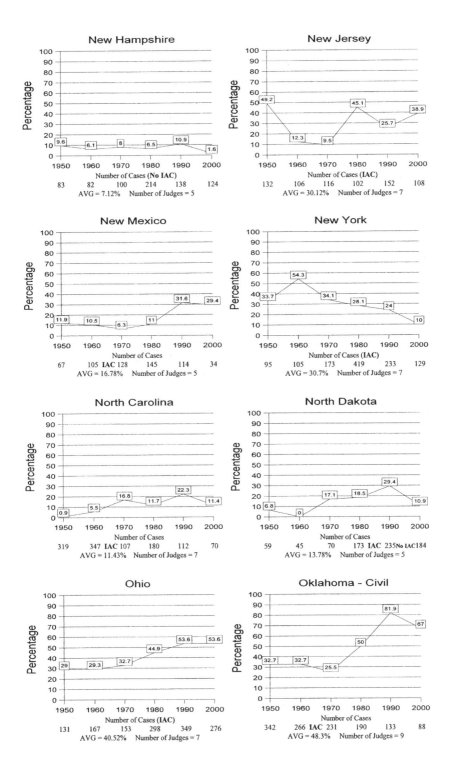

New Hampshire

Number of Cases (No IAC)
83   82   100   214   138   124
AVG = 7.12%   Number of Judges = 5

New Jersey

Number of Cases (IAC)
132   106   116   102   152   108
AVG = 30.12%   Number of Judges = 7

New Mexico

Number of Cases
67   105 IAC 128   145   114   34
AVG = 16.78%   Number of Judges = 5

New York

Number of Cases (IAC)
95   105   173   419   233   129
AVG = 30.7%   Number of Judges = 7

North Carolina

Number of Cases
319   347 IAC 107   180   112   70
AVG = 11.43%   Number of Judges = 7

North Dakota

Number of Cases
59   45   70   173 IAC 235No IAC184
AVG = 13.78%   Number of Judges = 5

Ohio

Number of Cases (IAC)
131   167   153   298   349   276
AVG = 40.52%   Number of Judges = 7

Oklahoma - Civil

Number of Cases
342   266 IAC 231   190   133   88
AVG = 48.3%   Number of Judges = 9

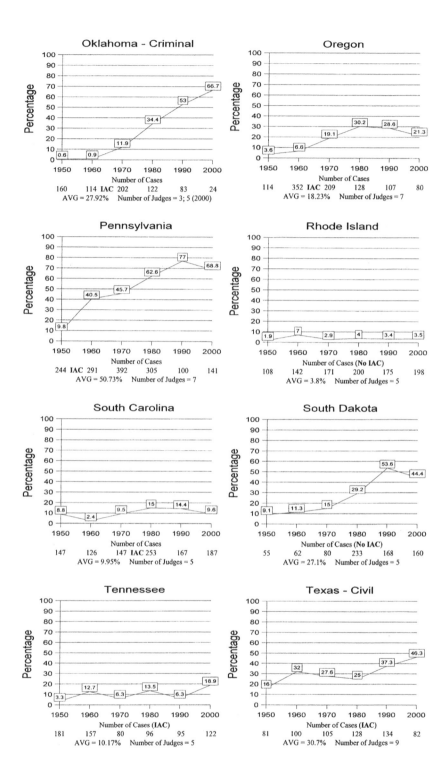

Oklahoma - Criminal

Percentage

1950	1960	1970	1980	1990	2000
0.6	0.9	11.9	34.4	53	66.7

Number of Cases

160   114 **IAC** 202   122   83   24
AVG = 27.92%   Number of Judges = 3; 5 (2000)

Oregon

Percentage

1950	1960	1970	1980	1990	2000
3.6	6.6	19.1	30.2	28.6	21.3

Number of Cases

114   352 **IAC** 209   128   107   80
AVG = 18.23%   Number of Judges = 7

Pennsylvania

Percentage

1950	1960	1970	1980	1990	2000
9.8	40.5	45.7	62.6	77	68.8

Number of Cases

244 **IAC** 291   392   305   100   141
AVG = 50.73%   Number of Judges = 7

Rhode Island

Percentage

1950	1960	1970	1980	1990	2000
1.9	7	2.9	4	3.4	3.5

Number of Cases (**No IAC**)

108   142   171   200   175   198
AVG = 3.8%   Number of Judges = 5

South Carolina

Percentage

1950	1960	1970	1980	1990	2000
8.8	2.4	9.5	15	14.4	9.6

Number of Cases

147   126   147 **IAC** 253   167   187
AVG = 9.95%   Number of Judges = 5

South Dakota

Percentage

1950	1960	1970	1980	1990	2000
9.1	11.3	15	29.2	53.6	44.4

Number of Cases (**No IAC**)

55   62   80   233   168   160
AVG = 27.1%   Number of Judges = 5

Tennessee

Percentage

1950	1960	1970	1980	1990	2000
3.3	12.7	6.3	13.5	6.3	18.9

Number of Cases (**IAC**)

181   157   80   96   95   122
AVG = 10.17%   Number of Judges = 5

Texas - Civil

Percentage

1950	1960	1970	1980	1990	2000
16	32	27.6	25	37.3	46.3

Number of Cases (**IAC**)

81   100   105   128   134   82
AVG = 30.7%   Number of Judges = 9

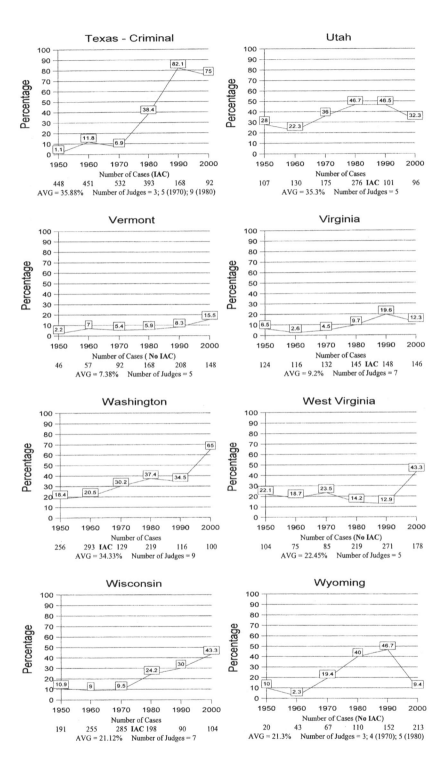

Texas - Criminal

Percentage

	1950	1960	1970	1980	1990	2000

1.1, 11.8, 6.9, 38.4, 82.1, 75

Number of Cases (IAC)
448   451   532   393   168   92
AVG = 35.88%   Number of Judges = 3; 5 (1970); 9 (1980)

Utah

Percentage

28, 22.3, 36, 46.7, 46.5, 32.3

Number of Cases
107   130   175   276 IAC 101   96
AVG = 35.3%   Number of Judges = 5

Vermont

Percentage

2.2, 7, 5.4, 5.9, 8.3, 15.5

Number of Cases (No IAC)
46   57   92   168   208   148
AVG = 7.38%   Number of Judges = 5

Virginia

Percentage

6.5, 2.6, 4.5, 9.7, 19.6, 12.3

Number of Cases
124   116   132   145 IAC 148   146
AVG = 9.2%   Number of Judges = 7

Washington

Percentage

18.4, 20.5, 30.2, 37.4, 34.5, 65

Number of Cases
256   293 IAC 129   219   116   100
AVG = 34.33%   Number of Judges = 9

West Virginia

Percentage

22.1, 18.7, 23.5, 14.2, 12.9, 43.3

Number of Cases (No IAC)
104   75   85   219   271   178
AVG = 22.45%   Number of Judges = 5

Wisconsin

Percentage

10.9, 9, 9.5, 24.2, 30, 43.3

Number of Cases
191   255   285 IAC 198   90   104
AVG = 21.12%   Number of Judges = 7

Wyoming

Percentage

10, 2.3, 19.4, 40, 46.7, 9.4

Number of Cases (No IAC)
20   43   67   110   152   213
AVG = 21.3%   Number of Judges = 3; 4 (1970); 5 (1980)

6

Contemporary United States Practice
Individual Style

I have been occupied in earlier chapters with the institutional style of presenting judicial opinions because it tells us something about how judging fits into the legal culture. I suggested that separate opinions have become a more accepted feature of the judges' institutional style—at least in courts of last resort where the results are more contentious—because Legal Realism acknowledges that the underlying source of law is a mixture of what was traditionally known as law and politics, and separate opinions enable judges to explain how their views fit into that complex legal landscape.

But what of the judges' individual style of presenting opinions? Judges communicate not only through an institutional style but also through their individual style; and both elements of style are related to the legal culture. Section A of this chapter defines what I mean by individual judicial styles—specifically, the different types of voice and tone. Section B provides an extended discussion of Judge Posner's majority opinions on the Seventh Circuit Court of Appeals to illustrate the use of a personal voice and exploratory tone. Section C explains why the personal/exploratory style ought to be used more often by contemporary U.S. judges.

An important inference from this chapter is that a change in individual judicial style requires an active judicial commitment to a new way of thinking about judging. Although U.S. judges have always had more freedom to choose their individual style—either because of their inherited seriatim tradition or because they are expected to play an important lawmaking role—the older judicial style of a technical/professional voice and an authoritative tone is likely to be resistant to change. This chapter makes the case for overcoming this resistance in favor of a more personal voice and exploratory tone.

A. Definitions of individual judicial styles

It is a "devil to define" style, as Posner says,[1] but it is important to make clear what I am talking about without worrying too much about whether my definition differs from others'. What I mean by judicial style is whatever in the judicial opinion seeks to persuade beyond the paraphrasable content of the decision. Judicial style consists of voice and tone. Voice refers to the author's relationship to the source of law; tone refers to the author's relationship to the audience. I therefore define style, not as writing skill, but as a method of conveying substantive ideas.[2]

In two respects, these categories are oversimplifications. First, an opinion can combine more than one voice and more than one tone. Second, the categories are extremes, with opinions often displaying some but not all of the qualities that characterize a particular style. Nonetheless, it is useful to identify elements of style in pure form for what such identification tells about how judges fit their opinions into a changing legal culture.

1. Voice

The three dominant judicial voices that impart a sense of the judge's relationship to a source of law are the technical/professional, magisterial, and personal.

a. Technical/professional

The technical/professional voice invokes legal expertise as the means to identify legal principle. The author of the judicial opinion comes across as a professional insider, expert in the internal workings of the law as a result of legal training. The classic example is Coke, whose reliance on artificial reason shunted aside King James's claim to know the law through natural reason.[3] And it is also apparent in Hale's assertion about the judicial role in statutory interpretation: "As to [the] exposition of [statutes] he that hath been educated in the study of the law hath a great advantage over those that have been otherwise exercised. . . ."[4]

Logic often characterizes an opinion in the technical/professional voice, which is what led to Justice Holmes's famous complaint that "the life of the law is experience, not logic"; and, less famously, Judge Hand's observation that statutes "should be construed, not as theorems of Euclid, but with some imagination of the purposes which lie behind them."[5]

> *Example 1.* An example of the technical/professional voice employing logic is the majority opinion in the 1920 Supreme Court case of Eisner v. Macomber.[6] The Court held that a common stock dividend (one share for every two held by the taxpayer) was not "income" within the meaning of the Sixteenth Amendment to the U.S. Constitution. The Court's initial and unwavering premise was that a corporation is legally separate from its shareholders. The logical conclusion that followed from this premise was that a common stock dividend paid to common stockholders could not be income to the stockholders because it separated nothing from the corporation's assets for the shareholders' benefit; it simply gave the shareholders another piece of paper. The government took a more pragmatic view of the concept of income—that taxing stock dividends was a proxy for taxing undistributed corporate profits—a view that implicitly rejected the notion that corporate law separating the entity and its owners was a premise necessarily incorporated into tax law. But the Court simply insisted on its legal premise that corporations were separate from the shareholders for all purposes —tax as well as corporate law—and that, therefore, their profits could not accrue to the owners prior to distribution.

b. Magisterial

A magisterial judicial voice speaks with what Benjamin Cardozo described (referring to Chief Justice Marshall) as "the mystery and the awe of inspired revelation."[7] The power of Marshall's magisterial voice was captured in the frustration of one of his critics, who lamented: "All wrong, all wrong, but no man in the United States can tell why or wherein."[8] The model for the magisterial voice is religious, as when a priest, prophet, or oracle transmits a message from a higher power. The magisterial voice contrasts with what Cardozo labeled the "demonstrative or persuasive" (which I take to be the technical/professional style) and which he said was "not unlike [the] magisterial," but more like a "scientific seeker for the truth and less reminiscent of the priestess on the tripod."[9]

The magisterial, like the technical/professional voice, draws on an external source of law, but with a sense of grandeur that is lacking in the professional model. In the early 19th Century, the magisterial voice was often associated with an appeal to natural law principles[10] or, in our fledgling republic, the people.

Marshall, though not alone in invoking natural law, did so with fervor in his dissent in Ogden v. Saunders:[11]

> In a state of nature, . . . individuals may contract, their contracts are obligatory, and force may rightfully be employed to coerce the party who has broken his engagement. . . . [I]ndividuals do not derive from government their right to contract, but bring that right with them into society; [the contractual] obligation is not conferred on contracts by positive law, but is intrinsic, and is conferred by the act of the parties. . . . These rights are not given by society, but are brought into it. . . . This reasoning is, undoubtedly, much strengthened by the authority of those writers on natural and national law, whose opinions have been viewed with profound respect by, the wisest men of the present, and of past ages.

And, in one of his most famous opinions, McCulloch v. Maryland,[12] Marshall relied on the "people" as the source of the Constitution he was expounding:

> [The draft constitution] was submitted to the *people.* They acted upon it in the only manner in which they can act safely, effectively and wisely, on such a subject, by assembling in convention. . . . The government proceeds directly from the people; is ordained and established, in the name of the people. . . . The assent of the states, in their sovereign capacity, is implied, in calling a convention, and thus submitting that instrument to the people. But the people were at perfect liberty to accept or reject it; and their act was final.

The magisterial and technical/professional voices can appear in the same opinion—as in Marshall's opinion in Marbury v. Madison[13] upholding the Court's power to declare a statute unconstitutional. Marshall is most famously known for the magisterial voice with which he asserted judicial power:

> If an act of the legislature, repugnant to the constitution, is void, does it, notwithstanding its invalidity, bind the courts and oblige them to give it effect? Or, in other words, though it be not law, does it constitute a rule as operative as if it was a law? This would be to overthrow in fact what was established in theory; and would seem, at first view, an absurdity too gross to be insisted on. . . . It is emphatically the province and duty of the judicial department to say what the law is.

But he goes on in a technical/professional voice to assert that this power is analogous to what judges routinely do when deciding which of two laws has priority:

> Those who apply the rule to particular cases, must of necessity expound and interpret that rule. If two laws conflict with each other, the courts must decide on the operation of each. So if a law be in opposition to the constitution: if both the law and the constitution apply to a particular case, so that the court must either decide that case conformably to the law, disregarding the constitution; or conformably to the constitution, disregarding the law: the court must determine which of these conflicting rules governs the case. This is of the very essence of judicial duty.

c. Personal

The judge who speaks with a personal voice relies on judicial insight into contemporary community values as the source of law and relies on that voice to converse with fellow members of that community. Justice Holmes's opinions provide the best examples of a personal judicial voice, often characterized by his reliance on aphorisms.

Example 2. "Three generations of imbeciles are enough."—Buck v. Bell, 274 U.S. 200, 207 (1927); "The most stringent protection of free speech would not protect a man in falsely shouting fire in a theatre and causing a panic."—Schenck v. U.S., 249 U.S. 47, 52 (1919); "Neither are we troubled by the question where to draw the line. That is the question in pretty much everything worth arguing in the law. Day and night, youth and age are only types."—Irwin v. Gavit, 268 U.S. 161, 168 (1925).

Perhaps the most interesting example of Holmes's personal voice is his down-to-earth insistence that "[t]he power to tax is not the power to destroy while this Court sits,"[14] which explicitly rejected as obsolete Marshall's magisterial assertion that the "power to tax is the power to destroy." Holmes attributes Marshall's perspective to an age when the law consisted of absolutes, not matters of degree: "In those days it was not recognized as it is today that most of the distinctions of the law are distinctions of degree."

In each of these illustrations, Holmes's language is direct, unadorned, and without artifice, neither magisterial nor professional. He uses language shared by a community that includes both the judicial author and the public audience. Perhaps for this reason, Holmes's aphorisms are among the very few that make it into common parlance, rivaled only by Justice Stewart's comment on obscenity—"I know it when I see it"[15]—and, perhaps, by some of Justice Jackson's statements—for example: "We are not final because we are infallible, but we are infallible only because we are final";[16] "There is danger that, if the Court does not temper its doctrinaire logic with a little practical wisdom, it will convert the constitutional Bill of Rights into a suicide pact."[17]

2. Tone: Authoritative or exploratory

Tone is different from voice—it establishes the author's relationship to the audience, not to the source of law. Tone can be either authoritative or exploratory. An authoritative tone speaks down to the audience. The technical/professional and magisterial voices are always authoritative in modern judicial usage—with the judge transmitting law to the reader from a vantage point between the source of law and the audience. By contrast, an exploratory tone draws the reader into a participatory community with the judge, wondering aloud about how to deal with the complexities of the case. The exploratory tone is an extension to the individual judge of the seriatim institutional style used by a court. Just as multiple judicial views characterize seriatim opinions, so an exploratory tone reveals the multiple perspectives occurring to an individual judge thinking about a case—what has been called by Posner a "back and forth" thought process.[18] It is well illustrated by Justice Stevens's explanation of how he uses legislative history: "I have often formed a tentative opinion about the meaning of a statute and thereafter examined the statute's drafting history to see whether the history supported my provisional conclusion or provided a basis for revising it."[19]

An exploratory tone can assume various guises. In its extreme version, the judge explicitly admits to being unsure of the result, an unusual but not unheard of occurrence. The following statement is especially unusual in that it comes from a case interpreting a statute, and a tax statute at that:

> We have now changed our minds. . . . We have struggled with [the question] unsuccessfully at least once, and it may, indeed, turn out that the United States Supreme Court will tell us that it is this opinion which is error. This is simply one of those cases—and there are more of them than judges generally like to admit—in which the answer is far from clear. . . . Law, even statutory interpretation, is not a science. It is merely an effort by human beings, albeit judges, to do their best with imperfect tools to arrive at a correct result.[20]

More often, the judge adopts an exploratory tone that is not so openly doubtful. One variation finds the judge considering multiple ways to analyze an issue—what I call exploring "horizontally." Judicial consideration of multiple lines of analysis increases the potential for an opinion to be exploratory because it makes it harder for the judge to insist that any single criterion is clearly dispositive.

Example 3. Judge Easterbrook's opinion in Matter of Erickson[21] is a good example of a "horizontal" exploratory opinion (which also admits to serious doubts about the result). The issue was whether a 1935 law exempting "mowers" from the bankruptcy claims of creditors applied to a haybine, which did not exist when the statute was passed and which did more than just mow. Easterbrook provides an extensive exploration of multiple approaches to interpreting the statute—namely: (1) the functional denotation of a word (how it works in a particular setting); (2) the statute's purpose (keeping a small farm in operation);

(3) an "equal value" principle that would limit a debtor's exemption to property with value close to 1935 value; (4) the canon that "remedial" statutes should be liberally interpreted; and (5) the contemporary law and economics approach, which worries about whether "helping" farm debtors with an exemption from creditors would hurt farmers when they tried to get credit. Finally, Easterbrook's conclusion explicitly expresses doubt: "To the extent there is doubt—and there is still substantial doubt . . .—we accept the decision of the bankruptcy and district judges. . . . The law has need of tie-breakers, and if this case be a tie (it comes close), the nod goes to the district court's construction."

Multiple lines of analysis will lead to an exploratory tone, however, only if the judge is inclined in that direction. An alternative way for the judge to deal with multiple lines of analysis is for the opinion to suggest that they all lead unproblematically to a common result, like good soldiers marching in lockstep, especially when the opinion is a committee product at the appellate level. When that happens, incorporating multiple points of view can result in the jarring inclusion of an argument that is dramatically out of step with the rest of an opinion.[22]

Another way in which the judge can adopt an exploratory tone is to explore "vertically"—up from the text to consider the intent or purpose underlying the legal rule, or down from the text to the facts to which the rule applies. Identifying the underlying intent or purpose of a rule opens up possibilities for uncertainty that would not otherwise exist, such as: difficulty in proving intent or purpose; argument about whether these considerations ought to prevail over the text of the rule; and the effect of a change of circumstances after the initial adoption of the rule on its meaning and survival. Similarly, the more elaborate the judge's consideration of the facts, the more likely it is that their relevance or weight will be called into question.

Hand's opinions provide good examples of exploring "vertically," although he was too complex to pigeonhole into a single approach. In his non-judicial writings, he sometimes sounded almost authoritarian, acknowledging that the judge "pos[es] as a kind of oracle," and counting it "among [man's] most dependable joys to impose upon the flux that passes before him some mark of himself, aware though he always must be of the odds against him."[23] But his opinions display little of the authoritarian tone that these quotes might imply. Hand's exploratory style was probably the result of his conception of judging as a craft,[24] wherein a person's "reward is not so much in the work as in its making; not so much in the prize as in the race. . . ."[25] An exploratory opinion allowed Hand to reveal how the judicial craft worked with complex and uncertain raw material, and he did this without regard to the political visibility of the issue—a tax or admiralty case would receive the same close attention as an anti-trust or free speech case—because the judicial craft is no more engaged in a publicly important case than in a case of lesser public significance. Illustrations from Hand's opinions are too long to excerpt, but his opinion in Fishgold v. Sullivan Drydock & Repair Corp.[26] is a good example of exploring vertically (upward) to try to identify what the legislature's rationale might have been for a statutory rule; and The T. J. Hooper v. Northern Barge Corp.[27] is a good example of exploring vertically (downward) through an exhaustive consideration of the facts to which admiralty rules might apply.

These descriptions of an exploratory tone suggest a possible criticism of its judicial use—the uncertainty it might create in the law. There are several versions of this criticism. First, an exploratory tone is often associated with the adoption of less clear standards (such as relying on statutory purpose to interpret legislation), rather than clear rules. And, as Schauer notes, judicially adopted, clear rules might serve the law better than more traditional common-law-like standards.[28] Whatever the merits of the rule vs. standard debate, however, an exploratory tone does not *necessarily* require a judicial standard rather than a rule. Judges can openly explore the uncertainties that lead to a decision, whether or not that decision eventually takes the form of a rule or standard. Moreover, even if an exploratory tone often correlates with less clear standards (as I have suggested), there is no reason why a standard should lack coherence, even if it is less clear than a rule. As we will see, Posner is the prime contemporary example of an exploratory judge who frequently rejects clear (sounding) rules, but he is also vehemently opposed to unclear multi-factor tests that completely fail to guide a judicial decision.[29]

Second, even if the conclusion is clear, an exploratory tone might be less useful to the professional audience, to the extent that it holds back the conclusion until the end of the opinion. Judge Wald made this point in her response to Posner's criticism of her writing style, when she suggested that stating a result up front provides the bar with more guidance (her term is "user-friendly"), in comparison to Posner's more discursive style that lingers over the reasoning process before crossing the finish line.[30] But it seems unlikely that the profession is deprived of the guidance that a judicial opinion can provide just because its holding is withheld until the end.

Third, an exploratory tone (like seriatim opinions) might contribute to a decision's fragility over time by encouraging limits on its reach or (perhaps) its overruling. Whether or not that is true (and such claims are very hard to prove),[31] that is not necessarily a fault. Some judicial law *should* be limited in future cases, and an exploratory tone makes that possibility transparent to the reader. Moreover, there are a variety of ways that an opinion can be exploratory (as the discussion of Judge Posner's opinions in Chapter 6B illustrates) without making the decision fragile.

3. Combining voice and tone

What combination of voice and tone can a judge employ? Modern usage associates the magisterial and technical/professional voices with an authoritative tone that speaks down to the audience. By contrast, a judge who speaks with a personal voice can adopt either an authoritative or an exploratory tone—authoritative by asserting the judge's knowledge of contemporary community values; or exploratory by engaging in a hypothetical dialogue that simulates intra-community deliberation.

A personal voice with an authoritative tone is a difficult judicial style to sustain, because there is a tension between claiming to be an ordinary member of the political community and speaking authoritatively for that community. Political leaders can often combine a personal voice with an authoritative tone, but only because they are open to popular rebuke; their authoritative claims to speak for the people can be rejected at the next election. But it is more difficult for a judge to claim authority to speak for the public, absent a willingness to have his or her views subjected to a popular vote. Justice Holmes was able to pull it off, but perhaps no one else could do it effectively. As Posner notes,[32] a careful analysis of Holmes's opinions reveals that he often put the rabbit in the hat and then pulled it out without much legal analysis. There is little in his brief opinions that smacks of an exploratory, deliberative reasoning process—a process that would recognize the complexities that underlie his straightforward conclusion. (I differ here from both Posner and

Cardozo regarding the characterization of Holmes's opinions. Posner attributes to Holmes what he calls an impure style—which is both personal and exploratory;[33] I hear Holmes's personal voice but not an exploratory tone. Cardozo puts Holmes in the laconic, sententious, conversational, homely category—that is, a personal voice; but Cardozo states that Holmes "make[s] us partners in the deliberative process," which is not apparent to me.)[34]

> *Example 4.* A good illustration of Holmes's personal/authoritative style is his opinion in Lucas v. Earl.[35] In this case, Holmes presents his basic premise with brevity—income is taxed to the person who earned it. He advances the alternative premise—taxing the person who enjoys the benefit of the income under the property law arrangements between the parties—but he dismisses that approach as an "attenuated subtlety." The only thing wrong with this statement is that the "benefit" principle is a perfectly respectable premise on which to define the income taxpayer, not an attenuated subtlety. Although there are good analytical and policy arguments to support Holmes's conclusion—for example, that the correct tax rate to apply to income is that of the primary family earner, rather than a member of the family with a lower tax rate—this argument does not appear in the opinion.

Holmes's reliance on a personal/authoritative style was ideally suited to a transitional period of declining faith in judicial ability to access first principles (associated with the growing influence of Legal Realism), while the judge still remained anchored in the older formalist vision of the law, in which courts declared the law.[36] But a personal/authoritative style attracts skepticism about whether the judge has special knowledge of what the political community prefers. There is a problem whenever the judge claims to know what the people want. When the U.S. Supreme Court did this is Chisholm v. Georgia[37] in 1793—concluding that the "people" had decided in the Constitution that states lacked sovereign immunity when sued in federal court—the people disagreed and amended the Constitution to override the decision, acting on a proposal that passed Congress almost unanimously within two months after the decision.[38] With the passing of legal formalism and the acceptance of democracy as the "central legitimating concept in American constitutional law" in the 20th Century,[39] an authoritative judicial tone becomes even more suspect, especially when it is grounded on what the people want. This may be one reason why Justice Black's personal voice[40] mixes so badly with the self-assuredness of his opinions; and why Justice Scalia's frequent use of a personal voice[41] seems so discordant with his authoritarian tone (for example, when he lectures us about the "wisdom of the ages" and prefers "justice" to "mercy, or compassion, or social utility"),[42] so that he comes across as the imperial judge that he so often derides.[43]

The problem is that an authoritative tone combined with any voice does not fit well with modern legal culture. Holmes's objections to the logical analysis associated with a technical/professional voice and to the absolutism inherent in the magisterial voice foreshadowed the Legal Realist insight into the relationship of judicial law and politics. And when that insight filters down into public and professional perception, it becomes difficult for a post-Holmesian judge to maintain a personal/authoritarian style. The modern suspicion of judicial claims to speak authoritatively suggests that judges should now make greater use of the combination of a personal voice and an exploratory tone.[44] But this possibility, to be viable, must be something more than a default position —that is, we need a more affirmative case for a personal/exploratory style than the fact that it seems to be what is left after Legal Realism has called into question an authoritative judicial tone. I will make that affirmative case in Chapter 6C, but first I will further illustrate its use in the next section with the purest example of which I am aware among current judges—Judge Posner's opinions. A more thorough review of that style will put us in a better position to evaluate how it fits into modern legal culture and will suggest how a judge can selectively adopt elements of that style, without going as far as Judge Posner.

B. Posner: Personal/Exploratory style

Judge Posner became a federal court of appeals judge on the Seventh Circuit in 1981, served as chief judge from 1993 to 2000, and now serves in retired status. Before (and after) becoming a judge, he taught at the University of Chicago Law School, where he pioneered the Law and Economics movement, bringing an economic perspective to all areas of law (not limited to subject matters where economics was traditionally relevant, such as anti-trust). He has also written extensively on judging[45] and his opinions bear the unmistakable mark of someone who is deeply concerned with how a judge should communicate his ideas.

In the remainder of this section, I present examples of Posner's personal/exploratory opinion-writing style.[46] The opinions are primarily from three groups of cases—the earliest opinions (from 666 F.2d 1112, Dec. 23, 1981 through 696 F.2d 544, Dec. 30, 1982); later 1998–1999 opinions (from 143 F.3d 545, May 4, 1998 through 176 F.3d 1012, May 7, 1999); and more recent opinions (from 356 F.3d 767, Jan. 18, 2004 through 404 F.3d 605, April 25, 2005). In addition, I examined some income tax opinions, using the Westlaw Key Search Number 220, and a few miscellaneous opinions with which I was familiar from other research.

The following presentation of quotations from opinions inevitably drains out much of their flavor, but I hope there is enough in my excerpts to convey a sense of what Posner is trying to say and do. In any event, I provide citations to the referenced cases in the text rather than in endnotes, so that the reader can easily find and read the complete opinion to get a better understanding of the way Posner writes. All but a few of the quotations are from majority opinions for the court because I am concerned with individual judicial styles that are in the mainstream and concurrences and dissents give judges freer rein to indulge an idiosyncratic writing style.

1. Personal voice

A judge using a personal voice speaks to an audience of fellow community members. Instead of transmitting law from a distant source—as when the judge uses a magisterial or technical/professional voice—the judge speaks to ordinary readers with whom he or she shares a common background. Several features of Posner's opinions illustrate a personal voice:

—using colloquial language;
—reducing legal language to everyday usage;
—presenting simplified examples;
—using a conversational style.

I did not, however, encounter Holmes-like pithy aphorisms to summarize legal conclusions, perhaps because the law is more complicated today and the reader expects something more (although I did come across a Holmes-like affirmation that moral intuition can be a basis for law).[47] The closest example I encountered was Posner's concluding statement in an opinion—"Three appeals in a case about a goatee are enough"[48]—which is an obvious echo of Holmes's statement that "[t]hree generations of imbeciles are enough."[49]

a. Using colloquial language

Chatty colloquial language abounds in Posner's opinions:

"We need not wrestle the issue to the ground."—397 F.3d 587, 592

"It would be positively Grinch-like for the President to say."—396 F.3d 887, 891

"jurisdictional hiccup"—393 F.3d 727, 731

"deliciously simple solution"—388 F.3d 1069, 1078

"booted a good Fourth Amendment claim"—387 F.3d 607, 609

"The immigration judge missed the boat."—376 F.3d 754, 756

"smelling a rat"—172 F.3d 520, 521

"spiel"—172 F.3d 467, 469

"chintzy"—171 F.3d 437, 439

"shenanigans," "cat's paw," "marionette"—170 F.3d 779, 783, 784

"monkey with"—168 F.3d 932, 935

"scotches [plaintiff's] argument"—166 F.3d 880, 884

"real gripe"—160 F.3d 1144, 1147

"We have before us a charming miniature of a case."—160 F.3d 358, 358

b. Reducing legal language to everyday usage

i. Translating legal jargon

Where possible, Posner gives us an ordinary-language translation of legal language, although he is aware that "[i]t is dangerous to take a legal term in its lay sense"—150 F.3d 729, 733:

"The word 'constructive' is a common legal term of art, but it should be avoided wherever possible. . . . When a court says that the defendant received 'constructive notice' of the plaintiff's suit, it means that he didn't receive notice but we'll pretend he did. . . . How much more illuminating it would be if the court said that notice isn't always required to make a person suable. . . ."—399 F.3d 876, 878

"due (= reasonable) care"—174 F.3d 842, 849

"For 'void' is just the name we give to those judgments that can be set aside without regard to the usual limitations on challenging judgments. . . ."—159 F.3d 1016, 1019

"assessed (demanded)"—926 F.2d 621, 622

"required to return [= report as income]"—792 F.2d 683, 688

"Fraud is just a name for the misrepresentations and omissions that legislators or judges want to punish. . . ."—694 F.2d 505, 509

"Tort law, unlike criminal law, does not punish 'inchoate,' which is to say purely preparatory, conduct. . . ."—686 F.2d 449, 453

ii. Legal argument in ordinary language

Legal argument is presented (again, where possible) in ordinary language, suggesting a minimal distance between the judge and the audience:

"symphony of frivolousness"—406 F.3d 453, 456

"the sheer injustice, at least as it would seem to a layman"—405 F.3d 488, 490

"a task for the agency, subject to light judicial review"—388 F.3d 251, 253

"[The taxpayer] cries foul."—248 F.3d 572, 576

The biblical story of Joseph hoarding grain is used to explain the difference between a dealer and a trader.—231 F.3d 1035, 1038

"In these circumstances, a light appellate touch is best."—182 F.3d 496, 498

"pull on one thread of a complex legal tapestry"—174 F.3d 842, 848

"That's an awful lot of compliance."—171 F.3d 1083, 1091

"weird result"—170 F.3d 747, 749

"[argument is] frivolous squared"—170 F.3d 691, 691

"whacky result"—168 F.3d 956, 958

"whiff of equitable estoppel"—165 F.3d 572, 575

"Waiver, however, differs by only a hair's breadth from estoppel."
—118 F.3d 522, 526

"The suggested anomaly is a bogey."—896 F.2d 218, 227

"Although there is a distinct echo in this of 'tie-in' sales and 'block booking.' . . , the echo is too faint to guide our interpretation of the Copyright Act."—693 F.2d 622, 626

c. Presenting simplified examples

Posner's opinions frequently use simplified examples so that the audience can easily understand the underlying events to which the law applies, even though he is well aware that examples can oversimplify ("This case is trickier than our example"—837 F.2d 309, 313).[50] The following are illustrative, along with additional cases cited in an endnote:[51]

"A numerical example, artificial only in irrelevant respects, may help to illuminate the issue."—263 F.3d 659, 661

To support a decision disallowing a deduction, the opinion explains the difference between gross and taxable income—viz., $100 gross income, with $25 spent to generate that income, yields $75 taxable income, not $75 gross income—259 F.3d 881, 883

d. Using a conversational style

Posner's opinions adopt a conversational style in a number of respects, giving the impression that he is speaking directly, almost intimately, with the reader.

i. No subdivisions

Unlike many other judges, Posner does not divide his opinions into Parts I, II, etc., or Subparts A, B, etc. This has the effect of a continuous, informal conversation, drawing the reader along as the judge's thoughts evolve.

ii. No footnotes

Posner refuses to use footnotes in his judicial opinions.[52] The aggressive absence of footnotes, even at the cost of placing long string citations in the text, is a conscious departure from "legal" writing and attempts to maintain a conversational style by not forcing the reader to glance up and down while trying to follow the author's thoughts.

iii. The beginning "but"

Posner frequently begins a sentence or paragraph with "but"—see, for example, 176 F.3d 1012, 1015–1016; 176 F.3d 952, 958. (Although I did not count, I would not be surprised if this occurred in a majority of his opinions.) The "beginning but" is the quintessential conversational style, often used in everyday discourse as a way of leading an audience through the speaker's thought processes.

iv. Use of contractions

Posner's opinions are replete with the use of contractions, which is typical of conversational language—see, for example: "won't"—161 F.3d 1117, 1119; "don't"—168 F.3d 1039, 1041; 159 F.3d 1016, 1019.

v. Speaking directly to reader

Posner uses several ways to create a sense that the judge is not remote but is instead engaged directly with the reader. For example, he often writes:

> "Remember that," "And remember," or some similar phrase—
> 392 F.3d 934, 938; 174 F.3d 870, 873; 162 F.3d 929, 933; 157
> F.3d 1092, 1098; 154 F.3d 404, 406; 151 F.3d 712, 715.
> "We come 'at last' to the merits of the case," "Another point and
> we are done," or some similar statement—371 F.3d 353, 359;
> 356 F.3d 767, 774; 148 F.3d 649, 655; 687 F.2d 899, 902; 686
> F.2d 550, 554; 683 F.2d 206, 213.

This way of writing gives the reader a sense of being carried along by the author in a shared venture, reinforcing an exploratory tone (discussed below). Indeed, sometimes Posner is quite explicit in bringing the reader along with him: "This discussion may seem to be leading ineluctably to [a particular] conclusion. . . . But not here."—395 F.3d 773, 778.

2. Exploratory tone

A judge who adopts an exploratory tone shares with the audience the difficulty of reaching a decision, rather than speaking down to the reader by adopting an authoritative tone. There are three ways in which Posner opinions are exploratory. The first is that he admits doubts about how to find the right answer. The second is that the opinion reads as though the author is thinking out loud about how to work through the issues—often speculating about questions that turn out not to be essential to dispose of the case but that are part of the judge's thought process.

The third way relates to the substantive criteria used to reach a decision. Posner rejects clear-sounding rules for deciding a case, such as textualism in statutory interpretation. Instead, he prefers more fuzzy standards (often the purpose of the underlying rule) or rules-with-exceptions, except when there are good pragmatic reasons for adopting a simple-to-apply rule.

I present examples of Posner's exploratory tone under the following headings:

—sharing doubts;
—thinking out loud;
—rejecting clear rules.

a. Sharing doubts

When Posner is sure of the answer, he tells us: "We are confident that he is wrong, although we cannot find any appellate case law directly on point"—157 F.3d 1092, 1094. But a remarkable number of his opinions admit doubts in the following three ways. Two direct ways are to indicate uncertainty about an answer and to specify that the answer falls in a gray area between two extremes. One less direct way is to suggest that the answer might be different if more information were available.

Occasionally, Posner hints at some of the reasons for judicial uncertainty. One reason is the nature of language: "We use with perfect clarity many words that we can't define, such as 'time,' 'number,' 'beauty,' and 'law' "—164 F.3d 337, 339. A second reason is the potential for personal predilection: "We must, so far as it is humanly possible to do, lay aside whatever personal reservations any of us may have either about abortion in general or about the decisions in which the Supreme Court has interpreted the Constitution as creating a right to abortion"—162 F.3d 463, 466. But usually, he is content simply to express doubts.

i. Unsure of answer

"How one translates all this vague information into a [legal conclusion] is a puzzler."—379 F.3d 457, 461

"The law is torn in two ways."—169 F.3d 1084, 1086

"This is a mysterious tort."—168 F.3d 1020, 1022

"We do not quite know."—150 F.3d 695, 703

"We are not experts in the investigation of violations of the commodity laws, so we may have overlooked reasons why, despite appearances, the effectiveness of the Commission's investigation of the appellants depends on its having access to their tax returns."—997 F.2d 1230, 1234

"We freely acknowledge that this is an uncertain area of law."—685 F.2d 192, 194

"Among other things that Congress was concerned with—at least ostensibly, and ostensible concerns are pretty much all a court can consider when construing a statute."—682 F.2d 1227, 1230

ii. Case falls between extremes

"The case just hypothesized . . . is intermediate between [two other examples.]"—109 F.3d 349, 353

"We have stated the issue of voluntariness as if it were a dichotomy, but, actually we are dealing with a continuum—with an issue of more or less."—49 F.3d 331, 334

"Ours is an intermediate case."—998 F.2d 513, 521

"[W]e recall Justice Holmes' admonition not to 'trouble ourselves with the thought that my view depends upon differences of degree. The whole law does so as soon as it is civilized.' "—687 F.2d 197, 202

"We do not want to pretend that the line between action and inac-

tion, between inflicting and failing to prevent the infliction of
harm, is clearer than it is."—686 F.2d 616, 618
"The present case is somewhere in between the two extreme situations discussed above."—676 F.2d 1139, 1143

Of course, the law might not leave it to the judge to eke out an answer in a gray in-between area but instead resolve the complexity with a
bright line rule. Thus, when a taxpayer receives a payment subject to an
obligation to repay, the "correct" result is to reduce the taxable receipt
by the value of the obligation to repay. But that is too difficult to do, so
"the court just asks how likely is repayment, and if the answer is, not
very, the receipt is treated as income"—792 F.2d 683, 690. Similarly,
Posner notes that the mechanically applicable grid used to identify
whether someone is disabled under the Social Security law produces a
borderline with close cases, but someone who falls on the wrong side of
the line presents "a 'hard' (harsh, not difficult) case"—670 F.2d 81, 84.

iii. Implying that more information could produce another result

Posner's opinions often suggest that he has done the best he could
with what he has, but that more information (either legal argument or
evidence) could lead to rethinking the result.

"[T]he parties have not suggested any better method."—388 F.3d
1069, 1079
"We have not been given enough information to enable us to do
this."—385 F.3d 1039, 1104
"[I]t is too remote a possibility [in this case], at least in the absence
of evidence that might make it plausible."—255 F.3d 394, 397
"Our system of judging is adversarial, and our judges are busy
people. . . . The plaintiff has to show that while her claim has
no basis in existing law, or at least the law's current pigeon-
holes, it lies in the natural line of the law's development."—168
F.3d 1039, 1042
"We can imagine an argument [etc.]" but, because the litigant did
not provide the factual groundwork, "we cannot evaluate the
argument."—154 F.3d 400, 403
"We are not pointed to any reason why."—147 F.3d 633, 635
"We do not pretend to be certain that this interpretation is correct. . . . But it is the best interpretation we can come up with

on the basis of the limited materials for decision."—990 F.2d
979, 984

b. Thinking out loud

Even when Posner does not suggest doubts about the result in a particular case, the opinion is often exploratory in another sense—thinking
out loud about legal issues not necessary for the specific decision. Posner's rejection of footnotes is closely related to this aspect of his exploratory style because he considers "[w]riting with footnotes, other than
purely bibliographic footnotes, [as] a lazy form of writing. . . . It enables the author to avoid having to decide whether a proposition is important enough to his argument to be integrated into it or sufficiently
dubious or marginal to be discarded."[53] The alternative he chooses is to
include the otherwise footnoted material in the text, thinking out loud
about its importance.

Posner's discussion of legal issues may be "unnecessary" in two
senses. First, the judge may speculate about a possible alternative line of
analysis that is not relied on to decide the case. My impression is that
Posner does this to a much greater extent than other judges. Examples
are presented in an endnote.[54]

Second, the opinion may adopt a position that is overbroad—that
is, more general than is needed to resolve the case—but is rejected as a
basis for decision on the facts of the case. For example, Posner asserts
that grandparents might have a liberty interest to prevent removal of
grandchildren from the grandparents' household under the due process
clause, but not on the facts of this case—669 F.2d 510, 513. As Posner
notes, some overly broad rationales are the basis of a decision; it is always up to the judge to decide how broadly to state a holding.[55] But
when the judge states a broad proposition that is inapplicable on the
facts and therefore not relied on to decide the case, the opinion is specu-
lative because it reaches out to discuss an issue whose disposition does
not help the litigant.

c. Rejecting clear rules

A third way in which Posner's opinions are exploratory relates to his
rejection of clear (sounding) rules. In this respect, Posner is different
from many judges influenced by law and economics, who opt for clear

rules to minimize judicial discretion. I do not mean that Posner has rejected law and economics insights—quite the contrary. His opinions are peppered with assumptions that people are likely to behave in "economic," self-aggrandizing ways. For example, in a case involving whether there was constitutionally adequate notice of a shortened filing period in an immigration case, he relies on the fact that

> [t]he bar is professionally and financially motivated to keep abreast of all changes of law as they occur. Its needs in turn create a demand for prompt publication in the print and electronic media. In highly specialized fields of federal law, such as tax, antitrust, and immigration, a specialized bar keeps an eagle eye on Congress and is assisted by a specialized press that churns out newsletters, loose-leaf services, and other legal bulletins in both print and electronic formats.—144 F.3d 472, 475

But clear legal rules are not an obsession: "There is a tradeoff between clarity and ease of application, on the one hand, and a tight fit between a legal rule . . . and its purpose, on the other. A simple, flat rule is deliciously clear and easy to apply, but it may be both underinclusive and overinclusive in relation to the purpose that animates it."—168 F.3d 956, 958

Posner often explains how choosing between a clear rule and a less clear standard requires subtle judgment. For example, a statute dealing with sale of a "security" did not apply to a sale by an entrepreneur owning 100% of a corporation's stock:

> There is a clear difference in principle between an investor and an entrepreneur; and while sometimes a person is both at once, often he is one or the other. . . . We agree that the costs of administering legal rules are a proper concern in designing those rules. But rarely will a net saving in those costs be produced by expanding liability, since even if the legal standard will be simpler and therefore cheaper to apply in each case the number of potential cases in which it will be applied will be greater. And if there were some net cost savings we doubt they could justify expanding liability to reach substantive evils far outside the scope of the legislature's concern.—687 F.2d 197, 200–02

But, in another context, Posner opted for a clear rule regarding jurisdiction:

Functional approaches to legal questions are often, perhaps generally, preferable to mechanical rules; but the preference is reversed when it comes to jurisdiction. When it is uncertain whether a case is within the jurisdiction of a particular court system, not only are the cost and complexity of litigation increased by the necessity of conducting an inquiry that will dispel the uncertainty but the parties will often find themselves having to start their litigation over from the beginning, perhaps after it has gone all the way through to judgment.—385 F.3d 737, 739–40

Posner's reliance on a standard is not to be confused with either a less open-ended rule-with-exceptions ("It is one thing to carve a hard-edged exception, necessary to avoid absurdity . . . ; it is another thing to replace [the rule] with a mushy, messy standard that would be hell [to apply]. A rule plus exceptions is not the equivalent of a standard."—168 F.3d 956, 959 [7th Cir. 1999]); or with a much-too-unstructured multi-factor test that completely fails to guide a judicial decision ("It is apparent that this test . . . leaves much to be desired—being, like many other multi-factor tests, 'redundant, incomplete, and unclear.' "—196 F.3d 833, 834–35 [7th Cir. 1999]).

Posner relies on standards to decide cases in (at least) the following three ways: (1) insisting that purpose rather than literalism or textualism is the right way to interpret legal documents (whether the Constitution, statutes, or regulations); (2) guessing about legislative intent rather than confidently identifying it; and (3) making sense of the law.

i. Purposivism vs. literalism

Posner is willing to consider purpose for interpreting all types of legal documents—such as the Constitution, statutes, and regulations.

(A) CONSTITUTION

"It has been a long time, however, since the contracts clause [of the Constitution] was interpreted literally."—148 F.3d 892

(B) STATUTES

"[Taxpayer] and the Tax Court have committed the common mistake of attempting to define a word without careful attention to its context; specifically they have attempted to define the word 'ownership' [in the tax code] without regard to the purpose of the statute."—873 F.2d 1018, 1023

"But there is no principle of interpretation that if the meaning of a word, phrase, or sentence plucked out of the heart of a statute seems clear if you do not read or think beyond it you must accept this as the meaning of the statute. . . . Surrounding sentences are context for interpreting a sentence, but so is the history behind the sentence—where the sentence came from, what problem it was written to solve, who drafted it, who opposed its inclusion in the statute."—17 F.3d 965, 967

"[L]egislative omniscience is not a realistic assumption. . . . [I]t belongs to a style of statutory interpretation—the rule-bound style rather than the purposive—that places greater emphasis on the text of statutes than on intentions behind them."—956 F.2d 703, 707

"[T]he present case is a textbook illustration of the deficiencies of literalism as a style of statutory interpretation. The idea that semantically unambiguous sentences—sentences clear 'on their face'—sentences whose meaning is 'plain'—can be interpreted without reference to purpose inferred from context is fallacious."—852 F.2d 1469, 1499 (concurring)

"In the absence of any contrary legislative history, so clear a statement in the principal committee report is powerful evidence of legislative purpose, which we are obliged to give effect to even if it is imperfectly expressed in the statutory language."—687 F.2d 194, 195

Other illustrations are cited in an endnote.[56]

(C) REGULATIONS

"It is very difficult to apply a regulation without a clue as to its purpose."—165 F.3d 1162, 1164

ii. Guessing about legislative intent

Another clear-sounding rule is deference to legislative intent, but it is often impossible to be sure what that intent would have been in the context of a particular case. Posner, of course, shares that scepticism: "That is not to say that the IRS's interpretation can be referred to legislative intent; probably Congress had no intent with regard to the question"—135 F.3d 457, 460. But Posner does not duck the difficult task of guessing about likely legislative intent (a fuzzy standard):

"[O]ur only job is to think our way as best we can into the minds of the legislators who enacted sec. 1326 and its predecessors back to 1918. We have to guess whether they would have wanted to complicate the statute and reduce its deterrent effect by including a state of mind requirement. . . ."—683 F.2d 1011, 1021 (dissenting)

"This background suggests that Congress probably wanted the courts to interpret the definitional provisions of the new act flexibly, so that it would cover new technologies as they appeared, rather than to interpret those provisions narrowly and so force Congress periodically to update the act."—693 F.2d 622, 627

And, sometimes, guessing about legislative intent means updating a law to fit the current legal landscape, even if that might not be something the historical legislature would have done: "The question is not whether Congress in 1933 or 1970 conferred any such remedies but whether it meant forever to preclude such remedies even if the result would someday be a bizarre discrepancy between the constitutional position of veterans and that of other citizens."—852 F.2d 1469, 1499 (concurring)

Guessing about legislative intent also leads Posner to rely on assumptions about how the legislative process actually produces a statute, illustrated by the cases cited in an endnote.[57]

iii. Making sense of the law

Another "fuzzy" standard on which Posner sometimes relies is making sense of the law. This is also a theme in Justice Scalia's opinions— "Making sense rather than nonsense out of the corpus juris"[58]—but the difference in judicial approaches lies in how broadly to define the circumstances in which to make the law make sense. Not surprisingly, a judge like Posner, who is suspicious of literalism and unwilling to be a "potted plant,"[59] is more willing than Scalia to make sense of the law, often appealing to common sense as an alternative basis for a decision.[60]

Posner's pursuit of a sensible result led a dissenter to argue that Posner had carried over his views on rational decision-making into statutory interpretation and to urge that "rationality is not to be expected;

that logic and justice are irrelevant; that tax law is 'positive law' in the classical sense of the term; and that nothing but the expressed will of the legislator is controlling. Tax law is a field where arbitrary fiat is king. . . ." But Posner responded that he could not "imagine a theory on which Congress could have desired [a contrary result]."—691 F.2d 1220, 1221.

No situation is more likely to illustrate the effort to make sense of the law than interpreting a statute specifying a time within which something must be done, when insistence on rigid adherence to the time limit makes little policy sense. That occurred in a case requiring a court filing within ten days in order to perfect an appeal, when the tenth (and last) day for filing fell on December 26th. The relevant portion of the filing rule stated that, when the last day for filing fell on a "legal holiday" (which included a day appointed as such by the President, Congress, or the state), that day would not be counted. Because the president had ordered all executive branch offices closed on December 26 (without declaring it a legal holiday), the chief judge of the district court followed suit and ordered the courts closed on that day. The chief judge made no provision for filing on December 26th, and specified that filings due on that date could be completed the following Monday. Posner concluded that the litigant should be excused for not filing by December 26th: "Considering the short period for filing [the motion] and the consequences of failing to file it on time, we think that [the rule] should be read to exclude any day on which the district court is either officially closed, as here, or (as also here) inaccessible as a practical matter without heroic measures."—149 F.3d 673, 674.

Another Posner opinion in the same vein interpreted the statutory language "before January 12" to apply to an event "on January 12," when no event would otherwise have been covered by the law: "But the general rule honored even by interpretive literalists is that if a literal reading would produce an absurd result the interpreter is free (we would say compelled) to depart in the direction of sense."—960 F.2d 1339, 1345. Consistent with this view, Posner also approved of Stevens's dissent in United States v. Locke,[61] which would have interpreted a law requiring filing "before December 31" to permit filing "on or before December 31," when a contrary result would have meant loss of a business and the statutory language seemed to be a scrivener's error.

C. Modern legal culture and individual judicial style

There should be enough in the prior pages to suggest that a personal/ exploratory style—or at least selected elements of that style—is doable for a judge who is so inclined. But is it a good idea? The initial thesis of this book was that judging must satisfy two political goals—the external projection of judicial authority to the public and the internal professional development of the law. English judges implemented these goals by developing a legal culture in which judicial law was derived from an external, substantive source and explained by judicial decisions. But they did not usually rely on an institutional style of presenting judicial opinions to enhance judicial authority because, in 18th-Century England, judicial law retained its preeminence without the aid of an authoritative "opinion of the court" or official reporting system. Instead, English judges continued to deliver oral seriatim opinions published in unofficial reports, which gave judicial law a flexibility that the profession knew how to exploit to adapt the law to change. U.S. judges inherited the English tradition but confronted a political system in which government authority was derived from the people and in which the legislature was the preeminent source of law. To meet this challenge to judicial authority, the U.S. judiciary evolved an institutional style that more closely approximated judicial opinions to legislation (namely, an officially published written opinion of the court), and an individual style that helped to project judicial authority (namely, a magisterial or technical/professional voice combined with an authoritarian tone).

The public projection of judicial authority through an authoritative institutional and individual style of presenting judicial opinions has always existed in tension with the internal professional reality that the development of the law is a messy task, fraught with conflict and uncertainty. And this has placed tremendous pressure in the Anglo-American tradition on the judicial opinion, which must implement the dual external and internal goals of preserving judicial authority and developing judicial law. That pressure has only increased in the modern legal culture where judges[62] acknowledge the intersection of law and politics, reject the older tradition of judges authoritatively declaring law derived from legal principle, and consider an institutional base for judging to be insufficient support for justifying judicial law in a legal system where democratic legislation is now the dominant source of law. The judge is no Hercules.[63]

This leaves modern judges with the difficult task of appealing to an external source of substantive law, without the protective armor of authoritative legal principle or a completely secure institutional base. My suggestion for responding to this difficulty, explained in the following pages, is to make greater use of a personal/exploratory style of presenting judicial opinions, as illustrated by Posner's approach. This style implements what I call "democratic judging," which is suited to a legal culture where law and politics are clearly related and in which a democratic process is essential to maintaining the authority of government institutions.

1. Democratic judging

The general idea behind "democratic judging" is that judges are members of the political community and should therefore be responsive to the political values that shape the law. This does not equate judging with democratic legislating or with a commitment to partisan politics. The values relevant to democratic judging can be more or less than those properly considered by a legislature. In other words, judicial responsiveness to political values does not mean that the judge can adopt political views the way a legislator can, only that the judge should be willing to consider such views when they are relevant to the law. The critical difficulty, of course, is to determine what is "relevant to the law." It goes without saying that this is a daunting task, requiring the judge to choose past, present, or future values without privileging any particular values in advance. But daunting or not, that is what judges do, and they must decide cases in a way that is faithful to "democratic judging" without at the same time claiming an authority that cannot be sustained.

Democratic norms insist on the inclusion of a variety of points of view in shaping the law, but the critical question is the process by which this occurs. There are strong reasons why the democratic process should not intrude too directly into judging—for example, through the electoral recall of either judges or judicial decisions. Otherwise, judging will be too receptive to popular points of view. But democratic participation remains an important value for modern judging. And the process by which this should occur is for the judge to reject an authoritative tone, even when using a personal voice. The judge should instead acknowledge the multiple values relevant to a decision and the resulting complexity and uncertainty in determining judicial law by adopting a tone that respectfully and deliberatively examines different principles and policies—that is, an exploratory tone.[64] And the judge should do this publicly and candidly so that discussion can occur about what happened in reaching a decision. Posner put in this way: "[The lower court judge] announced a conclusion, but gave no reasons for it, as we require. 'Legal rules committing decisions to judicial discretion suppose that the court will have, and give, sound reasons for proceeding one way rather than the other.' "[65]

The "democratic judging" argument for a personal/exploratory style is supported by Frank Michelman in his Harvard Law Review Foreword (entitled "Traces of Self-Government").[66] Michelman argues for the judge to engage publicly in "a process of normative justification without ultimate objectivist foundation—of justifying social choice, in the sense of satisfying all contenders without denying that their conflicts, of interest or of vision, are deep and possibly enduring." The judge "pick[s] out from the fullness of [the 'live detail' of a case] its normatively significant features—in a way that matches or appeals to the sensibilities of the audience or community." In a process Michelman describes as "dialogic," expressing a "vision of social normative choice as participatory, exploratory, and persuasive, rather than specialized, deductive, or demonstrative," the judge exercises an "enlarged mentality, always implicitly testing itself against the views of others."

In some respects, contemporary judicial use of a personal/exploratory style is a return to the early English judges' way of delivering individual opinions seriatim, but that comparison highlights the dilemma for modern judges. Early English judges, like modern U.S. judges, thought of themselves more in individual than in institutional terms because each judge was an expert oracle of the law, not its institutional source. As legal experts, they did their best to apply and explain legal principle. In that environment, individual seriatim opinions were intimate professional conversations among members of the bench and bar,[67] in which (unlike today) the technical/professional voice could comfortably combine with an exploratory tone. Consequently, the early English law reports reveal a conversational style in judicial opinions, as befits their oral presentation. For example, in the famous mid-18th-Century case of Millar v Taylor,[68] involving the English law of copyright, the judges converse with members of the bar by using a personal voice and exploratory tone. One judge asks, "What! is there no difference betwixt selling the property in the work, and only one of the copies?"; and later apologizes that "I should have here closed what I had to say; and am indeed ashamed to have taken up so much time. But the singularity of my opinion may seem to require some apology. . . ."[69] And Lord Mansfield tells the bar about the judges' failure to avoid dissent for the first time since he came on the bench: "We have all equally endeavoured at that unanimity, upon this occasion; we have talked the matter over, several times. . . . In short, we have equally tried to convince, or be convinced; but, in vain. We continue to differ. And whoever is right, each is bound to abide by and deliver that opinion which he has formed upon the fullest examination."[70]

Modern U.S. judges who seek to reestablish an exploratory tone have a more difficult task than an 18th-Century English judge. When they adopt a technical/professional voice, the tone is authoritative rather than exploratory, because they have lost the sense that they are engaging in a conversation with fellow members of the bar. Moreover, their participation in a broader political community working at the intersection of law and politics dramatically expands the range of controversial issues about which they are required to converse and requires democratic judging through adoption of a personal/exploratory style.

2. Judicial authority

The most fundamental question about adopting a personal/exploratory style in judicial opinions is whether it is incompatible with the external goal of projecting judicial authority as one of the three great departments of government. No one can seriously doubt that democratic judging is more honest about the internal development of judicial law. But can judging survive as a significant source of law if it fails to project its traditional authoritarian image? There is certainly an intuitive appeal to the idea that authoritarian judging serves the public's need for reassurance. Dostoevsky may have said it best when he has the Grand Inquisitor say that the people yearn for authority:[71]

So long as man remains free he strives for nothing so incessantly and so painfully as to find some one to worship. But man seeks to worship what is established beyond dispute, so that all men would agree at once to worship it. For these pitiful creatures are concerned not only to find what one or the other can worship, but to find something that all would believe in and worship; what is essential is that all may be together in it.

But the decline of the two traditional sources of judicial authority—(1) access to substantive legal principle through legal expertise and (2) an institutional base as one of the three branches of government—suggests that the public will not respond favorably to what it perceives as an unsustainable fiction of authoritarian judging, however much they might yearn for authority.[72] My own hunch is that democratic judging—expressed through a personal/exploratory style—is well suited to contemporary legal culture and is, therefore, likely to enhance rather than undermine the acceptance of judicial law.

There are even some signs that the U.S. Supreme Court wants to nurture a more open, less remote public image, despite its persistent opposition to permitting photographing or televising oral arguments and delivery of opinions.[73] First, Bush v. Gore has not been the only occasion in which the Court has permitted quick release of transcripts of oral arguments. That precedent has spawned several repeat performances—most notably in cases related to affirmative action, campaign finance, abortion, and university prohibition of campus recruiting by organizations that discriminate against gays. Second, since the mid-1990s, the audio portion of oral arguments has been fed into a room near the Court's chamber, permitting a greater audience to have access to the arguments in real time. Third, since 1998, reporters can listen to oral delivery of the opinions at the same time that they receive written copies, thereby facilitating their job in explaining the Court's work to the public. Fourth, from about November 2002, the prohibition of note taking by public spectators during oral argument was dropped. Fifth, Justices O'Connor and Breyer (but not Scalia) agreed to a rare interview on a Sunday morning network news show on July 6, 2003, discussing (among other things) how the Court arrives at a decision. Sixth, beginning with the October Term 2004, official transcripts of oral arguments will identify the Justices who ask questions. Although these will seem like minor steps to nonprofessional observers, they add up to a significant shift toward opening up the Court to public observation when measured against the Court's usual glacial pace of change.

In the final analysis, the case for a relationship between a personal/exploratory style of writing judicial opinions and judicial authority requires a more nuanced definition of the judges' audience. A plausible argument can be made that the general public will respond more favorably to democratic judging than to the traditional use of an authoritative tone. But it is still unlikely that the general public will pay much attention to the way judges write opinions. Few judges are remembered for their style of reasoning,[74] and what evidence we have on public acceptance of judicial opinions stresses substantive results, not judicial style, as the most important criterion in gaining public support.[75] Why then does individual judicial style matter, if the public impact is so uncertain?

Individual judicial style is important because the greatest risk to judging comes from cynicism bred within the legal profession. Institutions usually wear out from within—an idea popularized by Will Durant ("A great civilization is not conquered from without until it has destroyed itself from within").[76] When put under stress, an institution requires internal support to survive. Although it will be rare that a judge's individual style will undermine the authority of a single decision or the public's diffuse support for judging, a consistently fictional style of presenting judicial opinions can erode professional confidence in judging. This "termite" theory of the decline of government institutions posits the need for a profession that is not cynical about the judicial institution that it knows so well, because inevitable public dissatisfaction with particular decisions requires a professional defense. The hollowness of authoritarian judging will echo within the profession long before the institution crumbles, and a profession aware of its own posturing will provide a weak defense when confronted by a questioning public. Listen, again, to the Grand Inquisitor,[77] who is willing to accept "lying and deception" and who says that "only we, who guard the mystery, shall be unhappy." Perhaps the profession is strong enough to remain unhappy with a lie and preserve its own integrity. But it is difficult to sustain an institution over the long haul when its members know that it rests on a fiction, especially in a pluralistic and democratic society that values respect for inclusive public deliberation. Failure to pursue that ideal will undermine the professional confidence necessary to guard the law and judging.

There are two other important questions about the relationship of a personal/exploratory style to judicial authority. First, will that style loosen whatever restraints the law imposes on judging?[78] I think not. There is nothing in a personal/exploratory style that rejects or undervalues what counts as a "legal" restraint on judging, even though it legitimizes the introduction of criteria that might not traditionally fit into judicial law. Recognizing the intrusion of multiple legal values does not justify political partisanship or disregard for the legal values of stability, reliance, equal treatment, and concerns about institutional competence, even though it makes the value-laden content of existing doctrine more transparent and vulnerable to criticism. What Posner says about the pragmatic judge applies to a judge adopting the personal/exploratory style: "[T]he pragmatic judge will . . . recognize his ordinariness—. . . that he is not Apollo's oracle and thus is not merely a transmitting medium relaying to the public decisions made elsewhere, and that he must take responsibility for his decisions. . . . Who is more cocky—the dogmatist or the pragmatist?"[79]

Second, will a more candid personal/exploratory style undermine judicial authority in *particular* cases?[80] Imagine, for example, rewriting the opinion in Brown v. Board of Education in a personal/exploratory style. (Posner hints at what that might look like—for example, concern about the vagueness of the equal protection clause, respect for precedent and reliance interests, disdain for social science evidence, and judicial restraint when confronted with the argument that public education deserves special judicial attention.)[81] Although the Court's opinion in Brown v. Board of Education has elements of a personal voice—under Chief Justice Warren's leadership, it was written for lay consumption[82] and avoids legal jargon—its appeal to social science to support its conclusion that separate but equal "brands" one group as inferior flirts with a magisterial/authoritative appeal to "science" to support the conclusion. I suspect that the attempt to write for the lay public was as far as the Court thought it could go in abandoning the traditional trappings of an authoritative opinion. But, even assuming that some decisions require an authoritative tone to assure compliance, they are likely to be rare, just as the unanimous opinion is now rarely necessary for that purpose.

3. Obstacles to change

I do not mean that all judges should immediately embrace a personal/exploratory style or that any judge should do so in all opinions.

Indeed, there are formidable problems with the suggestion that judges adopt a personal/exploratory style.

First, not every case presents difficult enough issues to warrant more than a technical/professional voice and an authoritative tone.

Second, judges are lawyers who are trained in an authoritarian style,[83] with law review writing and lawyers' briefs as their models, and it is a lot of work for a judge to switch styles when doing so does not come naturally. In addition, the use of law clerks to draft opinions will probably dampen any inclination a judge might have to experiment with different styles.[84] And the judge may also be discouraged by the fact that, as one commentator has noted, "[g]reat [judicial] reputations are rarely based on opinions that are admittedly filled with cracks, crevices, and loopholes, and decisions reached by groping for light and by testing and re-testing hypotheses."[85]

Third, judging is an unsettling task—fixing losers and winners—and there is a psychological need for the judge to feel certain of the result,[86] which might in turn reinforce whatever other tendencies exist to adopt a more authoritative tone in the judicial opinion. I am not sure why this should be so. I am more confident of a result when I work through the doubts first, but then I went to college in the 1950s when existentialism was in the air, painting a (perhaps) romanticized image of making decisions in the face of uncertainty.

Fourth, the need to forge a majority opinion might suppress a more individual style of judging in many cases. Majority appellate opinions are committee products, and there will be pressure to default to the least controversial and most familiar and traditional way of writing opinions —which is the technical/professional voice and authoritative tone.

Fifth, many judges will lack the creative flair and raw brain power of a Judge Posner and might, therefore, be reluctant to attempt an unfamiliar personal/exploratory style. But that should not be a deterrent. It may take a Posner to introduce a new style of writing judicial opinions, but even those less proficient at its implementation would still do the legal system a favor by replacing a sterile and authoritarian style with a more tentative presentation of judicial law.

Sixth, a personal/exploratory style might be especially hard to adopt for the highest court in the jurisdiction where a personal voice might seem too intimate and an exploratory tone too tentative for a court that sits at the apex of a judicial institution. Justices on the U.S. Supreme

Court might feel especially burdened by their responsibility and anxious to project an air of authority that could be undermined by the familiarity and uncertainty of a personal/exploratory style. Political leaders often think that admitting a mistake would undermine rather than shore up public confidence, and high court judges may share that view.

A comparison of the opinion-writing styles of Justice Breyer and Judge Posner suggests both the reluctance and the potential for U.S. Supreme Court Justices to adopt a personal/exploratory style. Breyer seems to share with Posner a pragmatic conception of law, rejecting one-dimensional oversimplifying solutions in favor of multiple criteria, often without clearly indicating the weight of each criterion in the overall decision. For example, in a typical statutory interpretation case, Breyer will insist on considering purpose and legislative history as well as the text.[87]

Breyer's rejection of footnotes is also linked to uncertainty about judicial law, just as it is with Posner. Breyer states that "the major function of an opinion is to explain to an audience of readers why it is that the Court has reached [a] decision. It's not to prove that you're right; you can't prove you're right, there is no such proof. . . . [The job of the opinion] is to explain as clearly as possible and as simply as possible what the reasons are for reaching th[e] decision. . . . If you see the opinion this way, either a point is sufficient to make, in which case it should be in the text, or it is not, in which case, don't make it."[88]

But this shared vision of judicial law results in only a partial embrace of Posner's personal/exploratory style. The similarity is most apparent in Breyer's occasional expression of doubt about the result—that is, an exploratory tone—stating that the "answer is not obvious"; and "[t]he answers to the questions are not obvious."[89] This was sufficiently startling to warrant the following comment in a New York Times article by Linda Greenhouse: "Late in the Supreme Court term that ended last month, in the course of an opinion addressing Government regulation of indecent programming on cable television, Justice Stephen G. Breyer did something unusual. He acknowledged publicly that he was not sure how to decide the case."[90] A few other cases contain similar language by Breyer—for example: "We do not see any obvious answer to this problem";[91] "We do not raise these questions to answer them (for we do not have the answers). . . ."[92]

But Breyer has not gone further to adopt Posner's personal discursive voice, which speaks on a more intimate, nonprofessional level to the reader. When speaking for the Court, Breyer usually gives the conclusion at the very outset of the opinion (a difference from Posner that had attracted Judge Wald's criticism), and he uses dividers in his opinions (such as numbered and lettered divisions and subdivisions), unlike Posner. There is only an occasional tendency to be more direct with the reader—for example: "A description at the outset . . . will help the reader understand the significance of the complex factual circumstances that follow";[93] "we leave the interested reader to examine the case and draw his or her own conclusions"; "The reader can make up his own mind";[94] and "[c]onsidering the fact that those procedures seek to terminate a potential human life, our discussion may seem clinically cold or callous to some, perhaps horrifying to others. There is no alternative way, however, to acquaint the reader with the technical distinctions among different abortion methods and related factual matters, upon which the outcome of this case depends."[95] But there is nothing like the colloquialisms and self-conscious reduction of legal to everyday language that we find in Posner's opinions.[96]

The contrast between Breyer and Posner, despite their similar view of the complexity of judicial law, suggests that a judge might be drawn selectively to elements of the personal/exploratory style and especially to an exploratory tone that hints at uncertainty, rather than a personal voice that is too intimate with the reader. At least that might be true for the highest court in a jurisdiction; judges on intermediate appellate courts might be more willing to experiment with elements of a personal/exploratory style.

These comments suggest that it is difficult to change the way the legal culture influences the writing of judicial opinions. Judicial opinion-writing practices are "rules of the game" that give the judge a sense of appropriate participation in a common activity,[97] and judges (like participants in most group ventures) do not routinely think through the basic rules every time the game is played. But, assuming that my observations about the legal culture are correct and that there needs, in the long run, to be a proper fit between that culture and the judge's style of presenting judicial opinions, then it is important to encourage judges to adopt a personal/exploratory style.

But how best to provide that encouragement? How can we nudge judges into writing in a less familiar style? The best way is to provide examples of judicial writing in different styles—preferably to law students (who will become clerks and judges) before their ideas about how to write opinions become ossified, but at the very least to judges when they attend continuing legal education classes. That, however, is another book.

Postscript

We have come a long way from an age when confident, individual judges shared unofficially published oral opinions with fellow members of the bar, to a time when courts issued officially published opinions written in an authoritative tone (to provide a secure institutional foundation for judicial law when legislation was becoming the lawmaking norm), and, finally, to the present—when Legal Realism has led to skepticism about the judges' ability to access legal principles through legal training. If I am right in my original claim that the way judges present their judicial opinions is a response to a descending chain of concerns—political goals achieved through a legal culture expressed through an institutional and individual style of judging suited to that culture—then modern skepticism about authoritative judging should lead to a transformation in the way judges communicate their decisions. Separate opinions should become more common, and judges should write in a more personal/exploratory style, responsive to the multiple legal and political values inherent in making judicial law.

Not every legal system can be expected to absorb such skepticism into its style of presenting judicial opinions. The pull of legal tradition will often work against that result. For example, the Civil Law tradition calls for unsigned opinions of the court without dissents or concurrences, quite the opposite of the Anglo-American tradition. And these rival traditions are deeply rooted in varying theoretical conceptions of law—legislative supremacy in the Civil Law tradition denying an independent judicial power, in contrast to the Anglo-American common law tradition of judicial authority. In addition, more practical concerns are sometimes said to influence the Civil Law approach—for example, because judges lack life tenure, signed and/or separate opinions might expose them to political pressures on decision making that life tenured judges are less likely to experience.

But the creation in the 20th Century of new tribunals forces a re-thinking of judicial styles (whatever the legal tradition)—for example, international tribunals (such as the Permanent Court of International Justice and its successor the International Court of Justice), supra-national courts (such as the European Court of Justice and the European Court of Human Rights), and constitutional courts in different European countries (for example, Germany, Italy, Hungary), South Africa, and Asia.[1] Not surprisingly, these tribunals adopt a variety of institutional styles.

The Permanent Court of International Justice (PCIJ) (which heard its first case in 1922) and the International Court of Justice (which began in 1946) have always permitted and frequently used separate opinions, despite their judges serving for limited nine-year but renewable terms.[2] This may have been the result of U.S. and English influence over the creation of these courts;[3] although the United States did not become a party to the PCIJ statute or join its sister organization, the League of Nations, it always placed one judge on the court.[4]

By contrast, the European Court of Justice (ECJ) has always relied on unanimous and unsigned opinions of the court. This embrace of the Civil Law tradition may reflect the court's creation in the 1950s by the European Economic Community (which was the predecessor to the European Union), without English influence (England did not become a member until 1973). Moreover, the judges were limited to renewable six-year terms, raising the concern that loss of anonymity might have repercussions for the judges' future careers.

The pattern is more complicated for other courts. The dominant pattern in European constitutional courts is that of unsigned opinions without dissent,[5] although the German Constitutional Court (despite its Civil Law tradition and lack of life tenure) has employed dissents since 1971, albeit reluctantly and (as of 1997) in less than 10% of the cases.[6] By contrast, the European Court of Human Rights (ECHR) has allowed dissents and concurrences since its creation in 1959 pursuant to the 1950 European Convention for the Protection of Human Rights and Fundamental Freedoms by the Council of Europe.[7] This right to file separate opinions in the ECHR was affirmed in Article 45(2) of the Convention (now renumbered as Article 51[2]),[8] despite the judges serving for renewable nine-year terms. Perhaps the Civil Law tradition was less influential among the original ten members of the Council of Europe (Belgium, Denmark, France, Ireland, Italy, Luxembourg, Netherlands,

Norway, Sweden, and the United Kingdom) than it was for the ECJ; even a French participant in a conference preparatory to adoption of the ECHR argued that separate opinions had produced good results in the Hague Court of Justice.[9]

These variations among newer courts suggest that tribunals that are beginning to develop their own traditions should address the questions raised in this book about the institutional style of presenting judicial opinions. For example, should they adopt an opinion of the court? Should the opinion be signed? Should there be dissents and/or concurrences?[10]

As for the United States, judging seems ripe not only for an institutional style that places greater reliance on separate opinions but also for a more dramatic shift to an individual style that resorts to opinions written in a personal/exploratory style. Judging in our legal culture should be perceived as democratic judging, riddled with controversial legal and political value judgments. Consequently, the personal/exploratory style of writing opinions is more rather than less likely to foster acceptance of judicial authority.

Appendix 1
Law Reporting in Individual States, 1789–1860

This appendix discusses the rules and practices relevant to the institutional style of presenting judicial opinions in 15 states from 1789 to 1860. The statutes and law reports from which the material is taken are cited at the end of the text for each state in chronological order. Every effort was made to find all of the relevant legislation but some statutes were undoubtedly missed because the title did not always indicate that the law dealt with the reporting and writing of judicial opinions and because some material was buried in appropriations statutes. Chapter numbers in statute listings are given in arabic figures or roman numerals according to their original sources.

1. Connecticut

Connecticut adopted a statutory requirement that judges write opinions in 1784, well before it adopted an official reporting system in 1814. The 1784 law stated that its goal was to lay "a foundation . . . for a more perfect and permanent system of common law in this state." The law also required seriatim opinions, stating that "it shall be the duty of the judges of the Superior Court, in all matters of law by them decided . . . , each one to give his opinion seriatim, with the reasons thereof, and the same reduce to writing. . . ." However, judicial practice did not match the statutory mandate. According to one observer (Casto, *The Supreme Court in the Early Republic: The Chief Justiceships of John Jay and Oliver Ellsworth*, p. 110 [1995]), the judges in fact gave majority and dissenting rather than seriatim opinions. Later legislation seemed to waffle on this issue—an 1800 law did not require seriatim opinions and an 1806 law stated that the Supreme Court of Errors had to commit their reasons to writing "signed by *one* of the judges" (emphasis added), but an 1809 law required "each one [of the judges] to give his opinion. . . ."

The first unofficial reports were by Kirby, in 1789. Kirby's Preface stated that the 1784 writing requirement proved inadequate because the "the opinions were mislaid," the "arguments of the judges, without a history of the whole case, would not always be intelligible," and they would "become known to but few persons." This led to "uncertainty and contradiction attending the judicial decisions in this state, [which] have long been subjects of complaint." This was a serious defect, Kirby argued, in view of the fact that "deviation from the English laws [was] in many instances, highly necessary," because "the common law of England . . . was not fully applicable" in the United States. Kirby's successor, Root, also stated that law reports helped to develop U.S. common law.

There are also hints in Kirby's Preface of a concern with public understanding of his reports. He says that he avoided "technical terms and phrases as much as possible, that it might be intelligible to all classes of men." (Subscribers to Kirby's Reports included merchants as well as lawyers and public officials; Cohen & Seeman, "A Man without Qualities: Ephraim Williams, First Reporter of the Supreme Court," 9 *Massachusetts Legal History* 148 [2003].)

The unofficial reports must not have satisfied the need for judicial opinions—at least the need felt by judges. An 1804 law required the clerk of the Supreme Court of Errors to record the reasons given for reversal of decisions by the superior court and to distribute the original of those reasons to appropriate lower court officials.

Eventually, in 1814, an official reporter was required by law, with appointment to be made by the Supreme Court of Errors. The 1814 law had a four-year life, but was made permanent in 1818. None of the laws requiring appointment of a reporter said anything about the reporter's discretion in selecting cases to be reported.

The first official reporter (Day) exercised discretion regarding what lawyers' arguments to include. His Preface to Volume 1 of the Connecticut Reports stated that he aimed at "distinctness and conciseness" in presenting arguments of counsel, and sometimes "contented himself, especially where all the considerations urged are reviewed by the court, with mentioning [only] the names of counsel."

Both the 1814 and 1818 laws provided the reporter with $300 annual compensation; and an 1821 law left the compensation amount to the general assembly's discretion. These laws are silent about providing copies to the state and about ownership of the copyright and the reporter's retention of profits from sale.

None of these statutes contained any provisions to assure the quality of the reports (for example, specifying the size of type, quality of paper, etc.) or their timely publication.

Connecticut continuously tinkered with its written-opinion requirement. After the initial 1784 legislation, two subsequent laws (in 1800 and 1806) repeated the writing requirement. But two later statutes (in 1809 and 1815) replaced the writing requirement with a rule that each judge shall "give his opinion publicly, with the reasons thereof." The abandonment of a writing requirement seems to be confirmed by Day, when he states that "the opinions of the judges have been transcribed from their notes"—assuming that "notes" are not full opinions. Then, an 1820 law allowed the judges to provide opinions either in writing or by oral presentation—stating that when "the judges shall not publicly assign the reasons of their judgment, it shall be the duty of the judges to cause the opinion of the court to be reduced to writing" and filed with the court clerk. But the 1821 law restored the requirement that "the judges shall publicly assign the reasons of their judgment . . . ," seemingly dispensing with the writing mandate. An 1831 law then completely repealed prior law requiring the public assigning of reasons, perhaps because judges followed a practice of providing either an oral or written opinion, as appropriate, without a legal mandate. Finally, an 1858 law required the judges to prepare opinions in cases decided at the prior term and deliver them to the reporter. This last law sounds as though written opinions had become routine practice without a legal requirement and the law simply ordered their delivery to the reporter.

Throughout this period, there seemed to be difficulty getting the judges to render opinions in a timely fashion. The 1800 law required opinions to be filed with the appropriate clerk within six months of trial; the 1815 law required that the opinions be given "at the time [the judges] make known or pronounce their judgment"; the 1821 law stated that reasons must be assigned "at the term in which the cause shall be decided or at the next succeeding term"; and the 1858 law required delivery of opinions to the reporter in cases decided the prior term.

186 | *Appendix 1*

Statutes

1784—"An Act establishing the wages of the Judges of the Superior Court," cited as 3 State Rec., May, p. 9 (1784) in 1 Conn., at p. xxv, note (p) (1817)

1800—"An Act in addition to an Act, entitled, 'An Act for constituting and regulating courts, and appointing the times and place for holding the same,'" May, 1800, p. 525

1804—"An Act in addition to an Act, entitled, 'An Act for constituting and regulating courts, and appointing the times and place for holding the same,'" October, 1804, p. 681

1806—"An Act in further addition to and alteration of an Act for constituting and regulating courts and appointing the times and places for holding the same," May, 1806, par. 8, pp. 713, 716

1809—"An Act in addition to 'An Act for constituting and regulating courts, and appointing the times and place for holding the same,'" October, 1809, Ch. V, sec. 1, p. 22

1814—"An Act for the appointment of a reporter of judicial decisions," May, 1814, ch. 25

1815—"An Act in addition to an Act, for constituting and regulating courts and appointing the times and place for holding the same," May, 1815, Ch. I, p. 27

1818—"An Act for the appointment of a reporter of judicial decisions," May, 1818, Ch. 14, p. 308

1820—"An Act in addition to and alteration of an act, entitled 'An act in addition to an act for constituting and regulating courts, and appointing the times and places for holding the same,'" Ch. XVII, sec. 1, p. 393

1821—"An Act for constituting and regulating courts, and for appointing the times and places of holding the same," May, 1821, Title 21 (Courts), secs. 7, 8

1831—"An Act to repeal a part of an Act entitled 'An Act for constituting and regulating courts and for appointing the times and places of holding the same,'" June 1, 1831, Ch. IX, p. 318

1858—"An Act in alteration of 'An Act relating to courts,'" June 4, 1858, Ch. XXIII, sec. 1, p. 19

Law Reports Citations

Kirby, Reports of cases adjudged in the superior court, from the year 1785 to May, 1788, Preface, pp. iii–iv, xiii (1789)

Root, Reports of cases adjudged in the superior court and supreme court of errors, Vol. I, Introduction, p. xiii (1798)

Connecticut Reports (Day), Reports of cases argued and determined in the supreme court of errors, Vol. I, Reporter's Preface, p. xxvii (1817)

2. *Delaware*

Delaware was late in publishing reports—either unofficial or official. There was legislation in 1816 appointing a named individual to prepare a summary of cases interpreting statutes, along with a digest and index of state legislation, and to "lay the same before the legislature." But this law did not call for general publication, did not require inclusion of the judge's opinions, and did not cover cases other than those construing legislation.

There were two later legislative efforts to publish law reports (in 1830 and 1831), but they came to naught. In 1830, a resolution stated (in chatty tones) that a committee had conferred with the Chancellor, who was willing to act as the reporter of cases from the High Court of Errors and Appeals, if the state would advance him money for specified expenses; that the Chancellor affirmed that he had had access to opinions in cases "worthy of preservation" since he had become Chancellor; that he had notes of earlier cases in which he was counsel but that he expected to "be enabled" to "make true and full reports of [the earlier] cases" with the help of "other gentlemen, and with the aid of records." The resolution went on to state that the Chancellor would sell the volumes (including some to the state) and use the proceeds to reimburse the state (without interest), but that he "expects that no profit will be made but by the paper-maker, the printer and the book-binder." The resolution also provided for payment to the Chancellor of $300 "at such time or nearly so, as he shall have prepared for printing a volume of such reports," plus indemnity for any additional expenses. Then, in 1831, another resolution provided a similar arrangement as the 1830 resolution for another person, though without stating explicitly that the state would buy copies or that the sales proceeds would be used to reimburse the state for expenses. This arrangement for compensation, combined with the government advancing money to cover publication expenses that would be reimbursed by the reporter out of sales proceeds, created an arrangement similar to the modern salaried government employee, given the expectation that there would be no profits, except that the reporter was technically responsible for arranging for publication and sale.

Apparently, neither the 1830 nor the 1831 resolution was effective in obtaining the services of a reporter. In 1943, Daniel Boorstin observed that "[u]ntil 1837, when the first volume of Harrington's Reports was published, the Delaware lawyer had not a single volume of printed reports for his own state"; and that Boorstin's 1943 publication "comprise[d] virtually the only Delaware cases in print before 1814, and the only cases at common law before 1832."

Boorstin's Preface also contains some observations on how judges and lawyers recorded information about cases in the absence of published official or unofficial reports. He says that some of the judges' notes were more concerned with recording the evidence and lawyers' arguments for their own use than with preserving the judges' own opinion for posterity; that some lawyers' notebooks were copied by other lawyers, presumably because of their reliability (reminiscent of Plowden's experience in late 16th-Century England); and that some accounts of cases by different lawyers were contradictory.

Legislation in 1837 appointed the associate judge of the superior court residing in Kent County to report opinions from several courts, which led to Harrington's official reports of Delaware cases. The law gave the reporter discretion to report "on all such points as to him shall seem important to be known and understood by the people of this state," when enough of the cases had accumulated to form a "suitable volume." The legislation did not provide any rules to assure the quality of the law reports.

Regarding compensation, the 1837 law increased the judge-reporter's annual salary by $200 for performing the additional reporting tasks without making any provision about supplying the state with copies. Then, an 1841 law stated that Judge Harrington should continue his reports, deliver 100 copies to the office of the Secretary of State for distribution to selected officials, and receive (over and above the $200 supplement) additional salary in the form of $5 for each of the 100 copies.

There is nothing in the state legislation regarding ownership of the copyright or the reporter's retention of profits from sale.

There was no explicit statutory requirement that opinions be in writing, although Bates's Preface to his 1876 publication of chancery cases provides some evidence that chancery court judges wrote some opinions from 1814 to1833. Bates said that he "selected and prepared [cases] from manuscript notes of the Chancellors" and that "opinions have not, in every case, been published literally and fully, as they were found in manuscript." As for lawyers' arguments, Bates said that the

> arguments of counsel are not reported literally [because the] . . . notes of argument in a cause made by a Chancellor, for his own use only, would not bear a literal publication. They present but the thread of the argument, sufficient to refresh the memory of the Chancellor in his investigation of the cause, but meagre to the reader. . . . The arguments reported . . . are substantially as found in the manuscript notes; but they must of course fall short, both in force and fullness, of those actually made by counsel—able, and eminent in their profession, as all of the counsel were.

Statutes

1816—February 6, 1816, Ch. LXXXI, p. 146

1830—January 27, 1830, Ch. L, p. 39

1831—January 26, 1831, Ch. XCV, p. 82

1837—"An Act to secure a report of cases adjudged in this state," February 22, 1837, Ch. CXL, p. 188

1841—"An Act to continue the reports of adjudged cases and for other purposes," February 2, 1841, Ch. CCLXXVIII, p. 320

Law Reports Citations

Boorstin (ed.), Delaware Cases (1792–1830), Vol. 1, pp. III–VI (1943)

Harrington, Reports of cases argued and adjudged in the superior court and court of errors and appeals of the state of Delaware, Delaware Reports, Vol. I (1837)

Bates, Reports of cases adjudged and determined in the court of chancery of the state of Delaware, Opinions in chancery cases from 1814 to 1833, Preface, p. iii (1876)

3. *Georgia*

Unofficial reports date from 1824. The Preface to T.U.P. Charlton's 1824 volume suggests the financial difficulty that reporters encountered, stating that reports would have been published earlier "but failing the required number of subscribers, the plan was abandoned. . . ."

Prefaces to the unofficial reports stress the goal of improving knowledge of the law and the need for such knowledge to prevent conflicting judicial decisions. T.U.P. Charlton's Preface states: "Decisions . . . upon questions of first importance, are left to float upon memories of the gentlemen of the bar," leading to conflicting decisions. (Conflict among judicial decisions was likely in Georgia because there was no Supreme Court until it was established by state law in 1845, ten years after the Georgia Constitution authorized a state supreme court in 1835.) In a similar vein, G.M. Dudley's Preface to his 1836 unofficial reports stressed the value of "uniformity," which frees the judiciary from "suspicions of impartiality and restrains its power to oppress," and the usefulness of reports in "ensur[ing] greater deliberation and research in the adjudication of doubtful questions. . . ." And Robert Charlton's Preface to his unofficial 1838 reports states that "[i]t is all important to the citizens of a Republic that they should know the laws which control their property, liberty and lives. A general knowledge of the statutes is essential, and an acquaintance with the construction placed upon such statutes by the proper expositor is not a whit less necessary." (Robert Charlton also makes what must be the first reference to a judge as a "legal Hercules," whose conclusive fiat is unreviewable.)

It is unclear whether written opinions were common. T.U.P. Charlton's 1824 Preface states that "few opportunities are afforded for written decisions." But Robert Charlton's 1838 Preface notes that, although the constitution does not require written decisions except on motions for a new trial, "the practice in our circuit, (particularly of late years,) has been, to give written opinions in all matters, to which deliberate investigation has been bestowed."

In 1841, Georgia adopted an official reporting statute, which also required written decisions in certain cases:

> [I]t shall be . . . the duty of the Judges . . . to write out in a fair and legible hand, and place upon the minutes of [the] courts . . . , their decisions and judgments in full, in all cases of motions for new trials . . . and in all cases of decisions or judgments upon writs of certiorari, mandamus [etc.], as soon . . . as the nature and circumstances of the case will permit.

The 1841 law goes on to require government publication of law reports, rather than the appointment of an individual as reporter. The court clerks were required to transmit the written opinions to the Governor, who was required to publish them "whenever the same shall be of general interest . . . upon the cheapest and most advantageous terms." The law specified that the Governor should pay for publication expenses, provide copies to specified judges, and sell the remaining copies for the benefit of the state treasury. Publication was required to be within "August next ensuing the passage of the Act and annually thereafter." Surrency calls the reports published in compliance with the 1841 law one of the first examples of state government taking over the job of publishing judicial opinions; Erwin Surrency, *A History of American Law Publishing,* p. 41 (1990).

An 1845 law (adopted pursuant to Article III, sec. 1 of the state constitution creating the Supreme Court) revised the reporting requirement, reverting to the more traditional private entrepreneurial system and specifying that the judges of the Supreme Court should elect a reporter for a six-year term. The 1845 law repeated the 1841 law's requirement about writing opinions and added a requirement that they be delivered seriatim, "except in cases where [the judges] are unanimous." But the seriatim requirement was repealed on December 11, 1858.

The 1845 law fixed the reporter's compensation at $1,000 (with the proviso that a certain number of copies be delivered to various government officials); and the reporter was also allowed the copyright. Copies provided to the county clerks were available for free perusal by any person but had to be kept in his office, perhaps to preserve a market for the published volumes.

Later law suggests that compensation remained an issue. An 1847 law reversed a prohibition that had been contained in the 1845 law against the reporter appearing as counsel before the court and allowed such appearances; and it also required quarterly compensation payments to the reporter. A December 19, 1858 law added $3 to the reporter's compensation for "each copy" of the reports furnished to specified government officials, but was silent about ownership of the copyright or profits from sale.

Timely reporting was obviously a concern, as evidenced by the provision of the 1845 law that the reporter would forfeit one-fourth of his compensation if he did not publish the reports within four months after the session had ended, and another one-fourth for each additional tardy month, unless a majority of judges certified that the delay was not from the reporter's fault or neglect. There is nothing in the law to assure the quality of the reports, apart from calibrating compensation to account for delay.

The 1845 law required the reporter to attend all sessions and report "all the decisions there made, with the reasons therefor." (The 1847 law relaxed the attendance requirement, permitting nonattendance for "providential cause" or if relieved by the judge.) Although the reporter lacked discretion about which cases to report, he exercised discretion about what lawyers' arguments to include, noting that they were "valuable to the profession," even though some believed that they created a "useless expense." The inclusion of lawyers' arguments had apparently been controversial. Robert Charlton's Preface to his 1838 volume apologizes for "not mak[ing] the volume more perfect by adding . . . the arguments of counsel," because they were not in the records available to him and he "was unwilling to trust to the fading memory of counsel. . . ." And an 1850 law made it unlawful to insert lawyers' arguments beyond "a simple statement" of authorities cited and "points made," probably to keep down costs.

Statutes

1841—"An Act to require judges of the superior courts of this state to write out and place upon the minutes of said courts their decisions in full, etc.," December 10, 1841, p.132

1845—"An Act to carry into effect that part of the first section of the third Article of the Constitution, which requires the establishment of a Supreme Court, etc.," Acts of 1845, December 10, 1845, secs. 5, 12, pp. 18, 21, 23

1847—"An Act to amend the twelfth section of an act entitled an act to carry into effect that part of the first section etc.," December 24, 1847, pp. 81,82

1850—"An Act to amend the several acts in relation to the Supreme Court, so far as they relate to the reporter and assistant reporter," February 23, 1850, sec. 1, p. 140

1858—"An Act to repeal a part of the fifth section of the act, approved December 10, 1845, etc.," Law No. 63, sec. 1, December 11, 1858

1858—"An Act to allow and make compensation to the reporter, etc.," No. 140, December 19, 1858, p. 109

Law Reports Citations

T.U.P. Charlton, Reports of cases argued and determined in the Superior Courts of the Eastern District, etc., Book I, Preface, p. 4 (1824)

Dudley, Reports of decisions made by the judges of the superior courts of law and chancery, etc., Book I, Preface, p. 339 (1836)

Robert Charlton, Reports of decisions made in the superior courts of the Eastern District of Georgia, Book I, Preface, pp. 115–16 (1838)

Georgia Reports, Reports of cases in law and equity argued and determined in the supreme court of the state of Georgia, Vol. I, Preface, pp. v–vi (1847)

4. *Kentucky*

Unofficial reports began in 1803. Hughes's Preface to his 1803 reports (Volume 1) argued that publication would encourage uniform law about claims arising in Kentucky regarding lands carved out from the state of Virginia.

In 1804, the state legislature took the unusual step (for the early 19th Century) of requiring a government employee to perform law reporting tasks, instead of providing for appointment of a law reporter. The legislature required the clerk to make a copy of all decisions of the court of appeals since 1801 "in which the case was stated and the reasons of the court are given at large" and to deliver them to the public printer before April 1 next. The printer was required "to print the same with all convenient dispatch," and to deliver copies to various state officials, including the court clerk, so that the reports would be "free for the inspection of all persons who may wish to inspect [them] in the [clerks'] offices. . . ." Compensation was provided by increasing the clerk's salary for delivering reports to the printer at the rate of two cents per 20 words. The law stated that law reports were needed to provide "uniform" rules. The Preface to Volume 2 of the Kentucky Reports stated that it was the first volume published under this legislative authority.

The 1804 law also provided some public financial support for unofficial reports by requesting the Governor to buy a copy of Hughes's unofficial reports to be delivered to each court along with the statutes of the present session of the legislature, suggesting an analogy between law reports and legislation. (Hughes's Preface to Volume 1 had hinted at some financial difficulty, stating that it "was known [the work] would be expensive, and whether a sale of the book would or would not defray expense was uncertain.")

According to Hardin's Preface to Volume 3 of the Kentucky reports, the official reporting project undertaken pursuant to the 1804 law failed (he said that "the law it contained was hid in obscurity and trash"), and that Hughes had fallen several hundred dollars short of recouping actual expenses for his unofficial reports. This gave rise to a February 20, 1808 law, which made it lawful for the court of appeals to procure reports to be made of all decisions as shall be deemed useful. The court was "directed" to procure reports. Hardin states that the court asked him to do the job; that the 1808 law left the reporter discretion to select cases to be reported; and that lawyers' arguments were included if they were useful, until their inclusion made the reports too bulky, after which they were omitted. The 1808 law required the court to certify to the legislature a "reasonable compensation" for the reporter.

Hardin's Preface further observed that the legislature failed to carry out the 1808 law, but that this was remedied by an 1810 law, by which the general assembly authorized Hardin to publish his reports and provided for payment to him at the rate of $5 per volume upon delivery of 250 copies to the Secretary of State, based on a 600-page volume, with the compensation adjusted up or down for longer or shorter length; the law also left Hardin the copyright and all benefits accruing therefrom. The 1810 law imposed some quality control—by specifying the kind of type for the body of the work and for marginal material. The problem of delay was addressed by conditioning payment on depositing the reports with the Secretary of State by "the first day of January next." One commentator notes that the inadequate incentives to engage in law reporting resulted in Hardin publishing only one volume and that cases thereafter went unreported until 1815; Dietzman, "The Kentucky Law Reports and Reporters," 16 *Ky. L.J.* 16, 19 (1927–28) (hereafter "Dietzman").

The next statute dealing with law reports was passed in 1815. It changed the method of selecting a reporter, requiring the Governor to appoint a reporter with the advice and consent of the Senate, pursuant to which Bibb was appointed. The next year (1816), as a followup to the 1815 law, the legislature required the Secretary of State to deliver copies of Bibb's Reports to court clerks, who were required to keep them for use by the courts and for examination by others, and were subject to fine if they were "mislaid, abused, or written in."

The reporter had the duty to publish "the decisions," which may or may not have meant all decisions. The law also specified that arguments of counsel should be omitted. Compensation was at the rate of $5 per 600 pages, for delivery of 250 volumes for use of the commonwealth, and the reporter retained the copyright. Quality control measures included a requirement of printing in good type on good paper and well bound with a table of cases and index. In addition, the Secretary of State was to certify payment "if [he] shall find that the work is well done," and the Attorney General was authorized to make a motion in court to reduce payment if the work was not well executed.

Bibb's Introduction to his 1815 volume affirmed that the prior law reporting statutes were not working well. He said that the legislature had given "very limited encouragement to the publication of the decisions of our Courts," which he treated as "a warning to the reporter to contract his cases within the narrowest possible limits." He noted that Hughes (who had published Volume 1 of the Kentucky Reports) had not been reimbursed for "materials, press and engravings," and that Hardin still had on hand many copies of his earlier volume, which suggests inadequate demand.

Bibb stressed that "the decisions of the courts are not less operative than the acts of the legislature" and "ought, therefore, to be as public as the acts of the legislature." He also tied concern with knowledge of the law to "impartial" and "independent" judging—"If judges are ignorant and dull, they are more liable to the impressions of able and ingenious counsel. . . . If judges are learned, they are more likely to be impartial; prejudice and impartiality [sic] are the creature of ignorance. . . ."

Something must have gone wrong with the implementation of the 1815 law because, in 1822, the legislature repealed the prior law and stated that William Littell, who edited the laws of Kentucky, would receive $1 per hundred pages in each volume of law reports for the 250 copies that he delivered to the Secretary of State (a potential increase in compensation over $5 per 600 pages). (No mention is made of the ownership of the copyright or profits from sale in the 1822 law.) The reports had to be well bound and lettered, with letter and paper of the same size as Littell's editions of the laws of Kentucky; and payment was conditioned on the court of appeals certifying their approbation of the work. The 1822 law, like prior laws, required that arguments of counsel be omitted. Delay was discouraged by denying payment if the copies were not received by the Secretary of State within 60 days of the close of the term, unless Littell was unable to do so because he could not obtain paper or for some other reason beyond his control. The next year, an 1823 law added to the reporter's duties that he report previously unreported cases.

Still, there was a problem. An 1824 law authorized an advance payment to allow Littell to buy paper. At the same time, however, it repealed the requirement that reports be filed with the Secretary of State within 60 days after adjournment, requiring only that the reporter shall act "with all practicable dispatch."

The 1824 law also included legislative attention to the minutiae of reporting—prohibiting abstracts of cases except in the margin of the volume; and prohibiting publication of a table of cases cited or statutes expounded. It also qualified the 1823 requirement that Littell publish previously unreported cases, limiting the requirement to cases that settle some principle of law not settled in previously published reports. The 1824 law also required publication of the name of the judge who delivered the opinion as well as the judge whose decision was affirmed or reversed.

In 1825, apparently on the death of Littell, the legislature reinstated the provision of the 1815 law requiring the Governor to appoint a reporter with the advice and consent of the Senate (for two-year terms), with the same provision for compensation as applied to Littell in the 1822 law and subject to the duties provided by the 1824 law. It also reduced to 200 the number of copies to be delivered to the Secretary of State.

But, yet again, the legislature revised the system. An 1833 law repealed prior laws creating the office of reporter and authorized the court of appeals to consent to delivery of copies of reports to the Secretary of State, which in the opinion of the judges of the court, contained decisions "establish[ing] some new or settl[ing] some doubtful point, or otherwise by them deemed important to be reported. . . ." This indirectly gave the power to appoint a reporter to the court instead of the Governor. Compensation was set at $1 per 100 pages. The law also provided that the letter and paper be of the same size and quality as Hardin's reports; that the court certify that the work meets their approbation; and that 250 copies be delivered to the Secretary of State for use by the commonwealth. No mention was made of the copyright or profits from sale. In 1838, the legislature addressed the problem of delay by requiring the court of appeals to require the printing of reports by the beginning of the next term.

An 1851 law regularized the court of appeals' dominant role in official reporting. It required the court to appoint a reporter, and to direct which decisions should be published. It also required the reporter to print the reports on paper of proper size and superior quality, well bound in calf skin, and with good indexes and marginal notes. Compensation was set, as before, at $1 per 100 pages, assuming court certification that the reports met with their approval. Two hundred copies had to be deposited with the Secretary of State. The law was silent regarding the copyright and profits from sale.

As for lawyers' arguments, the 1854 Code of Practice specified that the reporter had a duty to report "the legal proposition made by counsel in the argument on both sides, with the authorities relied on for their support." One commentator says that these abstracts of arguments "were often of considerable length," and that an 1860 law restricted the reporter to "stating only the names of counsel and the authorities relied on for their support"; Dietzman, p. 25.

Throughout this period, Kentucky imposed a writing requirement for judicial opinions. Art. V, sec. 3 of Kentucky's first constitution in 1792 (as noted in Hughes's 1803 Preface) imposed an opinion-writing requirement—the court had to "state on the record, the whole merits of each case, the questions arising therefrom and the opinions of the court thereupon, and a summary of the reasons in support of those opinions." Then, a February 20, 1808 statute stated that the court of appeals "shall cause their decisions to be so recorded as to shew the governing principle or principles thereof," which the Reporter's Introduction described as an "arduous task." In 1823, the law was amended to reduce the burden on judges of preparing opinions in all cases, stating "[t]hat in future it shall not be the duty of the court of appeals to deliver written opinions in cases involving matters of fact only, or principles of law previously settled by said court; but it shall be sufficient . . . to state the principle or principles upon which the case may be determined, and to refer to the case or cases in which the said principle or principles may have been recognized."

Statutes

1804—"An Act concerning the promulgation of the opinions of the court of appeals," December 19, 1804, Ch. LXXI, p. 92

1808—"An Act amendatory of the law regulating the court of appeals," February 20, 1808, Ch. XII, p. 28

1808—"An Act to procure reports of the decisions of the court of appeals," February 20, 1808, Ch. XV, p. 32

1810—"An Act providing for the publication of Hardin's reports of the decisions of the court of appeals," January 25, 1810, Ch. CXLII, p. 81

1815—"An Act to provide for the further publication of the decisions of the court of appeals," February 8, 1815, Ch. CCLVI, p. 414

1816—"An Act for the distribution of Bibb's Reports," February 10, 1816, Ch. CCCXCII, p. 637

1822—"An Act to amend the several acts providing for the publication of the decisions of the court of appeals," December 11, 1822, Ch. DXXXVI, p. 244

1823—"An Act to prescribe the duties of the judges of the court of appeals, and for other purposes," December 29, 1823, Ch. DCXLIII, p. 372

1824—"An Act prescribing the duties of the reporter of the decisions of the court of appeals," January 7, 1824, Ch. DCLXXXII, p. 412

1825—"An Act to provide for reporting the decisions of the court of appeals," Ch. 86, January 3, 1825, p. 95

1833—"An Act to change the mode of publishing the decisions of the court of appeals," Ch. 52, January 4, 1833, p. 54

1838—"An Act concerning the court of appeals," February 8, 1838, Ch. 755, p. 159

1851—"Act of the General Assembly," November 6, 1851, Ch. XXII ("Courts"), Art. VI ("Concerning the reporting of its decisions"), p. 90

1854—Code of Practice of 1854, sec. 906 (published in an 1859 edition, by R. H. Stanton)

1860—"Duty of Reporter in reporting decisions of court of appeals," Title XXXIV, Court of Appeals, February 28, 1860

Law Reports Citations

Hughes, A Report of the causes determined by the late supreme court for the district of Kentucky and by the court of appeals, etc., Vol. 1, To the Reader, pp. v–vi (1803)

Sneed, Decisions of the Court of Appeals of the state of Kentucky, Century edition, Vol. 2, Preface, p. v (undated)

Hardin, Reports of cases argued and adjudged in the court of appeals of Kentucky, Vol. 3, Preface, p. iii (1810)

Bibb, Reports of cases at common law and in chancery argued and decided in the court of appeals of the commonwealth of Kentucky— Vol. 4, Dedication, pp. 3–6; Introduction, pp. 15–16 (1815)

5. Maryland

Unofficial reports date from 1809 to 1813, when Harris & McHenry published several volumes of cases decided from 1650 to 1799. Their Preface stressed the problem of contradictory decisions in the absence of reliable information about judicial decisions:

> This want of reports has been sensibly felt by the Bench and the Bar; and if the Courts, when obliged to rely on tradition, or the uncertainty

of memory, have been often embarrassed between the different asser-
tions of counsel, and hence have fallen into inconsistencies, it is evident
that these reports, when completed, will to a certain degree remove
such inconveniences, and prevent future contradictory decisions.

The 1824 legislature stated that it was "a matter of great importance
to the people of this state, that the decisions of the court of appeals
should be reported, in order that those rules and legal obligations, to
which the citizen is bound may be known and understood by him. . . ."
To that end, it adopted a resolution stating that "the publishers of the
Maryland reports [have] been deterred from a further prosecution of
their work by the expenses of publication, and the limited sale of same"
and that "the said decisions [could not] be reported and published by
individuals without the aid of the legislature." Consequently, "the Governor and council [were] authorised and required to contract with any
competent person or persons for reporting and publishing the said decisions in the manner which to them shall seem most expedient," agreeing
to buy no more than 200 copies "at a price not exceeding the usual
price of legal publications, and those copies to be at the future disposal
of the legislature." This is not usually considered the beginning of official reports in Maryland because the legislation refers to contracting
with a private publisher rather than appointing a reporter with compensation.

Writing judicial opinions had (according to the state legislature) become a common practice; the 1824 Resolution stated that "the court of
appeals have of late years reduced their opinions to writing." But opinions were apparently not written in every case. An 1833 law required
the court of appeals "to file the opinion of [the court], in all [equity appeal cases] when such determination shall be had upon argument, oral
or in writing, on [the] part of any of the parties in such cases."

The Maryland legislature continued to be concerned with subsidizing
publication of reports through state purchase after 1824. An 1839 law
provided for the purchase of as many copies of Bland's Chancery Reports as could be bought for $500. Two laws passed in 1852 provided
for payment by the state to purchase 200 copies of the sixth and seventh volumes of Gill's Reports of the Decisions of the Court of Appeals
covering 1847–49 and published in 1852, as well as 190 copies of Volumes 1 and 2 of Maryland Chancery Decisions (published by Woods
and Wingate) on condition that they contain not less than 600 pages

and that the cost be reduced to $5 per volume. And an 1853 law made a similar provision to purchase Volume 3 of the Wingate's Chancery Reports.

Official reports began in Maryland as a result of a provision in the 1851 Maryland Constitution, which imposed both a writing and a reporting requirement—specifying that "in every case decided, an opinion [of the court of appeals] in writing shall be filed, and provision shall be made by law for publishing reports of cases argued and determined by the said court." The reporting requirement was implemented by an 1852 law that required the judges of the court of appeals to appoint a state reporter to report "the cases argued and determined in the Court of Appeals as soon as possible, after the close of each session of the court."

The 1852 legislation was also concerned with the quality of the reports, stating that each volume had to "contain at least 600 pages, and . . . be printed on good paper, with clear type, and in size, form, quality of materials, and quantity of matter per page, . . . correspond[ing] as nearly as possible with" Volume 14 of the McFarland & Jencks New Hampshire Reports published in 1851. The price could not exceed $5 per volume, substantially bound, or $4.50, paper bound.

The 1851 Constitution and the 1852 law appear to require every court of appeals opinion to be reported, although they are not as explicit as the 1860 codification of Maryland laws—which states that the reporter "shall report all cases."

The reporter was entitled under the 1852 law to $500 annual compensation and the copyright. The state also agreed to take 200 copies, implying that it would purchase the copies rather than receive them without further payment. Although the law required that publication occur "as soon as possible" after each session, compensation was not explicitly conditioned on meeting a deadline.

Statutes

1824—"Decisions of the court of appeals," Resolution No. 50, January 31, 1824, p. 173

1833—"A Supplement to the Act, entitled, an Act to define and enlarge the powers of courts of equity," March 22, 1833, ch. 302, sec. 6, pp. 1093, 1094

1839—"Resolution authorising the librarian to purchase copies of

Chancellor Bland's Reports, etc.," April 4, 1839, Resolution No. 74, p. 1838

1851—Maryland Constitution of 1851—Art. IV ("Judiciary Department"), sec. 2

1852—"An Act entitled, an act to provide for publishing reports of cases argued and determined by the court of appeals," March 17, 1852, Ch. 55

1852—[Two statutes dealing with state purchase of reports]—"An act making appropriations, etc., March 30, 1852, ch. 119"; "An Act to purchase copies of the Maryland chancery reports, etc.," May 21, 1852, ch. 224

1853—"An Act to purchase copies of the third volume of Maryland chancery decisions, etc.," May 24, 1853, ch. 263, p. 365

1860—The Maryland Code, Public General Laws, Vol. I, Art. LXXX ("Reporter-State"), sec. 3, p. 553

Law Reports Citations

Harris & McHenry, Maryland Reports, being a series of the most important law cases argued and determined in the Provincial Court and Court of Appeals of the Province of Maryland (Volume 1), in the General Court and Court of Appeals of the State of Maryland (Volumes 2–4), Preface, p. iv (1809)

6. Massachusetts

In 1804, Massachusetts law provided that the Governor, with advice of the council, shall appoint a reporter. The statute was unclear about whether the reporter had discretion regarding what decisions to report —it says that he shall report "the decisions" of the court—but Ephraim Williams's 1805 Preface suggests that he had some discretion because he provides an explanation for including some cases about points of practice. Williams clearly exercised discretion about how to report arguments of counsel, of which he gave no "more than a sketch."

The 1804 law was not accompanied by a requirement that judges write opinions. Moreover, the fact that the 1804 law required the reporter "by his personal attendance, and by any other means in his power, to obtain true and authentic reports of the decisions" implies that many of the court's opinions were oral—hence the need for personal attendance (unless the reporter's attendance was needed to record lawyers' arguments). Ehpraim Williams's Preface to the first volume of official reports suggests that the norm was oral opinions when he stated that he felt "inadequate" to perform his job as a reporter because he did not take shorthand and that he was obliged to use his own language. The next volume (by Tyng), however, indicates that the reporter received a written opinion when it "has been prepared," and that the judges examined and corrected the reporter's notes for accuracy when the opinions had been delivered extemporaneously. And the report of one case, Woodbridge v. Brigham, 13 Mass. 556, 559–60 (1816), indicates that judges sometimes wrote opinions, though not necessarily for publication. In that case, the reporter had mistakenly published a judge's opinion as the opinion of the court even though it was counter to the court's actual decision. This occurred because the reporter had received the judge's papers containing the judge's written opinion in the case, which had in fact been rejected by the majority of the court and which the judge had abandoned.

The 1804 law provided for $1,000 compensation to the reporter, funded out of payments by attorneys admitted to practice before the court, without any provision that the reporter supply the state with copies. In addition, the reporter was entitled to the profits arising from publication. The law made no specific provision to assure the quality of the reports, except to require the reporter to be "learned in the law."

Tyng's 1808 Preface was somewhat unusual in noting an intra-professional educational role for law reports—helping the younger members of the bar learn about decisions involving points of practice, which (he acknowledges) may seem to more advanced members of the profession to unnecessarily swell the reports. Tyng also comments on the usefulness of law reports in conveying information about statutory and constitutional interpretation to citizens (besides those in the profession).

An 1826 law slightly changed the earlier law. It contained somewhat different wording regarding the reporter's discretion to report cases, although it may simply have enacted the practice followed by the reporter. It stated that the reporter "shall, at his discretion, report the several cases more or less at large, according to their relative importance, so as not unnecessarily to increase the size or number of the volumes of the reports." It also included a provision requiring written opinions in some cases, stating that "the court shall communicate to the reporter a statement in writing of their decision or opinion in the case" whenever judgment is entered other than at the term of the court. The implication is that written opinions had not yet become a uniform practice and that they were required to assure accurate reporting whenever judgments were delayed beyond the end of the term. The Revised Statutes of 1836 repeat the 1804 and 1826 laws, except for adding a provision that someone else "take notes of the decisions," if the reporter cannot attend the court.

Delay was apparently a problem, because an 1838 law stated that reports of cases argued and determined before September 1 in each year shall be published on or before that day.

Finally, in 1859, a law was enacted that (according to a 1916 ABA committee report) led to the "practice of writ[ing] opinions in practically all cases," although the version of the law I found was somewhat less expansive than what the ABA Report indicates; "Report of the Special Committee on Reports and Digests," 2 *A.B.A.J.* 618, 637 (1916). The version in the ABA Report says that the court shall "make and enter a proper order, direction, judgment or decree . . . or cause a rescript containing a brief statement of the grounds and reason of the decision to be filed therein"; the 1859 law I found says that the court shall issue a "rescript which shall also contain a brief statement of the grounds and reason of the decision announced."

Statutes

1804—"An Act for the appointment of a reporter of decisions in the supreme judicial court," March 8, 1804, Ch. LXVIII, p. 449

1806, 1810, 1815—"An Act for continuing an act entitled, etc." March 8, 1806, p. 496; March 3, 1810, p. 135 (extending time period of 1804 law); "An Act further continuing in force an act providing for the appointment of a reporter," February 3, 1815, p. 587 (extending reporter law indefinitely)

1836—Revised Statutes of 1836, Title I ("Of courts, and judicial officers"), Ch. 88 ("Of clerks, attorneys, and other officers of the courts"), p. 543 (discussing the contents of 1826 law)

1838—"An Act concerning the reports of the decisions of the supreme judicial court," April 12, 1838, Ch. C, p. 385

1859—"An Act establishing the superior court," April 5, 1859, Ch. 196, sec. 48, p. 351

Law Reports Citations

Williams, Reports of cases argued and determined in the supreme judicial court of the Commonwealth of Massachusetts, Vol. I, Preface, pp. iii, v (1805)

Tyng, Reports of cases argued and determined in the supreme judicial court of the Commonwealth of Massachusetts, Vol. II, Preface, pp. iii–v (1808)

7. *New Hampshire*

New Hampshire's first effort at official reporting was short-lived. An 1815 law required the supreme judicial court to "appoint some person, learned in the law" to be the reporter and required each attorney practicing in the court to contribute $5 per year to pay the reporter's "full" compensation; no mention is made in the law about copyright ownership or profits from sale, and it seems likely that "full compensation" meant only that no further payment from the state would be forthcoming, such as payment of expenses. However, the 1815 law was repealed the next year, leaving law reports to "the inclination and interest of private individuals;" "American Reports and Reporters," 22 *Am. Jurist* 108, 114 (1839). According to a Reporter's Note introducing Volume 49 of the New Hampshire Reports in 1872 (hereafter "Reporter's Note"), judges thereafter reported such cases as "taste, leisure and inclination might prompt," although the state provided some financial support by requiring the state treasurer to purchase a specified number of copies of the reports; see, for example, Ch. CCXXXV, June 27, 1835; Ch. 1152, July 5, 1851. (Perhaps that is why one commentator stated that a system of published reports of judicial decisions began in 1816; Albert Batchellor, "The Development of the Courts of New Hampshire," in

Vol. 4, *The New England States* [William Davis ed., 1897], Ch. 161, pp. 2295, 2309.)

Unofficial reports appeared in 1819. The Preface by the reporter (Nathaniel Adams) acknowledges the patronage received from the state legislature without further explanation. The Preface suggests that the reporter was motivated by a mixture of all three rationales for law reports —professional development of the law, projecting judicial power, and public accountability. He stressed professional concerns by noting that a correct report of judicial proceedings was important because legislatures settle only principle, not the application of law, and that application will benefit from knowledge of other decisions. Projection of judicial authority was suggested by his emphasis on a link between legislation and judging—"If . . . the law should be known, the decisions of the judges should be as carefully promulgated as the acts of the Legislature." And public accountability was served by reports that bring judging "under the controul and excitement of public opinion."

The reporters seem to have had routine access to written opinions, at least in most cases of any importance. Adams's Preface says that written opinions were communicated to the reporter in "every case," making the reports "in the highest degree authentick." But an 1872 Reporter's Note suggests that the practice might have been limited to important cases, stating: "For several years preceding [1816], the judges were in the habit, in specially important causes, of preparing carefully-considered, written opinions, more especially during the office of Chief Justice Smith."

The unofficial reporting system continued through the publication of Volumes 14 and 15 in 1851, but hit a serious snag thereafter, when the Secretary of State objected to the price (see the Memorandum in Volume 16). Despite three laws attempting to obtain publication of the volumes after Volume 15 (Ch. 1011, July 12, 1850, p. 972; Ch. 1152, July 5, 1851, p. 1089; Ch. 1458, July 2, 1853, p. 1364), Volumes 16–18 were not published until 1863, 1864, and 1865, respectively, which was after publication of the official Volumes 19 (1856) and 20 (1859).

The difficulty in obtaining the unofficial reports must have been apparent even before publication of Volumes 14 and 15 in 1851, because the New Hampshire legislature passed a law in 1850 creating the office of State Reporter for the superior court of judicature, to be appointed by the Governor with the advice and consent of the council. Volume 19, appearing in 1856, was the first to contain a reference to the "State Reporter" on its title page.

The 1850 law seems to have given little discretion to the official reporter about what cases to report, placing major responsibility on the judges; and it also imposed a written opinion requirement—"[E]ach justice . . . [shall] prepare for the press correct reports of all the cases in which the judgment of the court shall hereafter be pronounced by him, within six months from the time when such case shall be decided. . . ." (The Reporter's Note states that state laws on reporting made the reporter's duties "almost mechanical—practically those of a proof-reader. . . .") For their labors, the judges would receive $1.50 per page for reports "seasonably furnished." The judges had a duty to report the cases "more or less at length, according to their importance, so as not to unnecessarily increase the number or size of the volumes." The requirement that "all" cases be reported was relaxed in 1859—"Reports of such cases only shall be so prepared and furnished, as in the opinion of said judges establish some new or settle some doubtful point, not before adjudicated and reported among the decisions of the state, or as otherwise deemed by them important to be published." The 1850 law was silent concerning the quality of the reports, apart from concerns about delay and price.

The 1850 law provided the state reporter with a $400 annual compensation. Although nothing specific was said about the profits from sale, the reporter was apparently not expected to be an independent entrepreneur. He was to arrange for the sale of the reports or the copyright and pay over the proceeds, net of expenses, to the state treasury. The maximum price per volume was set at $3.50. In effect, the reporter had become a salaried government employee, with any sales proceeds being used to finance his publication expenses and any profits turned over to the government. This result is suggested by a complaint in the Reporter's Note (in 1872) that the payment to the reporter was a "beggarly pittance . . . —too much for droning laziness, and too little to be termed payment for honest work . . . [and] renders this office no inducement to any member of the profession, in active practice." (An 1855 law appears to adopt the same arrangement for the supreme judicial court, which was the successor to the superior court of judicature, although it does not clearly state that the sales proceeds, net of expenses, shall be turned over to the state by the reporter.)

Statutes

1815—"An Act to provide for publishing reports of the decisions of the supreme judicial court," June 26, 1815, Ch. XLVI, p. 16

1816—"An Act to repeal an act entitled 'An act to provide for publishing reports of the supreme judicial court,'" December 18, 1816, Ch. LXXXII, p. 75

1850—"An Act to establish the office of state reporter, and to define his duties," Ch. 961, July 12, 1850, p. 944

1855—"An Act to remodel the judiciary system, and for other purposes," July 14, 1855, Ch. 1659, secs. 32–33, pp. 1539, 1549

Law Reports Citations

Adams, Reports of cases argued and determined in the superior court of judicature for the state of New Hampshire, Vol. 1, Preface, p. iii (1819)

Reports of cases in the superior court of judicature in New Hampshire, Vol. XVI, page facing table of cases (1863)

New Hampshire Reports, Reports of cases argued and determined in the supreme judicial court of New Hampshire, Vol. 49, Reporter's Note, pp. v–vi, viii (1872)

Decisions of the Superior and Supreme Court of New Hampshire, from 1802 to 1809, and from 1813 to 1816, selected from the manuscript reports of the late Jeremiah Smith, Chief Justice of those courts, Preface, pp. v–vi (1879)

8. New Jersey

An 1806 statute required annual appointment of an official supreme court reporter by a joint meeting of the council and general assembly of the state. The law stated that the opinions would be "distributed in the same manner" as legislation, that the reporter was to be "skilled in the laws of this state," and, further, that the selection of cases should provide "useful information to the citizens of this state." The law gave the reporter discretion to choose such opinions for publication "as he shall think will tend to promulgate useful information to the citizens of this state" as well as in cases on "all other important and intricate subjects." The 1806 statute imposed a written-opinion requirement. Judges had to furnish the reporter with their reasons in writing in all certiorari cases and in other cases that were "important and intricate."

Ten years later, in 1816, Coxe's unofficial reports appeared (containing earlier cases from 1790 to 1795), addressed to the "learned profession." He also stated that he was presenting a concise rather than lengthy version of the lawyers' arguments because of the expense, indicating that the "modern practice of introducing the arguments of counsel at length, seems, in some instances, to have been carried to an extreme not warranted by any corresponding advantage." Anticipating some complaint from lawyers, he says that "their professional character is built upon foundations too solid" to result in "the slightest injury" from this plan.

A March 13, 1832 statute adopted similar official reporting and written-opinion requirements for equity cases as for law cases. The legislation stated that the cases "should be promulgated and rendered equally accessible to citizens, officers and professional men," and "should be known and understood to the end that the rules of property may remain stable and uniform." Although written opinions were to be provided by the judges in all cases, the reporter had a duty to include only cases that were "important or intricate" or would "tend to promulgate information useful to the citizens of this state." (This law leaves out the "as [the reporter] shall think" language in the 1806 statute, but there appears to be some reporter discretion in deciding which cases should be published.)

An 1845 law provided for a court of errors and appeals as a court of last resort and required opinions in writing by the judges of the court from whom an appeal was taken. An 1846 law adds a provision requiring the writing and reporting of all opinions from the court of errors and appeals, rather than leaving the selection of reported cases to the reporter's discretion.

Compensation was periodically adjusted. The 1806 law dealing with law reports specified $100 annual compensation, and this amount was raised in 1818 to $150. An 1820 law provided $250 compensation "for the present year," although it required appointment for a five-year term, and (according to the author of a later commentary on state law reports) compensation for the two years after 1820 was $200 per year;

"American Reports and Reporters," 22 *Am. Jurist* 108, 123 (1839). No mention was made of providing copies to the state or about ownership of the copyright or profits from sale. The 1832 law dealing with reports of equity cases did not fix a dollar compensation but left the amount to be determined by the legislature.

Numerous state laws and resolutions not only provided for appointing a printer but also provided financial help to the reporter by paying the cost of printing. The 1806 law stated that the reporter should furnish the opinions to the state printer, who would be compensated in the same manner as for printing state legislation. The 1832 law dealing with chancery reports required use of a printer appointed by the legislature or, if none was appointed, the printer of state legislation, but left compensation to later legislation. Thereafter, several resolutions (between 1832 and 1839) appointed a named printer for both the law and equity reports and provided for specific dollar payments per page. The 1846 law required use of a printer appointed by the legislature and the 1849 statute required the law and equity reporters to appoint the printers, at such rates as the legislature shall direct (which I assume meant state payment to the printer). Then, a March 15, 1855 law reverted to the earlier practice of specifying a named printer for a set amount per page.

A March, 19, 1857 law changed the method of compensation significantly. It required the law and equity reporters to arrange for printing at their own expense, but it also required the reporters to deliver 300 copies to the state treasurer in exchange for $3 per copy (which was an increase in compensation). The law was silent about copyright ownership and profits from sale.

Some of the state laws tried to assure the quality of the reports and their timely publication. The 1806 law made a nod in this direction, specifying that "cases and opinions [provided to the state printer shall be] regularly digested with a proper index." Numerous later resolutions (1832–1835) contained specifications about the quality of the reports—for example, "large octavo page." An 1849 law specified that no compensation was due either the law or equity reporters until delivery to the state treasurer of the "authorized number of copies." The 1855 law stated that each book should be "trimmed and bound in workmanlike manner." And the March 19, 1857 law made it the reporter's duty to arrange for printing "without delay, . . . upon good paper," with payment of a specified sum per copy for each volume (of not less than 600 pages).

Statutes

1806—"An Act for the publication of law reports," March 12, 1806, Ch. CXV, p. 688

1818—"A supplement to the act entitled 'An act for the publication of reports,'" February 12, 1818, p. 104

1820—"A supplement to the act entitled 'An act for the publication of reports,'" March 1, 1820, p. 54

1832—"An Act for the publication of reports of cases decided in the court of chancery, and other purposes," March 13, 1832, p. 156

1832—Resolution, March 16, 1832, p. 198

1833—Resolution, February 27, 1833, p. 170

1834—Resolution, February 24, 1834, p. 179

1835—Resolution, March 2, 1835, p. 172

1835—Resolution, November 10, 1835, p. 31

1838—Resolution, February, 28, 1838, p. 261

1839—Resolution, February 14, 1839, p. 240

1845—"An Act to regulate the proceedings of the court of errors and appeals," April 5, 1845, sec. 4, pp. 157, 158

1846—"An Act for the publication of chancery and law reports," Approved April 17, 1846, found in Digest of the Laws of New Jersey (4th ed. 1868), secs. 1–4, pp. 815–16

1849—"A supplement to the act entitled, 'An act for the publication of chancery and law reports, approved April 17, 1846,'" March 1, 1849, p. 244.

1855—"An act relative to the public printing," March 15, 1855, Ch. CV, p. 267

1857—"An act regulating public printing," March 11, 1857, Ch. LIII, p. 175

1857—"A supplement to the act entitled, 'An act for the publication of chancery and law reports, approved April 17, 1846,'" March 19, 1857, Ch. C, p. 293

Law Reports Citations

Coxe, Reports of cases argued and determined in the supreme court of New Jersey, Vol. I, p. 3 (1816)

9. New York

The first law authorizing an official reporter was passed by both houses of the New York legislature in March, 1804 and was allowed to become law by the Council of Revision in April, 1804.

New York had earlier unofficial reports but their date is unclear, and there is some dispute over whether Johnson or Coleman predated Caines (who was the first official reporter in 1804).* In any event, the statements made in the Prefaces by Johnson, Coleman, and Caines all occur at around the same time and are indicative of the attitude toward early law reporting in New York, whether the publications were official or unofficial.

The Prefaces written by Johnson and Caines unmistakably stress the goal of developing indigenous U.S. law. Johnson's Preface to Volume 1 of his 1808 reports reminds the reader that no English cases are law in New York "until they have been recognized and sanctioned by our own courts." And the Preface to his 1807 Volume states that law reports are "far more necessary in [the United States than in England], where new questions every day arise, in the decision of which, English adjudications cannot always afford a certain guide." Consequently,

> [w]e must look . . . to our own courts, for those precedents which have the binding force of authority and law. But how are their decisions to be known? . . . No man doubts of the propriety or necessity of publish-

---

* Caines's Preface to his first volume is dated February, 1804, which predates passage of the official reporting law, but he is considered the first official reporter appointed pursuant to the 1804 law; Langbein, "Chancellor Kent and the History of Legal Literature," 93 *Colum. L. Rev.* 547, 575 (1993) (hereafter "Langbein"). Caines may simply have written his Preface in anticipation of the law's passage. Johnson replaced Caines as the official reporter in 1805, probably because Kent thought that Caines was incompetent; Langbein, pp. 578–79.

Frederick Hicks, *Materials and Methods of Legal Research*, p. 135 (3d ed. 1942) (hereafter "Hicks"), gives a 1799 publication date for Johnson's Reports but Langbein gives 1808 as the date when Johnson cobbled together 1799–1803 cases; Langbein, p. 579. The Preface to Johnson's Reports indicates that Langbein is right because it refers to the 1804 official publication—consequently, Johnson's reports could not have predated Caines's 1804 official reports; Preface to Vol. 1 of Johnson's 1808 Reports. An earlier 1807 publication of Johnson's Reports of cases, Vol. I, Preface, p. 4, also refers to the 1804 legislation resulting in official reports. Coleman's Reports published in 1801 were therefore the first unofficial New York reports, and this is corroborated by a later commentator who says that Coleman was the first New York reporter; "American Reports and Reporters," 22 *Am. Jurist* 108, 119 (1839).

ing the acts of the legislature. As the rights and interests of every individual may be equally affected by the decisions of our courts, one would naturally imagine, that it would be equally a matter of pubic concern, that they should be made known in some authentic manner to the community.

In a similar vein, Caines states that "every member of th[e] profession" laments the "want of a connected system of judicial reports," and that, without law reports, determinations do not extend "beyond the circle of" litigants, and "points adjudged have been often forgotten." His Preface "present[s] the book to the profession."

The 1804 law authorizing the first official reporter in New York stated that "it shall and may be lawful for the justices of the supreme court of judicature . . . to appoint . . . a person as reporter. . . ." The law gave the reporter discretion to report cases he "deemed important to be reported." (This also seems to have been Johnson's practice—in the Preface to his 1808 reports, he claimed not to have "intentionally" omitted "decision[s] of any importance.")

The 1804 law fixed the annual compensation at $850 (referred to by Johnson in his Preface to the third edition as a "moderate salary"), which was raised to $1,250 in 1809. It also specified that publication should occur "as soon as conveniently may be after the expiration of each term." (The Preface to Johnson's 1807 reports had expressed a preference for "speedy publication" over accuracy.) However, the law did not condition compensation on compliance with this requirement. The reporter was also required to deliver enough copies to the Secretary of State at his own expense for distribution to courts in the various counties. No mention is made of ownership of the copyright or profits from sale.

In 1814, a statute required the law reporter to report equity cases as well (that is, cases from the chancery court) and Johnson was the first official reporter; Langbein, p. 579. In this instance, however, the Chancellor (Kent) determined which cases were of "sufficient importance" to be published, leaving the reporter no discretion. The reporter's compensation was raised to $1,500, but only because his reporting duties covered both law and equity cases, and (again) no mention is made of copyright ownership or profits from sale. This amount was raised to $2,000 in 1816, but was cut in half in 1820 and again in 1821, leaving $500 compensation; Moore, "One Hundred Fifty Years of Official New

York Reporting and the Courts in New York," 6 *Syr. L. Rev.* 273, 289 (1954–55) (hereafter "Moore").

Two later laws changed the appointment process for reporters. An 1823 law gave the power to appoint the reporter for both law and equity cases to the president of the Senate, the Chancellor, and the Chief Justice. An 1825 law gave the Chancellor the power to appoint a reporter for equity cases and this law appears to separate the law and equity reporting duties. The 1825 law also specified $500 compensation for the reporter of equity cases, so that the law and equity reporters each received $500; Moore, p. 290. No mention is made in the 1825 law of copyright ownership or delivery of copies to the state.

The reporters' approach to the inclusion of lawyers' arguments varied. Coleman and Johnson were tentative about including lawyers' arguments in the reports. Coleman's 1801 Preface indicated that in a future work he would "endeavor to give the arguments of the counsel more at length than I felt authorized to do in a work which professes to state no more than notes of practice." Johnson's Preface to his 1808 reports said that "[f]or obvious reasons, the arguments of counsel, except in a very few instances, are not inserted," although he gives no reasons. Johnson's Preface to the third edition of Volume 1 is more equivocal. He apologized for errors because, "[u]nused to the practice of shorthand writing, [he has] been obliged to rely on a quick pen and on memory" when "stating the arguments of counsel, in those causes in which they were deemed important." But Caines's 1804 Preface presented the conventional case for including lawyers' arguments before the judges' opinions were more thorough; he says that "[t]o omit altogether what the advocate has urged . . . has more than once been suggested," but that the arguments are presented in condensed form because "the reasonings of the barrister [form] the link which connects the case with the decision." Finally, in anticipation of modern practice, Johnson's Preface to his official Reports of Chancery cases noted the "almost entire omission of the arguments of counsel" because the opinions provide a "full discussion" of their content and because "steady and constant attendance on the court" would have been necessary for the purpose of recording lawyers' arguments.

Writing judicial opinions appears to have been the practice in early New York cases. Coleman's Preface suggests that he often received written opinions; he states that "large extracts from [the Chief Justice's] early minutes written with his own hand . . . have [been] committed to the press as I received them," but that, in other cases, he "assumed the liberty of . . . amending the phraseology, so as to meet my own conceptions of what was most precise and accurate." Johnson implies that opinions were written routinely in most cases. The Preface to Johnson's 1807 reports stated: "An object of . . . importance was to state the opinions delivered by the court exactly as they were pronounced. By the kindness of the judges . . . [who] have communicated to me their written opinions and notes, without reserve, I have been relieved from all solicitude as to the due performance of this part of my labors." And the Preface to his 1808 reports stated that "[t]he opinions of the judges are taken from their own manuscripts, and, in almost every case, are given exactly as they were pronounced." Caines's Preface also stated that the judges "have unreservedly given their written opinions." And Caines's Preface to his second edition refers to cases being recorded "from manuscript notes lent to him . . . by the Chief Justice" and then copied ("nearly the whole") in shorthand.

Whatever may have been the practice with the early law reports, the later reports of equity cases simply transcribed the judge's written opinions. One observer states that Chancellor Kent began the practice of providing written opinions (Henry Scott, *The Courts of the State of New York*, p. 261 [1909]), and the reporter (Johnson) stated that the opinions were "given exactly as delivered in writing, so that all danger of error . . . is entirely avoided."

Chancellor Kent's dominance of the equity reports—writing all opinions and determining which ones to publish—reminds us that law reporting helped to project judicial authority. (Kent had also insisted on preparing written opinions while a New York Supreme Court judge; Langbein, p. 572.) Kent was obviously making use of a judge-reporter collaboration to further his goal of creating judge-made law in the United States. In this respect, Kent was much like Story. Both wrote treatises that helped to create U.S. judicial law, both maintained close relationships to reporters to assist in that goal (Story with Wheaton and Kent with Johnson), and both sought the reporter's advice about opinions; Langbein, pp. 578, 582.

In 1847, the New York legislature substantially altered its official reporting system in the direction of the modern reporter-as-government-employee approach, acting pursuant to the mandate in the 1846 Constitution that "the legislature shall provide for speedy publication of such judicial decisions as it shall deem expedient"; Moore, p. 290. The law created the office of state reporter, appointed by the Governor and lieutenant governor. The reporter was explicitly denied any pecuniary interest in the reports, and was not allowed to practice in any court. The law makes no specific provision to compensate the reporter and payment may have been provided in an appropriations resolution; Surrency, p. 46, notes that some provisions regarding reporters were buried in appropriations acts. Publication of the reports was by the Secretary of State under the reporter's supervision and pursuant to a contract with a public printer, under a March 5, 1846 law dealing with public printing. The printer was obligated to provide a number of copies to the Secretary of State, and to sell the volumes (bound in leather) at the lowest possible price, according to the pages therein contained. Two later laws made it clear that the reporter did not own any copyright in any portion of the reports: an 1848 law said that neither the reporter "[n]or any other person" had any copyright in the reports, notes, or references, "but the same may be published by any persons"; and an 1850 law explicitly gave the copyright in notes and references made by the state reporter to the Secretary of State for the people's benefit.

The 1847 law required the reporter to publish "every cause argued and determined" that the court directed him to publish, but he also retained discretion to publish "such others as the public interests shall, in [the reporter's] judgment require to be reported," thereby combining judicial control and reportorial discretion. For the first time of which I am aware, New York law was explicitly concerned with timely publication and, to some extent, with the quality of the reports; the reporter was required to report each case within three months of decision and to prepare such "digests and tables of contents as are usually prepared for similar reports." The court was required to tell the legislature if the reporter was not doing his job faithfully, so that he could be removed from office.

The 1847 law also required the judges to deliver written opinions to the reporter in all cases in which oral opinions were not delivered in open court "to enable [the reporter] to perform his duty." This suggests that, whatever the prior practice regarding written opinions, the reporter was expected to transcribe at least some opinions that were orally delivered in court.

The 1848 law made a few amendments to the 1847 law. First, the Attorney General joined the Governor and lieutenant governor to appoint the reporter. Second, the publishing contract was entered into by the Secretary of State, reporter, and comptroller (not just the Secretary of State), after consideration of all publication proposals (not necessarily with the public printer); in addition, the price was set at no more than $3 for a volume of 500 pages. Third, the law required reporting "as soon after [a decision] as practicable," implying that the earlier three-month requirement was too rigid. Fourth, it specified that the judges "shall deliver to [the reporter] such written opinions as they shall prepare upon questions of law," which further suggests that the judges were not required to write opinions in every case.

Statutes

1804—"An Act to authorize the supreme court to appoint a reporter," April 4, 1804, Ch. LXVIII, p. 234

1809—"An act to amend and continue in force an act, entitled, 'An Act to authorize the supreme court to appoint a reporter,'" March 27, 1809, Ch. CXXIV, p. 117

1814—"An act relative to the salary of the reporter appointed by the justices of the supreme court," April 15, 1814, Ch. CXCIII, p. 243

1823—"An Act concerning the supreme court, etc.," April 17, 1823, Ch. CLXXXII, sec. III, pp. 208, 209

1825—"An Act to provide for reporting the decisions of the court of chancery," April 20, 1825, Ch. CCLXIII, p. 385

1846—"An Act to provide for the public printing," March 5, 1846, p. 20

1847—"An Act in relation to the judiciary," May 12, 1847, Ch. 280, sec. 73, pp. 319, 342

1848—"An Act to provide for the publication of the reports of the court of appeals," April 11, 1848, Ch. 224, p. 335

1850—"An Act to amend the act to provide for the publication of the reports of the court of appeals, passed April 11, 1848," April 9, 1850, Ch. 245, p. 479

Law Reports Citations

Coleman, Cases of practice adjudged in the supreme court of the state of New York, Preface, p. 29 (1801)

Caines, New York Term Reports of cases argued and determined in the supreme court of the state, Vol. I, Prefaces to first (1804) and second (1813) edition, pp. iii–vi

Johnson, Reports of cases argued and determined in the supreme court of judicature, etc., Vol. I, Preface, 3d ed., pp. 3–4 (1807)

Johnson, Reports of cases adjudged in the supreme court of judicature, etc., Vol. I, Preface, p. 215 (1808).

Johnson, Reports of cases adjudged in the court of chancery of New York, Vol. I, Preface, p. 5 (1816)

10. North Carolina

Unofficial reports began with the publication of Martin's Reports in 1797; Hicks, p. 132. Some years later, a law passed at the 1818 legislative session required appointment of an official reporter by the judges of the state Supreme Court. It provided for $500 annual compensation, with delivery of a specified number of copies to certain officials without further expense to the state; no mention is made of the ownership of the copyright or profits from sale.

An 1822 law modified the compensation arrangement so that the reporter's annual compensation was reduced to $300, but the copies provided to government officials (considerably more than were required by the 1818 law) were to be printed at state expense. (An 1836 law further increased the number of copies to be provided to state officials.) Both the 1822 and 1836 laws allowed the reporter to obtain the copyright at his own expense (thereby allowing him to print, publish, and sell at his own expense any additional copies not provided to the government).

The 1818 law conditioned compensation on delivery to the state official within nine months of the decisions being made. An 1821 law changed the publication date to three months after the end of the term (extended to five months by an 1831 law). Another provision in the 1818 law required the reports to be "in a neat type and on good paper."

Nothing was said explicitly in these laws about the reporter's discretion in selecting either cases or lawyers' arguments for publication. The 1818, 1821, and 1822 laws (and a later 1836 law) only refer to reporting "the" decisions of the court. But the 1822 law adds that the reporter shall "report the decisions of the present Supreme Court, which have not already been reported," and the July, 1823 Preface to Volume 8 of the North Carolina Reports says that the reporter had no discretion about what cases to report—"To some it may seem necessary to explain the insertion in [Volume 8] of cases apparently unimportant. . . . The act under which the Reporter is appointed leaves him no discretion, but enjoins the publication of *all* cases."

Nothing was said about requiring judges to write opinions until 1836. An 1836 law imposed a duty on the judges "to deliver their opinions or judgments in writing, with the reasons at full length upon which they are founded." (One commentator says that the legislature gave the court discretion about whether to write opinions, but does not cite the law that granted this permission. Walser, "Some Thoughts about Law Reports and Law Reporting," 1 *N.C.J.L.* 114, 118 [1904].) The law also ordered the clerk not to enter decisions on the record until one of the judges "shall have delivered publicly and in open court the opinion of [the] court, stating at length the ground and argument upon which such opinion shall be founded and supported," as well as providing the clerk with the written opinion—presumably to prod the judges into giving the reasons for their decisions as publicly as possible.

Both the 1821 and 1836 laws imply some difficulty in filling the reporter's job because they provide for the clerk of the court to perform the reporter's duties if "no suitable person should offer to fill" the reporter's position.

Statutes

1818—"An Act supplemental to the act concerning the supreme court," Ch. II, sec. XIII, pp. 5, 8

1821—"An Act to amend an act supplemental to the act concerning the supreme court," Ch. XIV, p. 16

1822—"An Act to repeal the thirteenth section of an act, passed in the year 1818, entitled 'an act supplemental, etc.,'" Ch. XX, p. 21

1831—"An act to extend the time within which the reports of the supreme court shall be published," ch. XXXIX, p. 32

1836—"An Act concerning the Supreme Court," January 17, 1836, No. LXVI, secs. 13, 16–17, pp. 96, 99, 100–01

11. *Pennsylvania*

Hopkinson's Judgements in the Admiralty of Pennsylvania, containing only six cases, is sometimes said to be the first of the state law reports (in 1789), beating out Kirby's Connecticut Reports by one month; Hicks, p. 132, n.4. In any event, significant reports of Pennsylvania cases soon appeared in 1790 in Volume 1 of Dallas's U.S. reports, which contained only Pennsylvania cases. Dallas's Preface states his purpose as "preserving the principles on which the future judgments of our courts are founded."

Until 1845, Pennsylvania had only unofficial reports, but there was earlier legislation dealing with written opinions. An 1806 statute required judges to give a written opinion with their reasons, "if either party by himself or council require it." And an 1812 law required written opinions when required by plaintiff, defendant, or "any third person interested in the event of the cause." These laws might have been a response to a 1784 statement by the judges of the Pennsylvania Supreme Court "that the judges do not hold themselves bound to assign any reasons for their judgments"; Respublica v. Doan, 1 U.S. 86, 89 (Pa. 1784). They appear to be a modest effort to provide interested parties with reliable information about what the judges decided, rather than to facilitate publication of law reports.

Some of the prefaces to early unofficial reports imply that judges wrote opinions, at least sometimes. Binney's 1808 Preface to Volume 1 of his reports stated that he had "access to notes and opinions of the justices." (Binney, like early English reporters, says that he began to keep notes of the arguments and decisions of the supreme court for his own use and "not with any fixed view to publication.") And Sargeant & Rawle's 1818 Preface to Volume 1 of their reports stated that the opinions of some justices who had died had "been mislaid."

The reporters were also concerned about how thoroughly to report the arguments of counsel. Binney's Preface apologized for the "imperfect report of [lawyers'] arguments," and Sargeant & Rawle said that "the arguments of counsel, have in many instances been unavoidably omitted" and they apologized for the "imperfect manner in which they are sometimes given" in other cases. A later unofficial reporter (Grant, in 1859) also apologized for omitting some lawyers' arguments because the older files contained only the "opinion of the court." (Grant explained that private enterprise was still needed to publish supplemental volumes containing cases nearly all of which had been "marked to be reported," but which had not previously appeared because of a two-volume-per-year limit.)

In 1845 legislation was passed requiring appointment by the Governor of an official reporter, with "experience and learning in the law." (Fifteen years earlier there had been a proposal to finance official reports through a tax on writs of error but the money was used for other purposes; Fishman, "The Reports of the Supreme Court of Pennsylvania," 87 *Law Library J.* 643, 657 (1995) [hereafter "Fishman"].) The 1845 law required the reporter to publish all opinions "endorsed [by the court to be] of sufficient importance for publication" and such "others as he shall deem necessary and important for publication," providing a combination of judicial control and reporter discretion regarding publication. Reporter discretion also persisted regarding lawyers' arguments—Barr's Preface to Volume 1 of the first official reports remarks that the "arguments of counsel . . . may seem too much compressed; but it will be seen that the substance has been preserved. . . ."

The 1845 law contained several provisions to assure the quality of the law reports—for example, that the type and paper should be as good as prior unofficial reports and bound in law calf binding, with no less than 550 pages per volume. And an 1858 law permitted binding in "good substantial law sheep." In addition, the reporter was limited to two volumes per year.

The 1845 law gave the reporter the copyright in the reports and no other provision was made for compensation. If the sales price exceeded $4 per volume, the reporter was subject to a $200 fine.

The legislature indicated its concern about the reporter discharging his responsibilities by requiring a $10,000 bond, with at least two sureties, "for the correct and faithful performance of his official duties," and also required that he take an oath or affirmation before a judge that he will perform his duties "with correctness, impartiality and fidelity."

The 1845 law also contained an unusual provision prohibiting publication of minority opinions, but this prohibition was relaxed by an 1868 law permitting publication of dissents on constitutional matters. (There had been complaints about the frequency of dissents [Fishman, pp. 657–58], and a 1916 Report to the ABA stated that "the dissenting opinion, except in rare cases, should not be published"; "Report of the Special Committee on Reports and Digests," 2 *A.B.A.J.* 618, 621 [1916].) In any event, prohibitions on dissents were often disregarded, and dissents on both constitutional and nonconstitutional issues were published before and after 1868; Simpson, "Dissenting Opinions," 71 *Pa. L.Rev.* 205, 208 (1923).

Statutes

1806—"An Act to alter the judiciary system of this commonwealth," Ch. CXXII, sec. 25, pp. 334, 345

1812—"An additional supplement to an act, entitled, Act to alter the judiciary system of this commonwealth," March 6, 1812, Ch. LIII, p. 82

1845—"An Act to provide for the appointment of a reporter of the decisions of the supreme court of the commonwealth of Pennsylvania," April 11, 1845, No. 250, p. 374

1858—"A Supplement to an act to provide for the appointment of a reporter of the decisions of the supreme court of the commonwealth of Pennsylvania," February 22, 1858, No. 50, p. 40

Law Reports Citations

Dallas, Reports of cases ruled and adjudged in the court of Pennsylvania, etc., Preface, 1 U.S. (1 Dall.), p. vii (1790)

Binney, Reports of cases adjudged in the Supreme Court of Pennsylvania, Preface, Vol. I, p. vii (1808)

Sargeant & Rawle, Reports of cases adjudged in the Supreme Court of Pennsylvania, Preface, Vol. I, pp. iii–iv (1818)

Pennsylvania State Reports (Barr), containing cases adjudged in the Supreme Court, Preface, Vol. I, p. 3 (1846)

Grant, Reports of cases argued and adjudged in the Supreme Court of Pennsylvania, Preface, Vol. I, p. iii (1859)

12. Rhode Island

The first published law reports were official—pursuant to an 1844 law. The law required appointment of an official reporter by the General Assembly and specified that the reporter shall make a "true report of the decisions of the supreme court, on all legal questions that shall be argued by counsel and shall publish them annually," which suggests that the reporter lacked discretion about what cases to report. The law said nothing about maintaining the quality of the law reports.

The 1844 statute mandated written opinions if requested by the reporter; the law stated that the "court shall, when requested by the reporter, communicate to him in writing a statement of their decision or opinion in any case." It is unclear whether it was common for judges to write opinions before the 1844 law. Angell stated in an advertisement to Volume I of the official reports that he was including cases decided prior to his appointment (they went back to 1828) when he "succeeded in finding . . . written opinions," and he noted that these opinions "were not prepared by the judges with a view to publication." I cannot tell whether Angell's difficulty arose because old written opinions were hard to find or because they did not always exist.

The 1844 law provided $100 annual compensation to the reporter plus profits from publishing the reports, and provided for purchase by the state of 125 copies at market price for distribution. A memoir of the first reporter Angell, at the beginning of Volume I of the official reports, complained that this mode of compensation was the "wors[t] arrangement for the reporter" that could be imagined, because it left him with the risks of publication but destroyed the chance of sale to other parties. The implication—which is that the distribution of state-purchased copies might undermine the reporter's potential for profit—suggests that the legal availability of profits was not always realistic and that a compensation-plus-profits arrangement for the reporter might be the equivalent in some states of the reporter being a salaried employee without further financial risk or opportunity.

An 1845 law altered the appointment method from the General Assembly to the judges of the Supreme Court, specifying that the reporter could not be one of the Supreme Court judges. Then, an 1857 law shifted back to General Assembly appointment, permitting Supreme Court justices to be appointed.

Statutes

1844—"An Act in relation to the supreme court," Revised Statutes of 1844, secs. 19–22, pp. 88, 94

1845—"An Act in amendment of 'An act in relation to the supreme court,'" January, 1845, p. 62

1857—"An Act in amendment of 'An act in relation to the supreme court,'" January, 1857, p. 12

Law Reports Citations

Rhode Island Reports, Reports of cases argued and determined in the supreme court of Rhode Island, Vol. I, Advertisement, pp. xxi–xxii; Memoir of Joseph K. Angell, p. xviii (1847)

13. South Carolina

Bay's unofficial reports appeared in 1809. The Preface to Book 1, Volume 1 of Bay's Reports stated that cases were selected on the basis of "novelty and importance" and when they "tended to the enlargement and stability of our system of jurisprudence," relying on the reporter's discretion to choose cases for publication. The reporter noted that, although the opinions often repeated English common law, the principles had more weight coming from "our" courts. The Preface also stated that the reports provided only a "sketch" of lawyers' arguments and did not always provide a full report of the judge's opinion.

The date on which South Carolina first had something we might call official reports is unclear. A 1799 law required judges to deliver their written opinions seriatim and required the court clerk to keep these opinions with the records of the case. An 1811 law added the same requirement for equity cases. But these laws did not authorize official reports.

An 1816 law adopted an official reporting system, but did not appoint a reporter from the bench or bar. Instead, it imposed a duty on the judges to select for publication all important opinions and directed the clerk to transmit them to the state printer for publication with the state statutes. It provided payment to the clerk for delivering selected opinions to the printer in the same manner as for providing copies of records in other cases.

Apparently, the reporting system provided in the 1816 law was not implemented. Nott & McCord, in the Preface to their 1820 reports, stated that "such a publication would have been out of the question"— explaining that the 1816 law was a useless provision because it made access to the opinions very difficult, "without an index and without corrections." Consequently, the state printer "adopted the plan presented in this volume," which presumably meant that the opinions were delivered to Nott & McCord for publication instead of the state printer. (This explains why some of McCord's later volumes—such as Book 5, Volumes I and II—state on the title page that the reports were published "pursuant to the Act of Assembly of 1816.")

Nott & McCord's 1820 Preface justified their law reports as a way to help the state develop indigenous U.S. law and to prevent the common occurrence of the judges being unclear about points "decided but a year before." They noted that, without reports, the courts were forced to rely on English law, because they had nothing else. They also indicated that "[s]ome cases have been omitted" and they lamented not having had access to the lawyers' arguments because they were needed for a full understanding of the law. They also complained that reports were not likely to be routinely forthcoming because the compensation "scarcely . . . [equals that for] one or two cases of slander or trespass," without explaining what that compensation might be; perhaps appropriations legislation that I did not discover provided compensation, or perhaps they were referring to meager profits.

Desaussere's Preface to his 1817 Volume of unofficial reports of equity cases argued that opinions should be published "to enable the people to know what the law is"; and that "this knowledge is equally important to the judges" to prevent contradiction and uncertainty.

In 1823, South Carolina repealed its 1816 law dealing with publication of judicial opinions and provided for an official reporter (in an appropriations law); John O'Neall, *Biographical Sketches of the Bench and Bar of South Carolina*, Vol. I, p. 271 (1859). Compensation for one year was set at $1,000 (an 1824 appropriations law provided the same amount), and the reporter was required to deposit one set of the reports with the clerk of the court in each district. No mention was made of copyright ownership or profits from sale. Selection of the reporter was by joint ballot of both houses of the legislature. The reporter's duties were "to report the judicial decisions . . . and such arguments and statements of fact as shall be necessary to a correct understanding of said decisions. . . ." The shift to an official reporter is indicated by the description in the front of the volumes—Book 6, Volume II refers to McCord only as a member of the bar, but Book 6, Volume III refers to McCord as the State Reporter; and an 1827 law refers to the State Reporter.

The 1816 law mandated written opinions: "the opinion . . . shall be written by one of the judges [of the court], and read at the time the decision shall be made. . . ." It also required the judges to sign their names to signify concurrence with the court's opinion. However, the law did not take the further step of requiring seriatim opinions (unlike the 1799 law) and, in fact, explicitly stated that "it shall not hereafter be necessary for the judges . . . to give separate opinions in cases decided by them, except where they shall think proper so to do. . . ." (Bay's 1809 Preface had stated that he reported the opinions seriatim when there "has been occasionally any difference of sentiments on the bench, or where the novelty and importance of the points decided, made it proper," implying that seriatim opinions were a common if not universal practice.)

Bay's Preface implied that the judges sometimes wrote opinions, stating that many cases were reported in the judges' own words, and that, in other cases (where the opinions were mislaid or lost), the reporter used his own notes. Treadway's Preface stated that published reports would reduce the inconvenience experienced by the bar in reading manuscripts of opinions, suggesting that the judges wrote opinions. McCord says in his 1822 Volume that the reporter applied for copies of judges' opinions but they came too late (after completion of the volume), strongly suggesting that the judges wrote opinions in many cases; and his 1826 Volume also says that some manuscripts arrived too late for inclusion.

Statutes

1799—"An Act supplementary to an act entitled 'An Act to establish an uniform and more convenient system of judicature,'" December 21, 1799, secs. XIV, XL, pp. 293, 295, 300

1811—"An Act to regulate the courts held by the associate judges of this state at the conclusion of their respective circuits, etc.," December 21, 1811, secs. II, IV, pp. 311, 312–13

1816—Act of 1816, December 19, 1816, p. 18

1823—"An Act to make appropriations for the year 1823; and for other purposes," December 20, 1823, secs. XV, XVI, pp. 228, 233

1824—"An Act to make appropriations for the year 1824; and for other purposes," December 18, 1824, pp. 256, 257

1827—"An Act to regulate the sittings of the Court of Appeals, etc.," December 19, 1827, sec. III, p. 332

Law Reports Citations

Bay, Reports of cases argued and determined in the superior courts of law in the state of South Carolina, Book 1, Vol. I, Preface, pp. vii–viii (1809)

Desaussere, Report of Cases argued and determined in the Court of Chancery of the state of South Carolina, etc., Vol. I, Preface, p. xxii (1817)

Nott & McCord, Reports of cases determined in the constitutional court of South Carolina, Book 4, Vol. I, Preface, pp. iii–iv (1820)

McCord, Reports of cases determined in the constitutional court of South Carolina, Book 5, Vol. I, Advertisement, p. iii (1822)

Treadway, Reports of judicial decisions in the constitutional court of the state of South Carolina, Book 3, Vol. I, Preface, p. iv (1823)

McCord, Report of Cases argued and determined in the Court of Appeals of South Carolina, Book 6, Vol. III, Notice, p. iii (1826)

14. *Vermont*

Publication of unofficial reports dates from 1793; Hicks, p. 135. Nathaniel Chipman's Preface to Book 1 stated that these reports were needed to develop U.S. law because the "english common law writers fail us, in many instances," and because judges and lawyers could not rely on memory alone. Chipman also says that "[i]t was not practiced for the judges to give their opinions seriatim," a point he felt necessary to mention because his audience might think he had omitted the argument of his brethren on the bench.

The expenses of publication led Brayton to observe (in the Preface to his 1820 Volume of unofficial reports) that continuation of his series depended on the expenses being paid—which may explain the passage in 1823 of a statute providing for official reports. Daniel Chipman's 1824 Preface to his official reports supports this implication—noting that unofficial reports had been issued at "great intervals of time."

The 1823 law required the Governor, with the advice of the council, to appoint a "suitable person" who was "learned in the law" to report the decisions of the Supreme Court. Chipman's Preface to the official reports emphasized the importance of reports in limiting judicial discretion. He stated that "under any Judiciary system, it is necessary that reports of all decided cases be made, and published for the direction of the Courts, and for the information of the people." Acknowledging that the "judge has discretion in ascertaining what the law is," he argued that, "when ascertained, [the judge] is bound by it," or else "the discretion of the Judge is unlimited; and the Judge governs, not the law." Reports of cases would prevent unlimited discretion by enabling the judge to advert to prior decisions.

An 1827 law changed the method for obtaining law reports and relied on the Secretary of State instead of an appointed reporter, rejecting the traditional private enterpreneurial model for law reporting in favor of a government publication. The law imposed a duty on the justices of the Supreme Court to provide a true copy of decisions to the Secretary of State "subject to the order of the general assembly." But relying on the Secretary of State apparently did not work, because an 1829 law required appointment by the Governor of a reporter, who is now described as a "suitable person," without the "learned in the law" specification.

The laws about reporter discretion to report cases varied over time. The 1823 law gave the reporter discretion to publish those opinions "as he shall think of sufficient importance." The 1827 law referred to the judges' duty to report "all decisions . . . proper to be reported." But the 1829 law was less clear, stating that the reporter had a duty to prepare "reports of cases decided in the supreme court."

An 1837 law shifted the power to appoint the reporter from the Governor to the legislature. This law also eliminated doubts about the reporter's discretion, explicitly imposing a duty to report "all cases that may hereafter be decided," as well as cases "already decided and not reported."

Compensation provisions also varied over time. The 1823 law provided $400 annual compensation for the reporter, plus profits from publication, and was silent regarding copies for the state. The 1827 law, requiring the justices to deliver copies of decisions to the Secretary of State, provided an additional $125 compensation per justice per year. The 1829 law provided that the reporter would "receive such compensation as the general assembly shall direct" for arranging to deposit 500 copies with the Secretary of State "for the benefit of this state," and that the Secretary of State was required to sell the reports at a price that would defer the "whole expense" of publication. The 1829 law was silent regarding the copyright and the right to profits, but the large number of copies (500) delivered to the Secretary of State for sale to defray all publication expenses suggests that the reporter did not have the right to profit from further sales, making him the equivalent of a salaried government employee.

The 1837 law reverted to the traditional entrepreneurial approach, providing the reporter with $700 compensation per year plus the proceeds of sale. The compensation was higher than in 1823, perhaps because all decisions were now required to be reported. In exchange, the reporter was required to publish ("at his own expense") 200 copies, 50 of which were to be provided to the Secretary of State "for the use of the state." In addition, the reporter had to publish and deliver one copy for each organized town in the state (for which the state would pay the actual cost of publication). An 1839 law reduced compensation from $700 to $450, perhaps because it deleted a requirement found in the 1823 law that the reporter personally attend court sessions.

Later law (in 1847) added 35 more copies to be delivered to the Secretary of State above those already required, but provided for reimbursing the reporter for the additional expense. And an 1858 law required delivery of a total of 100 copies to the Secretary of State, for all of which the state would pay the cost of publication, binding, and transportation, which meant that the reporter's compensation and proceeds of sale would be supplemented by the state paying for its copies at cost.

The laws said nothing about the quality of the reports. As for delay, the laws required the judges to deliver their opinions to the Secretary of State (1827) and to the reporter (1837) "on or before October 1 in each year," but these laws did nothing to assure the timely action by the reporter. In 1843, the reporter was required to publish and distribute all cases within one year after decisions were made.

Initially, judicial opinions were not routinely written. Brayton's Preface to his unofficial reports states that he relied on the manuscript "notes" of a former Chief Justice for 1816–17 cases and that, because the opinions of the "several Judges, or of the Court, were not *written,* [he] could not attempt to furnish the reasons and arguments of each judge, or of the court, at length." Chipman's Preface to his official reports refers to a 1797 statute requiring written opinions but says that the law "neither was nor could be complied with in any case," given the demand on the judges' time from riding circuit to each county.

Later law is less clear on whether written opinions were becoming more common. The 1823 statute creating an official reporter stated that the reporter should "obtain true and authentic reports" either "by his personal attendance, and by any other means in his power," which implies that written opinions might sometimes have been available, even if not required or routinely anticipated. The 1827 law required the justices to "make true and authentic reports [of decisions] . . . as soon as may be after such decisions shall have been made . . . [and] furnish a true and correct copy of such reports to the Secretary of State," which suggests written opinions. The 1837 law repeated the requirement that the reporter personally attend the court but then imposed a duty on the judges to "prepare and furnish to the reporter . . . correct reports of the opinions by them severally given," which suggests that personal attendance may have been only for the purpose of obtaining reliable information about lawyers' arguments and that written judicial opinions were available. In any event, the 1839 law deleted the requirement of personally attending court sessions, perhaps because written decisions were sufficient for the reporter to do his job.

Statutes

1823—"An Act to provide for reporting the decisions of the supreme court of judicature," October 28, 1823, Ch. 12, p. 9

1827—"An act to provide for reporting the decisions of the supreme court of judicature, and for other purposes," November 13, 1827, Ch. 7, No. 4, p. 6

1829—"An Act, providing for the publication of the reports of the supreme court," October 29, 1829, Ch. 7, No. 3, p. 5

1837—"An Act, to provide for reporting the decisions of the supreme court," November 1, 1837, No. 9, p. 7

1839—"An Act, in alteration of the act providing for the reporting of the decisions of the supreme court, approved November 1, 1837," November 19, 1839, No. 2, p. 4

1843—Joint Resolution No. 44 of 1843, p. 34, referred to in Compiled Statutes of the State of Vermont (1851), sec. 67, footnote †, p. 86

1847—No. 32 of 1847, referred to in Compiled Statutes of the State of Vermont (1851), sec. 68, pp. 86–87

1858—"An Act relating to the reports of the supreme court," November 20, 1858, No. 41, p. 46

Law Reports Citations

Nathaniel Chipman, Reports and Dissertations in two parts, Part I (Reports of cases determined in the supreme court of the state of Vermont, etc., Book 1, Preface, pp. 4–5 (1792))

Brayton, Reports of cases adjudged in the supreme court of the state of Vermont, Book 1, Preface, pp. iii–iv (1820)

Daniel Chipman, Reports of cases argued and determined in the supreme court of the state of Vermont, Book II, Vol. I, Preface, pp. 30–31, 34 (1824)

15. Virginia

Virginia had a number of unofficial reporters predating appointment of an official reporter in 1820. Wythe issued reports of chancery cases in 1795. Reports of court of appeals cases followed, the earliest by Bushrod Washington in 1798. (For a description of early Virginia courts, see Brockenbrough, "Decisions of the General Court of Virginia," 2 *Virginia Reports Annotated* [2 Va. Cas.], Preface, pp. 101–03 [1826].) The early reporters said that they got help from the judges in the form of "notes," which are probably not the same as written opinions. Bushrod Washington's statement "To the Reader" thanked the judges for their "notes," which enabled him to correct "those cases in which I had misconceived the opinions which had been delivered." And Hening & Munford's 1808 Preface stated that they had access to "the notes of the judges (which they were so obliging as to furnish). . . ."

It is unclear how much discretion these early reporters exercised in choosing which opinions to report, but it is clear that they were very concerned about reporting lawyers' arguments. Hening & Munford explained the dilemma in their 1808 Preface—"[T]o give [the arguments of counsel] at large . . . would swell the volume to an enormous size. To omit them altogether . . . would not only convey a very inadequate idea of the merits of the several speakers, but often leave the case perfectly unintelligible." They therefore decided to pursue a "middle course." Alert to lawyers' sensitivities, they hoped that "the gentlemen of the bar" would accept their "apology for the brevity with which their arguments are reported." They also apologized to their readers for those few cases where the need for speedy publication resulted in including arguments "nearly as they were delivered," making the reports "too lengthy."

Unofficial reports were so often delayed that the judges petitioned the speaker of the Virginia House of Delegates to provide for "public patronage" of the law reports; 12 Virg. (1 Robinson) 6 (1843) (reporter's Preface quotes judges' communication to the Virginia legislature). The legislature responded with an 1820 law requiring the court of appeals to appoint a reporter. This was not the only time the judges used their influence to improve state reporting. The Preface to Brockenbrough's 1826 Decisions of the General Court states that the "Judges came to the resolution that their Decisions should be" published and "the task . . . devolved on me."

Prior unofficial reports had a less exalted pedigree. Wythe's reports of Chancery cases were, according to a memoir of the author, intended to "vindicate the decisions of the author from the opposite opinions of the Appellate Court. . . ." And Bushrod Washington in his statement "To the Reader" in his Volume 1, said that he originally gathered the information "for my own use" and published it when he "despaired" of others doing so. But Hening & Munford's Preface to the first edition of their Volume 1 stated that, to the contrary, the "authors cannot resort to a very usual apology, 'that the notes were taken merely for their own private use.'"

The 1820 law gave the reporter no discretion about what cases to report—any one judge of the court could designate which cases were "worth reporting." Moreover, the judges apparently followed a practice of writing their opinions, without a legal mandate. The first official reporter (Gilmer) stated that he was "relieved from a great portion of his responsibility by the circumstance of the Judges having selected the cases to be reported; and in every case writing their own opinions at large." However, the reporter retained discretion regarding publication of lawyers' arguments, as Gilmer explicitly noted along with the usual concern about the lawyers' reaction:

> To give [the arguments of counsel] at length, was the only way to do justice to their ability, but that would have made the volume a book of speeches rather than reports. To omit them altogether, would have excluded many valuable references; [the reporter] chose therefore, to insert just enough to embrace the law adduced on each case. No idea can be formed of the ability, and much less of the eloquence of the respective counsel, from their arguments as now presented.

The 1820 law was also concerned with the quality of the reports, specifying that they be "well printed on good paper, large octavo, and bound in calf." Timely publication was also required—by Jan. 1, 1821 and annually thereafter.

The 1820 law provided the reporter with compensation at the rate of 83 1/3rd cents "for every one hundred pages contained in each copy." The reporter had to deliver 600 copies to the government for distribution to selected officials, with the undistributed copies sold for public benefit at $1 per copy. Although the law says nothing explicit about copyright ownership, it states that the reporter could print an additional 400 copies on his own account, which indicates that he could obtain the profits from sale in addition to other compensation; and that was the understanding of the law by Robinson, a later reporter writing in Volume 12 of the Virginia reports. An 1828 law added to the reporter's task—ordering him to include "all the cases decided by the general court" since publication of Volume 2 of the Virginia cases.

There was obviously some difficulty in implementing the 1820 law because an 1821 law deleted the annual publication requirement and stated that 1820 cases should be published when the reporter was ready, for which purpose $1,000 would be advanced to cover publication costs, to be deducted from future compensation. The 1821 law also stated that, in lieu of the government distributing copies to government officials, the copies should be sold and the proceeds paid to the state treasury.

An 1829 law specifically required the reporter to "secure the copyright of any volume or volumes hereafter to be published for the benefit of the commonwealth." Denial of the copyright to the reporter does not legally mean that the reporter could not sell the reports at a profit—New York, by contrast, denied both a pecuniary interest and the copyright in the reporter—but it diminishes the opportunity to do so. The law also increased to 700 the number of copies to be delivered to the state, and specified that neither the reporter nor anyone else could publish more than 700 copies per year within 14 years of publishing any volume of reports, which meant that the reporter could not profit from selling additional copies.

Some years later, as the preamble to an 1842 law stated, the legislature had become dissatisfied with "the present mode of publishing the reports [because it was] attended with more expense than is necessary." The 1842 law provided that the Secretary of the Commonwealth should arrange for the printing and binding of 700 copies of the reports, with the reporter charged only with preparing the manuscript and "carefully examin[ing] and correct[ing]" the proof sheets. In addition, the law ordered the court (not any one judge) to select cases for publication, still denying the reporter discretion about what cases to report. The 1842 law also changed compensation from the per page method to a $1,500 annual compensation. This combination of government responsibility for printing 700 copies, along with the reporter receiving compensation, strongly suggests that the reporter had been reduced to a salaried government official with no risk or opportunity for profit.

Despite state laws dealing with official reports, there was at least one additional example of semi-unofficial reports in mid-19th-Century Virginia, as a result of an 1848 law establishing the Special Court of Appeals to deal with a backlog of cases. That law authorized the court to approve any person to report its decisions, free of charge to the state. This task was discharged in 1856 by Patton & Heath—whose Preface states they were appointed by the court "on our own motion," as was the "English" way. As for lawyers' arguments, the reporters explain that "[i]n reporting the arguments of counsel, we have been guided rather by the interests of the subject-matter discussed, than by the ingenuity and learning of counsel." In addition, the reporters call attention to a change in judicial practice since the first term of the Special Court, whereby only one opinion is usually delivered for the court, unless there is a dissent.

Statutes

1820—"An Act making provision for publishing reports of the decisions of the court of appeals," February 24, 1820, Ch. XVII, p. 16

1821—"An act to amend the act, entitled, 'An Act making provision for publishing reports of the decisions of the court of appeals,'" March 5, 1821, Ch. 30, p. 31

1828—"An act to amend the laws in relation to the jurisdiction of the court of appeals, and for other purposes," February 27, 1828, Ch. 25, p. 20.

1829—"An act concerning the reporter to the court of appeals," February 27, 1829, Ch. 9, p. 11

1842—"An Act changing the mode of compensating the reporter of the court of appeals, and for other purposes," March 24, 1842, ch. 88, p. 51

1843—"An Act concerning the decisions of the general court," February 27, 1843, ch. 39, p. 29 (adding general court cases to the reporter's duties)

1848—"An Act concerning the jurisdiction of the general court and diminishing the number of judges thereof," March 31, 1848, ch. 68, p. 51

Law Reports Citations

Wythe, Decisions of cases in Virginia by the high court of chancery, 1 Virginia Reports Annotated, Memoir of the author, p. 90 (1795)

Washington, Reports of cases argued and determined in the court of appeals of Virginia, 1 Virginia Reports Annotated (1 Wash.), "To the Reader," p. 354 (1798)

Hening & Munford, Reports of cases argued and determined in the supreme court of appeals of Virginia, 4 Virginia Reports Annotated (1 Hen. & M.), Preface to the first edition, p. 4 (1808)

Hening & Munford, Reports of cases argued and determined in the supreme court of appeals of Virginia, 4 Virginia Reports Annotated (2 Hen. & M.), To the Public, p. 282 (1809)

Gilmer, Reports of cases decided in the court of appeals of Virginia, 1 Virginia Reports Annotated, Advertisement, p. 786 (1822)

Brockenbrough, Decisions of the General Court of Virginia, 2 Virginia Reports Annotated (2 Va. Cas.), Preface, p. 99 (1826)

Robinson, Reports of cases decided in the supreme court of appeals and in the general court of Virginia, 12 Virginia Reports Annotated (1 Rob .), Preface, p. 6 (1843)

Patton & Heath, Reports of cases decided in the special court of appeals of Virginia, 2 Virginia Reports Annotated (1 Pat. & H.), Preface, pp. 419–20 (1856)

Appendix 2

Two Measures of Increase in State Nonunanimity Rates
[1950, 1960, 1970, 1980, 1990, 2000]

State	AVG nonunanimity rate (%) during study period	Each of last 3 yrs > Each of first 3 yrs	AVG of last 3 yrs > AVG of first 3 yrs
(1)	(2)	(3)	(4)
Alabama	22.35%	Yes	
Alaska[a]	18.34%	No	Yes
Arizona	20.47%	Yes	
Arkansas	24.01%	Yes	
California	48.92%	Yes	
Colorado	20.2%	No	Yes
Connecticut	12.02%	Yes	
Delaware	11.38%	No	
Florida	39.07%	Yes	
Georgia	20.6%	Yes	
Hawaii[a]	13.1%	No	Yes
Idaho	28.82%	Yes	
Illinois	23.25%	Yes	
Indiana	27.2%	No	Yes
Iowa	14.05%	No	
Kansas	15.7%	No	Yes
Kentucky	24.25%	Yes	
Louisiana	35.18%	Yes	
Maine	4.87%	No	Yes
Maryland	13.9%	Yes	
Massachusetts	5.87%	Yes	
Michigan	43.17%	Yes	
Minnesota	14.22%	Yes	
Mississippi	21.28%	Yes	
Missouri	18.83%	Yes	
Montana	26.13%	No	
Nebraska	11.08%	No	Yes
Nevada	10.88%	Yes	
New Hampshire	7.12%	No	
New Jersey	30.12%	No	Yes
New Mexico	16.78%	No	Yes
New York	30.7%	No	
North Carolina	11.43%	No	Yes
North Dakota	13.78%	No	Yes
Ohio	40.52%	Yes	

(continued)

Two Measures of Increase in State Nonunanimity Rates
[1950, 1960, 1970, 1980, 1990, 2000] (continued)

State	AVG nonunanimity rate (%) during study period	Each of last 3 yrs > Each of first 3 yrs	AVG of last 3 yrs > AVG of first 3 yrs
Oklahoma			
—Civil	48.3%	Yes	
—Criminal	27.92%	Yes	
Oregon	18.23%	Yes	
Pennsylvania	50.73%	Yes	
Rhode Island	3.8%	No	
South Carolina	9.95%	Yes	
South Dakota	27.1%	Yes	
Tennessee	10.17%	No	Yes
Texas			
—Civil	30.7%	No	Yes
—Criminal	35.88%	Yes	
Utah	35.3%	No	Yes
Vermont	7.38%	No	Yes
Virginia	9.2%	Yes	
Washington	34.33%	Yes	
West Virginia	22.45%	No	Yes
Wisconsin	21.12%	Yes	
Wyoming	21.3%	No	Yes

a Alaska and Hawaii did not become states until after 1950. With only five years in the study, the last two years are compared to the first two years (for column 3). Also, the average of 1980, 1990, and 2000 is compared to the average of 1960, 1970, and 1980 (for column 4).

Research Design and Search Techniques to Identify State Unanimity Rates

It is hard to obtain reliable data about nonunanimity rates in state courts. States do not routinely keep this information, as I found out by inquiring from state law libraries. Because it was too laborious to read a significant number of cases from all 50 states, I used a Westlaw search to identify nonunanimous decisions in the highest state court as a percentage of total cases in all 50 states. By nonunanimous decisions, I mean cases in which at least one judge expresses a separate view that does more than simply sign on to the majority opinion—including a dissent, a concurrence in the judgment, a separate concurrence with the majority opinion, and a simple "concur in the result." This measure is more inclusive than the Harvard Law Review measure of nonunanimity for the U.S. Supreme Court, which counts only dissents and concurrences in the judgment as evidence of nonunanimity, not a separate concurrence with the majority opinion. I used a broader measure because I am interested in whether judges express an independent view instead of silently going along with the majority.

My search technique identified decisions in which at least one judge stated a view separate from the majority for six different years—1950, 1960, 1970, 1980, 1990, and 2000 (beginning in 1960 for Alaska and Hawaii). This limitation in the years for which data were gathered made the research manageable, but there is a risk that the data were not representative of the surrounding years. For example, Henry R. Glick & George W. Pruet, Jr., "Dissent in State Supreme Courts: Patterns and Correlates of Conflict," in *Judicial Conflict and Consensus: Behavioral Studies of American Appellate Courts,* Ch. 9, p. 203 (Goldman & Lamb eds., 1986), report a dissent rate of 46.5% for Michigan in 1966, but my data report separate opinions of only 15.6% and 36.9% in 1960 and 1970, respectively.

I used the following Westlaw search technique (with modifications where appropriate for a particular state):

da({date}) and
ci{tation} ({west reporter cite, for example, "n.e."}) and
sy{llabus} ({"highest court of state," for example, "supreme court" or "court of appeals"} and concur! or dissent!) and
co{urt} ({"highest court of state" with the proper abbreviation, for example, "n.y." for the New York Court of Appeals } % [but not] {"lower appellate court," for example, "mass.app."}).

I used "app." in the "but not" field to exclude lower appellate court cases whenever Westlaw included that designation in the court field. Where no such Westlaw designation for a lower appellate court appeared, I omitted any reference in my search to a lower court, except for three states—Pennsylvania ("pa.super"); New Jersey ("n.j.super."), and Delaware ("del.ch."). It is possible that a few lower appellate court cases snuck through these filters.

The general idea was to identify lack of unanimity by finding cases from the highest court of the state in which the syllabus stated that at least one judge of that court separately concurred with or dissented from the majority opinion. I read the syllabus field for each reported case to exclude false positives—for example, where the reference to a dissenting opinion was only to an opinion in the lower court from which an appeal had been taken; or where the reference to "dissent!"

was to a dissenting shareholder; or where the reference to "concur!" was to concurrently served sentences, concurrent jurisdiction, or concurrent negligence.

I identified the total number of cases by replacing the words "and concur! or dissent!" in the syllabus field with "+15 held"—which meant that the word "held" came no more than fifteen words after the reference to the highest court of the state. This identified cases in which the syllabus field contained a statement such as "the supreme court, with judge [name] concurring, held," and should have excluded decisions that were too unimportant to contain a full written majority opinion. There is a risk that a few important cases were omitted because the text in the Westlaw syllabus field might use some verb other than "held" to describe what the court did.

It was necessary to exclude cases from intermediate courts of appeals by using the Westlaw "but not" code [%], because the syllabus for these lower court cases might contain a statement about what the highest court of the state held or whether its judges concurred or dissented.

The search techniques described above were used after a considerable amount of experimenting and tweaking. Inaccuracies that were corrected did not usually have a large effect on the data. For example, measuring total cases by counting cases with "+15 held" in the syllabus field (after originally using a lower number) changed the data count by only a very small amount. Reading the syllabus to exclude false positives had a more substantial effect in some states.

Appendix 3
Impact of Operational Factors on State Nonunanimity Rates

A. Intermediate Appellate Court (IAC) and Workload

State	First year of study with IAC	Nonunanimity rate every year after IAC > rate every year before IAC	Average nonunanimity rate after IAC > average rate before IAC	Workload change after IAC
(1)	(2)	(3)	(4)	(5)
Alabama	1950	—	—	—
Alaska	1990	No	No	Down
Arizona	1970	No	Yes	Almost same[a]
Arkansas	1980	Yes	—	Almost same[a]
California	1950	—	—	—
Colorado	1970	No	No	Down
Connecticut	1990	Yes	—	Down
Delaware	No IAC	—	—	—
Florida	1960	No	Yes	Down
Georgia	1950	—	—	—
Hawaii	1990	No	Yes	Down
Idaho	1990	No	Yes	Down
Illinois	1950	—	—	—
Indiana	1950	—	—	—
Iowa	1980	No	No	Almost same[a]
Kansas	1980	No	Yes	Down
Kentucky	1980	Yes	—	Down
Louisiana	1950	—	—	—
Maine	No IAC	—	—	—
Maryland	1970	No	Yes	Down
Massachusetts	1980	Yes	—	Down
Michigan	1970	Yes	—	Down
Minnesota	1990	Yes	—	Down
Mississippi	2000	Yes	—	Down
Missouri	1950	—	—	—
Montana	No IAC	—	—	—
Nebraska	2000	No	No	Down
Nevada	No IAC	—	—	—
New Hampshire	No IAC	—	—	—
New Jersey	1950	—	—	—

(continued)

A. Intermediate Appellate Court (IAC) and Workload (continued)

State	First year of study with IAC	Nonunanimity rate every year after IAC > rate every year before IAC	Average nonunanimity rate after IAC > average rate before IAC	Workload change after IAC
New Mexico	1970	No	Yes	Same[a]
New York	1950	—	—	—
North Carolina	1970	Yes	—	Down
North Dakota	1990-IAC	Yes[b]	—	Up (then down)[b]
Ohio	1950	—	—	—
Oklahoma				
—Civil	1970	No	Yes	Down
—Criminal	1970	Yes	—	Almost same[a]
Oregon	1970	Yes	—	Down
Pennsylvania	1960	Yes	—	Almost same[a]
Rhode Island	No IAC	—	—	—
South Carolina	1980	Yes	—	Up
South Dakota	No IAC	—	—	—
Tennessee	1950	—	—	—
Texas				
—Civil	1950	—	—	—
—Criminal	1950	—	—	—
Utah	1990	No	Yes	Down
Vermont	No IAC	—	—	—
Virginia	1990	Yes	—	Almost same[a]
Washington	1970	Yes	—	Down
West Virginia	No IAC	—	—	—
Wisconsin	1980	Yes	—	Down
Wyoming	No IAC	—	—	—

[a] Arizona (129 vs. 124); Arkansas (340 vs. 349); Iowa (235 vs. 242); New Mexico (105 vs. 105); Oklahoma—Criminal (108 vs. 114); Pennsylvania (246 vs. 244); Virginia (147 vs. 145).
[b] An increase occurred when North Dakota temporarily adopted an IAC in 1990, but then a drop occurred in 2000 to 1/3rd of the 1990 nonunanimity rate, when there was no IAC.

B. Number of High Court Judges

State	AVG nonunanimity rate (%) during study period	Number of judges on highest court for 1950 (1960 for Alaska, Hawaii) (date of change, if any)	AVG nonunanimity rate (%) before/ after change of at least 2 judges
(1)	(2)	(3)	(4)
Alabama	22.35%	5; 9 (1970)	4.6/31.3
Alaska	18.34%	3; 5 (1970)	10.5/20.3
Arizona	20.47%	3; 5 (1960)	6.2/23.3
Arkansas	24.01%	7	—
California	48.92%	7	—
Colorado	20.2%	7	—
Connecticut	12.02%	7; 6 (1970); 7 (1990)	—
Delaware	11.38%	6; 3 (1960); 5 (1980)	44.4/.95/7.3
Florida	39.07%	7	—
Georgia	20.6%	7	—
Hawaii	13.1%	5	—

B. *Number of High Court Judges* (continued)

State	AVG nonunanimity rate (%) during study period	Number of judges on highest court for 1950 (1960 for Alaska, Hawaii) (date of change, if any)	AVG nonunanimity rate (%) before/ after change of at least 2 judges
Idaho	28.82%	5	—
Illinois	23.25%	7	—
Indiana	27.2%	5	—
Iowa	14.05%	9	—
Kansas	15.7%	7	—
Kentucky	24.25%	7	—
Louisiana	35.18%	7; 8 (2000)	—
Maine	4.87%	6; 7 (1980)	—
Maryland	13.9%	5; 7 (1970)	4.7/18.5
Massachusetts	5.87%	7	—
Michigan	43.17%	8; 7 (1970)	—
Minnesota	14.22%	7; 9 (1980); 7 (1990)	6.0/11.9/27.7
Mississippi	21.28%	6; 9 (1970)	4.5/26.7
Missouri	18.83%	7	—
Montana	26.13%	5; 7 (1990)	27.6/23.3
Nebraska	11.08%	7	—
Nevada	10.88%	3; 5 (1970)	3.4/14.6
New Hampshire	7.12%	5	—
New Jersey	30.12%	7	—
New Mexico	16.78%	5	—
New York	30.7%	7	—
North Carolina	11.43%	7	—
North Dakota	13.78%	5	—
Ohio	40.52%	7	—
Oklahoma			
—Civil	48.3%	9	—
—Criminal	27.92%	3; 5 (2000)	20.2/66.7
Oregon	18.23%	7	—
Pennsylvania	50.73%	7	—
Rhode Island	3.8%	5	—
South Carolina	9.95%	5	—
South Dakota	27.1%	5	—
Tennessee	10.17%	5	—
Texas			
—Civil	30.7%	9	—
—Criminal	35.88%	3; 5 (1970); 9 (1980)	6.5/6.9/65.2
Utah	35.3%	5	—
Vermont	7.38%	5	—
Virginia	9.2%	7	—
Washington	34.33%	9	—
West Virginia	22.45%	5	—
Wisconsin	21.12%	7	—
Wyoming	21.3%	3; 4 (1970); 5 (1980)	—

Source of information about state intermediate appellate courts and number of judges in highest court of state: "The Book of the States, The Council of State Governments":

     1950–51   Classification of Courts, etc., p. 507
                   Salaries of Judges, p. 510
                   Highest Courts of Appeals, p. 514
     1960–61   Table 1—Classification of Courts, etc., p. 104

Notes

NOTES TO CHAPTER I

1. See Henry Hallam, *The Constitutional History of England,* Vol. I, p. 335 n.* (Garland Pub. Co. 1978) (1846).

2. Richard A. Posner, "Blackstone and Bentham," 19 *J. L. Econ.* 569, 585 (1976).

3. Hans W. Baade, "The *Casus Omissus:* A Pre-History of Statutory Analogy," 20 *Syr. J. Int'l L. & Comm.* 45, 90 (1994) (hereafter "Baade, Casus Omissus").

4. David Lieberman, *The Province of Legislation Determined: Legal Theory in Eighteenth-Century Britain,* p. 55 (1989).

5. Gerald J. Postema, *Bentham and the Common Law Tradition,* pp. 30–31 n.65 (1986).

6. Quoted in Baade, Casus Omissus, p. 84.

7. This description comes from William Blackstone, *Commentaries on the Laws of England,* Vol. I, p. 69 (hereafter "Blackstone, Commentaries").

8. See D. B. Swinfen, *Imperial Appeal: The Debate on the Appeal to the Privy Council, 1933–1986,* p. 224 (1987) (hereafter "Swinfen, Imperial Appeal"); Karl L. ZoBell, "Division of Opinion in the Supreme Court: A History of Judicial Disintegration," 44 *Cornell L.Q.* 186, 188 (1959); Edward McWhinney, "Judicial Concurrences and Dissents: A Comparative View of Opinion-Writing in Final Appellate Tribunals," 31 *Canadian Bar Rev.* 595, 596–99 (1953). Holdsworth notes three cases in which a dissent was published in the mid-19th Century. William S. Holdsworth, *A History of English Law,* Vol. I, p. 519 n.11 (hereafter "Holdsworth, History").

9. Stewart Jay, "Servants of Monarchs and Lords: The Advisory Role of Early English Judges," 38 *Am. J. Legal Hist.* 117, 130 (1994) (citing, among others, multiple pages of Edward Turner, *The Privy Council of England in the Seventeenth and Eighteenth Centuries, 1603–1784,* Vols. I & II [1927 & 1928]). But see Swinfen, Imperial Appeal, pp. 4–8 (noting that Privy Council panels often failed to include trained judges, even though they were eligible to sit).

10. Holdsworth, History, Vol. I, p. 518; W.F. Finlason, *The Judicial Committee of the Privy Council,* p. 73 (1877).

11. Holdsworth, History, Vol. I, p. 519.

12. John William Wallace, *The Reporters*, p. 172 (1882) (hereafter "Wallace, Reporters").

13. Percy H. Winfield, *The Chief Sources of English Legal History*, p. 335 (1925) (hereafter "Winfield, Chief Sources").

14. John P. Dawson, *The Oracles of the Law*, p. 77 (1968) (hereafter "Dawson, Oracles"); James Oldham, *English Common Law in the Age of Mansfield*, p. 30 (2004) (hereafter "Oldham, English Common Law").

15. Richard J. Ross, "The Commoning of the Common Law: The Renaissance Debate over the Meaning of Printing English Law, 1520–1640," 146 *U. Pa. L.Rev.* 323 (1998).

16. Dawson, Oracles, pp. 73, 75.

17. Blackstone, Commentaries, Vol. I, pp. 10–11.

18. Daniel J. Boorstin, *The Mysterious Science of the Law* (1941).

19. Roscoe Pound, "Common Law and Legislation," 21 *Harv. L.Rev.* 383, 384 (1908) ("coming to be a science of legislation").

20. Blackstone, Commentaries, Vol. I, pp. 59–62, 87–92.

21. David Lieberman, "Blackstone's Science of Legislation," 27 *J. of Brit. Studs.* 117, 121 (1988).

22. See G.I.T. Ian Machin, *The Rise of Democracy in Britain, 1830–1918* (2001) (hereafter "Machin, Democracy"). See also Lord Irvine of Lairg, "Sovereignty in Comparative Perspective: Constitutionalism in Britain and America," 76 *N.Y.U. L.Rev.* 1, 12–13 (2001) (hereafter "Irvine, Sovereignty").

23. Speech by Lord Chancellor Westbury in the House of Lords, June 12, 1863, "Revision of the Statute Law," p. 776 (hereafter "Lord Westbury speech") ("The Statute Law is in a great measure supplemental to the Common Law.").

24. James Oldham, *The Mansfield Manuscripts and the Growth of English Law in the Eighteenth Century*, Vol. I, p. 197 (1992) (hereafter "Oldham, Manuscripts").

25. Louis Blom-Cooper & Gavin Drewry, *Final Appeal: A Study of the House of Lords in Its Judicial Capacity*, p. 80 (1972) (hereafter "Blom-Cooper, Final Appeal"). See also Oldham, Manuscripts, Vol. I, p. 47, where the author notes Burrow's comment that "the degree of unanimity was high" from 1756 to 1770, when only two cases evoked dissent, and adds that thereafter dissents were more common (perhaps 20 reported cases and some other unreported cases).

26. Holdsworth, History, Vol. XII, p. 111.

27. Holdsworth, History, Vol. XII, pp. 111, 494–503.

28. Wallace, Reporters, p. 29.

29. James Burrow, *Reports of Cases Argued and Adjudged in the Court of King's Bench*, Vol. I, p. v (1756).

30. Holdsworth, History, Vol. XII, p. 116. But see Wallace, Reporters, p.

446, where the author says that Burrow made the reports for the purpose of publishing them.

31. See Oldham, English Common Law, p. 33; James Oldham, "Judicial Activism in Eighteenth-Century English Common Law in the Time of the Founders," 8 *Greenbag* 269, 273 (2005) (noting the objections of Lord Camden). See also Lord Ellenborough's opinion in DeHavilland v. Bowerbank, 1 Camp. 50, 50–51, 170 Eng. Rep. 872, 873 (1807) ("I want very much to lay down a certain rule respecting the payment of interest. . . . My great object is, to have a fixed rule, and to exclude discretion.").

32. Winfield, Chief Sources, p. 190.

33. See, for example, James Oldham, "Law Making at *Nisi Prius* in the Early 1800s," 25 *J. Leg. Hist.* 221, 223–24 (2004) (discussing Lord Campbell's reports of Lord Ellenborough's decisions).

34. William S. Holdsworth, "Law Reporting in the Nineteenth and Twentieth Centuries," in *Anglo-American Legal History Series*, Series 1, Number 5, p. 1 (1941).

35. Daniel Duman, *The English and Colonial Bars in the Nineteenth Century*, pp. 6–8, 16–29 (1983) (figures show anywhere from a doubling to a tenfold increase in barristers during the 19th Century; changes in their social, occupational, and educational background are less clear).

36. "Report of a Special Committee on the Law Reporting System, 1849," in W.T.S. Daniel, *The History and Origin of the Law Reports*, p. 5 (1884) (hereafter "Daniel, History").

37. Daniel, History, pp. 16, 19.

38. Daniel, History, p. 30. See also Lord Westbury speech, p. 782 ("But a judicial opinion is also a legislative enactment. It decides a particular case, and it sets a precedent for all future cases. Therefore the Judges become legislators. . . .").

39. Daniel, History, p. 31. See also Lord Justice Lindley, "The History of the Law Reports," 1 *L. Q. Rev.* 137, 137 (1885).

40. Daniel, History, p. 24.

41. The semi-official status of the English law reports was also evidenced by the following: they were not a monopoly; not all opinions had to be published; and the judge was not required to submit a written opinion to the reporters (although that practice eventually developed). Some of the opposition to government control also rested on concern about the effect of government patronage on the quality of reporters and on a desire by existing reporters to keep their jobs.

42. Irvine, Sovereignty, pp. 12–13; Machin, Democracy, p. 152.

43. Material in this and the following paragraph relies on Robert Stevens, *Law and Politics*, pp. 29, 34, 47–67, 90–98, 191–282, 303–04, 325, 337 (1978) (hereafter "Stevens, Law and Politics").

44. Swinfen, Imperial Appeal, pp. 4–8.

45. Frederick N. Judson, "A Modern View of the Law Reforms of Jeremy Bentham," 10 *Colum. L.Rev.* 41, 45 (1910).

46. See generally Michael J. Klarman, "The Judges Versus the Unions: The Development of British Labor Law," 75 *Va. L.Rev.* 1487 (1989).

47. Steve Hedley, "Words, Words, Words: Making Sense of Legal Judgments, 1875–1940," in *Law Reporting in Britain*, p. 183 (Stebbings ed., 1995).

48. Stevens, Law and Politics, p. 304 (Lord Parker's view that *stare decisis* and literal interpretation tend to go together).

49. Even Lord Reid, who did not shy away from admitting that judges made law, thought that Parliament was the right place for doing what the ordinary man thinks is controversial. Lord Reid, "The Judge as Lawmaker," 12 *J. Soc'y Public Teachers of Law* 22, 23 (1972) (hereafter "Reid, Judge").

50. [1932] A.C. 562.

51. Frederic Reynold, *The Judge as Lawmaker*, p. 9 (1967) ("The orthodox, popular conception of the existing law . . . was [contrary to the majority's decision].").

52. (1861) 9 H.L.C. 274, 338–39, 344, 349, 353.

53. [1898] A.C. 375, 379.

54. Compare Bright v. Hutton (1852) 3 H.L.C. 341, 388 (Lord Chancellor —can overrule) with id. at 391 (Lord Campbell—only Parliament can override House of Lords decision).

55. (1861) 9 H.L.C., at 338–39.

56. [1898] A.C. at 380.

57. *The Law Commission and the Scottish Law Commission, Interpretation of Statutes* (1969), pp. 15–17, paras. 25–28 (hereafter "Law Commission").

Of course, no theory of statutory interpretation could attract unanimous consent. For example, Lord Shaw took a more expansive view of the judge's role in statutory interpretation. See Lord Shaw, *Legislature and Judiciary*, pp. 13–14, 31–33, 49–50, 78–79 (1911); Stevens, Law and Politics, pp. 249–53 (discussing Lord Shaw).

58. Stevens, Law and Politics, pp. 219–22 (Lord Haldane), pp. 233–35 (Lord Birkenhead), pp. 330–35 (Lord Simon), pp. 337–41 (Lord Jowitt), pp. 341–54 (Lord Simonds). See also Lord Evershed, "The Impact of Statute on the Law of England," 42 *Procs. Brit. Acad.* 247, 258 (1956) ("some judicial utterance can be cited in support of almost any proposition relevant to the problems of statutory interpretation").

59. See, for example, Rupert Cross, *Precedent in English Law* (2d ed. 1968) (hereafter "Cross, Precedent"); Gerald Dworkin, "*Stare Decisis* in the House of Lords," 25 *Mod. L.Rev.* 163 (1962); Arthur L. Goodhart, "Precedents in the Court of Appeal," 9 *Camb. L.J.* 349 (1949); Arthur L. Goodhart, "Determining

the *Ratio Decidendi* of a Case," 40 *Yale L.J.* 161 (1930); Julius Stone, "1966 and All That! Loosing the Chains of Precedent," 69 *Colum. L.Rev.* 1162 (1969).

60. Cross, Precedent, pp. 136–37; Peter Wesley-Smith, "The *Per Incuriam* Doctrine," 15 *J. Soc'y Public Teachers of Law* 58 (1980); D. G. Valentine, "The Meaning of '*Per Incuriam*,'" 18 *Mod. L.Rev.* 602 (1955).

61. Some contemporary judges, who defend sticking to the text, argue that earlier examples of judicial literalism were cases in which the Law Lords did not really rely on the text, but instead invoked clear statement rules (that is, substantive canons of interpretation) grounded in a "Victorian Bill of Rights." See Lord Devlin, "Judges and Lawmakers," 39 *Mod. L.Rev.* 1, 14 (1976).

62. Compare Blom-Cooper, Final Appeal, p. 317 (from 1952 to 1968, about 30% of the English civil appeals in the House of Lords were revenue cases) with Gavin Drewry & Louis Blom-Cooper, "The Appellate Function," in Paul Carmichael & Brice Dickson, *The House of Lords: Its Parliamentary and Judicial Roles,* pp. 116–17 (1999) (two of 54 cases were revenue appeals in 1997). Stevens traces modern pro-taxpayer literalism to the high tax rates introduced in the early part of the 20th Century; Stevens, Law and Politics, pp. 170–71.

63. In Inland Revenue Commissioners v. Duke of Westminster [1936] A.C. 1 (H.L.), the taxpayer was allowed to convert nondeductible wages for personal servants into deductible "covenanted payments." The Law Lords held that these payments were deductible, stating that the Duke was entitled to the letter of law, rejecting the substance-over-form doctrine, and refusing to embrace the "uncertain and crooked cord of discretion" rather than the "golden and straight mete wand of the law."

64. The Law Lords often issued anti-labor decisions. When legislation tried to override early 20th-Century tort law decisions that exposed unions to damages resulting from strikes, the courts interpreted the law to minimize protection for the unions; for example, an important 1909 decision by the Law Lords reversed the Court of Appeals and interpreted a statute to deny union immunity from suit. Conway v. Wade [1909] A.C. 506. However, the interpretation of Workers Compensation statutes did not seem hostile to labor. In Trim Joint District School v. Kelly [1914] A.C. 667, the Law Lords generously interpreted the statutory phrase "accident arising out of and in the course of employment," even to the point of attracting a comment in the Law Quarterly Review, 31 *L. Q. Rev.* 8 (1915), that the "opinion of the majority gives effect . . . to what Parliament did mean; but we also think it attains that end by doing such violence to the words of the Act as may prove a dangerous example."

65. *The Preparation of Legislation, Report of a Committee Appointed by the Lord President of the Council, Chairman, Sir David Renton,* p. 135, para. 19.2 (1975) (Cmnd. 6053); Lord Diplock, *The Courts as Legislators,* p. 11 (1965) (hereafter "Diplock, Courts"); Lord Evershed, "The Judicial Process in

Twentieth-Century England," 61 *Colum. L.Rev.* 761, 766 (1961); Law Commission, pp. 3–4, para. 5; Stevens, Law and Politics, p. 100.

66. Gregory v. Helvering, 293 U.S. 465 (1935) (detailed tax rules dealing with corporate reorganizations interpreted in light of their purpose).

67. See Law Commission, pp. 3–4, para. 5.

68. Furniss v. Dawson [1984] 1 All E.R. 530, 533.

69. Brian Abel-Smith & Robert Stevens, *Lawyers and the Courts: A Sociological Study of the English Legal System, 1750–1965,* p. 294 (1967) (hereafter "Abel-Smith & Stevens, Lawyers").

70. Reid, Judge, p. 22. See also J.A.G. Griffith, *The Politics of the Judiciary,* pp. xiii–xiv (5th ed. 1997) (judges were roused from their torpor by Judge Reid in the 1960s).

Not everyone agreed with the public admission of judicial lawmaking. Lord Radcliffe insisted that it was better to fool the public into thinking that judges do not make law than to admit the exercise of judicial discretion. "We cannot run the risk of finding the archetypical image of the judge confused in men's minds with the very different image of the legislator. . . . Personally, I think that judges will serve the public interest better if they keep quiet about their legislative function." Lord Radcliffe, "The Lawyer and His Times," pp. 14, 16 in *The Path of the Law from 1967* (Arthur Sutherland ed., 1968).

71. Reid, Judge, p. 29.

72. Diplock, Courts, pp. 21, 23.

73. Stevens, Law and Politics, pp. 347–48 (Lord Simonds).

74. Diplock, Courts, pp. 5–6.

75. Abel-Smith & Stevens, Lawyers, pp. 285–89. See also Stevens, Law and Politics, p. 415.

76. Blom-Cooper, Final Appeal, p. 15.

77. Alan Paterson, *The Law Lords,* p. 163 (1982) (hereafter "Paterson, Law Lords") (eight cases overruled in the period from 1966 to1980).

78. Law Commission, p. 3 (percentage of House of Lords cases dealing with statutory interpretation increased from 57% in 1905 to 75% in 1965; for other courts, the comparable data are 42% [1905] and 56% [1965]).

79. The new realism in statutory interpretation was apparent in the admission that determining statutory meaning was a craft as much as a science (Law Commission, p. 5, para. 6), and in the startling statement by Lord Reid that he would *not* favor abandoning *stare decisis* for cases interpreting legislation *because* there is no right answer ([1972] A.C. 944, 966).

80. Law Commission, p. 6, para. 9.

81. Law Commission, pp. 7–8, para. 11, and pp. 48–49, para. 80.

82. Law Commission, pp. 19–20, para. 33, pp. 21–22, para. 35, and pp. 30–31, para. 52.

83. Law Commission, p. 5, para. 8.

84. Law Commission, p. 18, para. 31.

85. [1981] 1 All E.R. 865, 873.

86. [1984] 1 All E.R. 530, 533.

87. See Ensign Tankers (Leasing) Ltd. v. Stokes [1992] 2 All E.R. 275, 289.

88. See Pepper v. Hart [1993] 1 All E.R. 42. According to David Robertson, *Judicial Discretion in the House of Lords,* p. 157 (1998) (hereafter "Robertson, Judicial Discretion"), one Law Lord routinely read Hansard prior to the decision in Pepper v. Hart. See generally, Kenny Mullan, "The Impact of Pepper v. Hart," in Paul Carmichael & Brice Dickson, *The House of Lords: Its Parliamentary and Judicial Roles,* pp. 213–38 (1999).

For recent doubts about how broadly to apply Pepper v. Hart, see Lord Steyn's views in McDonnell v. Congregation of Christian Brothers Trustees, 2004 1 A.C. 1101 (2003) (HL), and Lord Steyn, "Pepper v Hart: A Re-examination," 21 *Ox. J. L. Studs.* 59 (2001).

89. Black-Clawson International Ltd. v. Papierwerke Waldhof-Aschaffenburg [1975] A.C. 591, 638 (H.L.).

90. See, for example, Note, "Why Learned Hand Would Never Consult Legislative History Today," 105 *Harv. L.Rev.* 1005 (1992).

91. The academic landmarks are: James Landis, "Statutes and the Source of Law," in *Harvard Legal Essays,* p. 213 (1934); Roscoe Pound, "Common Law and Legislation," 21 *Harv. L.Rev.* 383 (1908); Roscoe Pound, "Spurious Interpretation," 7 *Colum. L.Rev.* 379 (1907). The leading Supreme Court decision is: United States v. American Trucking Associations, Inc., 310 U.S. 534 (1940).

92. Abel-Smith & Stevens, Lawyers, pp. 26, 166.

93. Richard L. Abel, *The Legal Profession in England and Wales,* pp. 263, 265–66 (1988).

94. See Dawson, Oracles, pp. 96–97 (judges sometimes cite living authors but judges still look down on academics); Reid, Judge, p. 22 (blind eye to old rule not to cite living author); Paterson, Law Lords, pp. 13–20 (some increase in the Law Lords citations and use of academic commentary). For House of Lords references to living authors, see Woolwich Building Society v. I.R.C., 1993 A.C., at pp. 163–64, 166; Regina v. Secretary of State [2001] 2 A.C., at p. 532.

95. Peter Birks, "Adjudication and Interpretation in the Common Law: A Century of Change," 14 *Legal Studs.* 156, 166 (1994) (discussing Lord Goff); Diplock, Courts, p. 1 ("It is, I think, one of the weaknesses of the law in England that here, more than in any other country, there seems to be a gulf between those who teach and study it in the Universities and those who practice and administer it in the Courts.").

96. Current Law, Statutes 1998—Vol. 3, c. 42 (Humans Rights Act 1998).

97. The House of Lords recently made news with an 8–1 decision in A v. Secretary of State for the Home Department, [2004] UKHL 56 (Dec. 16, 2004),

declaring under the Human Rights Act 1998 that portions of the English Terrorism Act 2000 were incompatible with certain articles of the European Convention on Human Rights.

98. Scotland Act, 1998, c. 46 (Eng.); Government of Wales Act, 1998, c. 38 (Eng.); Northern Ireland Act, 1998, c. 47 (Eng.).

99. Robert Stevens, "A Loss of Innocence? Judicial Independence and the Separation of Powers," 19 *Ox. J. L. Studs.* 365, 375, 398 (1999).

100. *Modernising Parliament: Reforming the House of Lords,* Cmnd. 4183 (1999).

101. Paterson, Law Lords, pp. 98, 107.

102. Paterson, Law Lords, pp. 183–84.

103. Morris v. C.W. Martin & Sons [1966] 1 Q.B. 716, 730.

104. Robertson, Judicial Discretion, pp. 26, 77–78.

105. See Blom-Cooper, Final Appeal, pp. 93–95; Stevens, Law and Politics, pp. 567–68. See also Rupert Cross, "The *Ratio Decidendi* and the Plurality of Speeches in the House of Lords," 93 *L. Q. Rev.* 378 (1977).

106. [1973] A.C. 15, 94.

107. I am aware of three other joint opinions from the Law Lords, all delivered by Lord Blackburn, none of which was for a unanimous court: 1869–70 L.R. 4 H.L. 414 (for five judges, with four other opinions); 1868 L.R. 3 H.L. 17 (for three judges, with five other opinions); 1866 L.R. 1 H.L. 93 (for three judges, with three other opinions).

108. The ideal way to measure the lost potential for an opinion of the court would be as follows. (1) Identify the total number of judges sitting in a case. (2) Then subtract (a) those "opinions" that do nothing but concur in what another judge says (a "pure" concurrence), and (b) those opinions that clearly express an alternative concurrence or a dissent. This isolates those seriatim opinions that could be aggregated into a single opinion. For example, if there were five judges in the case, one of whom said nothing except to concur with another judge (a "pure" concurrence that was a seriatim opinion in form only), one of whom concurred in the judgment on alternative grounds, and one of whom dissented, that would leave two judges who could have aggregated their "seriatim" views into a single opinion. (3) In order to identify the lost potential for writing a single opinion, subtract "one" from the number of seriatim opinions that could be aggregated into one opinion—because one author would be expected to write the court's opinion. Reverting again to the prior illustration where there were two seriatim opinions that could be aggregated into an opinion of the court, the lost potential to aggregate these seriatim opinions is "1"—that is, the two seriatim opinions minus one. (4) The lost potential for an opinion of the court can be quantified as the lost potential to aggregate seriatim opinions into an opinion of the court divided by the total number of judges in the case—1/5

(.2) in the prior example. Similarly, if four of five judges simply say "I concur" in a single opinion written by the fifth judge, there is no lost potential for an opinion of the court (0/5), and the decision is in effect a unanimous opinion of the court, despite the seriatim form.

Making these calculations turned out to be more difficult than I anticipated. It was too difficult to identify when concurrences were on alternative grounds. In conformity with the seriatim style, opinions did not routinely come marked as separate concurrences in another opinion. Consequently, all opinions were considered as having the potential to be aggregated into an opinion of the court, *except* for one majority opinion, one dissent (if any), and those that were a "pure" concurrence with another judge (either the majority or dissent). I still had to make one judgment call—whether a brief concurring opinion of a few sentences was a "pure concurrence" or a separate seriatim opinion.

I looked at every House of Lords case in the annual Reports of Appeals Cases (A.C.) for some older and some newer cases—older cases in 1892 and 1902, and newer cases for 1952, 1962, 1972, 1982 and 1992–2001. The designated year refers to cases with an A.C. citation, not necessarily to cases decided in those years. A.C. refers to Appeals Cases, reported by the Law Council. The Weekly Law Reports, which are also published by the Law Council, contain additional cases, some of which are considered too unimportant to make it into the A.C. volumes. Another series of law reports—the All England Reports—are also more inclusive than Appeals Cases. A.C. cases are, therefore, probably more controversial than the entire body of Law Lords decisions. On the reasonable assumption that the more controversial cases are more likely to attract multiple opinions, any bias in my study from the omission of cases is likely to be in the direction of understating the extent to which the Law Lords have shifted away from seriatim opinions.

109. Another sign that the Law Lords acted institutionally as a court is noticeable in the 1952 data. In 1892 and 1902, cases could have four, five, six, or seven judges, but from 1952, almost every case had no more than five judges (fewer than five was possible if a judge died or became ill). The only exceptions were the use of seven judges in two cases in 1972 (where overruling a prior case was at issue); one case in 1993 (in which the court considered departing from historical practice to use legislative history); and one case in 2000 (involving the extradition of Pinochet).

110. This discussion of French law and practice relies primarily on the following secondary sources: John Dawson, *Oracles of the Law* (1968); Mitchel de S.-O.-l'E. Lasser, "Judicial (Self-) Portraits: Judicial Discourse in the French Legal System," 104 *Yale L.J.* 1325 (1995); Jean Louis Goutal, "Characteristics of Judicial Style in France, Britain, and the U.S.A.," 24 *Am. J. Comp. L.* 43 (1976); F. H. Lawson, "Comparative Judicial Style," 25 *Am. J. Comp. L.* 364

(1977); Vernon Valentine Palmer, "From Embrace to Banishment: A Study of Judicial Equity in France," 47 *Am. J. Comp. L.* 277 (1999) (hereafter "Palmer, France").

111. Palmer, France, p. 283.

112. Dawson, Oracles, pp. 413–14.

NOTES TO CHAPTER 2

1. See generally, Alexander Hamilton, *Federalist Papers # 79,* pp. 403–04. All references to "Federalist Papers" are to Max Beloff ed., 2d ed. 1987.

2. Madison, *Federalist Papers # 47,* p. 247; Plaut v. Spendthrift Farm, Inc., 514 U.S. 211 (1995).

3. Mark Kozlowski, *The Myth of the Imperial Judiciary,* Ch. 2 (2003).

4. Shannon Stimson, *The American Revolution in the Law,* pp. 133–36 (1990).

5. See Madison, *Federalist Papers # 47,* p. 246 (referring to Montesquieu as the "oracle" of separation of powers).

6. Cited in Robert J. Pushaw, Jr., "Justiciability and Separation of Powers: A Neo-Federalist Approach," 81 *Cornell L.Rev.* 393, 400 n.22 (1996).

7. Baron de Montesquieu, *The Spirit of the Laws,* p. 157 (Cohler, Miller, & Stone ed. & trans., 1989) (hereafter "Montesquieu, Spirit").

8. Montesquieu, Spirit, p. 157.

9. William Blackstone, *Commentaries on the Laws of England,* Vol. I, p. 269 (hereafter "Blackstone, Commentaries").

10. John Henry Merryman, "The French Deviation," 44 *Am. J. Comp. L.* 109, 109–10 (1996).

11. Montesquieu, Spirit, pp. 158, 160

12. Montesquieu, Spirit, p. 163.

13. Montesquieu, Spirit, p. 158.

14. M.J.C. Vile, *Constitutionalism and the Separation of Powers,* pp. 103–05 (1963) (hereafter "Vile, Constitutionalism").

15. Blackstone, Commentaries, Vol. I, p. 267.

16. Blackstone, Commentaries, Vol. III, p. 327.

17. Blackstone, Commentaries, Vol. I, p. 269.

18. Blackstone, Commentaries, Vol. I, p. 69.

19. Blackstone, Commentaries, Vol. I, p. 61.

20. See generally Willi Adams, *The First American Constitutions,* pp. 266–71 (1980) (hereafter "Adams, First American").

21. See Adams, First American, Ch. VI, pp. 129–49.

22. "Maryland, 1776 Constitution, Declaration of Rights, Art. III," in *The Federal and State Constitutions and Other Organic Laws of the United States* (Benjamin Poore, 2d ed. 1878), p. 817 (hereafter "Poore, Constitutions").

23. Charles M. Cook, *The American Codification Movement*, p. 3 (1981). See also Francis R. Aumann, "American Law Reports: Yesterday and Today," 4 *Ohio St. L.J.* 331, 334 (1938) (despite prohibitions against citing English cases, there was a need for English legal materials).

24. Madison, *Federalist Papers # 47*, p. 249.

25. Articles II, III, VI, Poore, Constitutions, pp. 280, 281, 283.

26. Articles VIII, IX, XX, Poore, Constitutions, pp. 1312, 1313.

27. The "whereas" clause objecting to merger of powers, is at Poore, Constitutions, p. 1329; the Council of Revision provision appears in Art. III, Poore, Constitutions, p. 1332; and the provision for an appellate court appears in Art. XXXII, Poore, Constitutions, p. 1337.

28. Plan or Frame of Government, sec. 2, Poore, Constitutions, p. 1542. The Georgia Constitution of 1777 also provided for a unicameral legislature, Arts. II, III, Poore, Constitutions, p. 378, but makes reference to "legislative, executive and judiciary departments" in Art. I, Poore, Constitutions, p. 378.

29. Plan or Frame of Government, secs. 2, 3, Poore, Constitutions, p. 1542.

30. Art. V, sec. 1, Poore, Constitutions, p. 1552.

31. Sec. IV, Poore, Constitutions, p. 1541. Nonetheless, despite Pennsylvania's rhetorical downplaying of a separate judiciary, judges in the higher courts had fixed salaries, served for seven years, and could not hold another office— giving them an independence in fact without explicit mention of a judicial power; Adams, First American, p. 261.

32. Art. V, Poore, Constitutions, p. 958.

33. 1776, Art. II, Poore, Constitutions, p. 1617; 1778, Arts. II, XI, Poore, Constitutions, pp. 1621, 1622.

34. Art. III., sec. 1, Poore, Constitutions, p. 1631.

35. Compare New Hampshire, 1776, Poore, Constitutions, p. 1280, with New Hampshire, 1784, Art. XXXVII, Poore, Constitutions, p. 1283 (Bill of Rights). In W.B. Gwyn, *The Meaning of Separation of Powers*, p. 5 (1965), the author notes that the term "executive" had a broader meaning from 1650 to 1750 than it does today, including both executive and judicial powers.

36. Massachusetts, Art. XXX, Poore, Constitutions, p. 960 (Declaration of Rights). The other five provisions are:

Georgia, Art. I, Poore, Constitutions, p. 378 (in the body of the Constitution, not in a separate declaration or bill of rights) ("The legislative, executive, and judiciary departments shall be separate and distinct, so that neither exercises the powers properly belonging to the other.").

New Hampshire, 1784, Art. XXXVII, Poore, Constitutions, p. 1283 (Bill of Rights) ("[T]he three essential powers thereof, to wit, the legislative, executive and judicial ought to be kept as separate from and independent of each other, as the nature of a free government will admit or is consistent with that chain of connection that binds the whole fabric of government in one indissoluble bond of union and unity."). In addition, the 1784 New Hampshire Constitution referred to "legislative power," "executive power," and "judiciary power" in the "Form of Government" part of the constitution; Poore, Constitutions, pp. 1284, 1287, 1290.

North Carolina, Art. IV, Poore, Constitutions, p. 1409 (Declaration of Rights) ("That the legislative, executive, and supreme judicial powers of government, ought to be forever separate and distinct from each other.").

Maryland, Art. VI, Poore, Constitutions, p. 819 (Declaration of Rights) ("That the legislative, executive and judicial powers of government, ought to be forever separate and distinct from each other.").

Virginia, para. 2, Poore, Constitutions, p. 1910 (in the body of the constitution, not a separate declaration or bill of rights) ("The legislative, executive, and judicial department, shall be separate and distinct, so that neither exercises the powers properly belonging to the other. . . .").

37. Jackson Turner Main, *The Sovereign States, 1775–1783,* pp. 206–09 (1973).

38. North Carolina, sec. IV; Maryland, sec. IV; Massachusetts, sec. XXX; New Hampshire, 1784, Art. XXXVII (all cited in note 36 *supra*).

39. Blackstone, Commentaries, Vol. I, p. 269.

40. Gordon S. Wood, *The Creation of the American Republic 1776–1787,* p. 301 (1969) (hereafter "Wood, Creation").

41. Morton Horwitz, *The Transformation of American Law, 1780–1860,* p. 5 (1977). See also Wood, Creation, p. 304 n.75 (Jefferson's concern about equitable construction).

42. Madison, *Federalist Papers* # 47, p. 248.

43. Jonathan Elliot, *The Debates in the Several State Conventions,* Vol. II, p. 438 (1836) (hereafter "Elliot's Debates").

44. Charles Warren, *The Making of the Constitution,* p. 42 (1967) (hereafter "Warren, Making") (letter dated Feb. 21, 1787 to John Adams).

45. Warren, Making, p. 46 (letter dated Aug. 18, 1786 to Thomas Jefferson).

46. Virginia (1776), para. 2, Poore, Constitutions, p. 1910; Massachusetts (1780), Declaration of Rights, Art. XXX, Poore, Constitutions, p. 960.

47. Gerhard Casper, "An Essay in Separation of Powers: Some Early Versions and Practices," 30 *Wm. & Mary L.Rev.* 211, 221 (1989) (hereafter "Casper, Essay").

48. Poore, Constitutions, p. 4.

49. See, for example, Massachusetts (1780), Frame of Government, Poore, Constitutions, p. 968.

50. *Department:* (1) Georgia, 1777 Constitution, Art. I, Poore, Constitutions, p. 378 ("The legislative, executive, and judiciary departments, shall be separate and distinct, so that neither exercises the powers properly belong to

the other."); (2) Massachusetts, 1780 Constitution, Declaration of Rights, Art. XXX, Poore, Constitutions, p. 960 ("[T]he legislative department shall never exercise the executive and judicial powers, or either of them; the executive shall never exercise the legislative and judicial powers, or either of them; the judicial shall never exercise the legislative and executive powers, or either of them. . . .").

Powers: (1) North Carolina, 1776 Constitution, Declaration of Rights, sec. IV, Poore, Constitutions, p. 1409 ("That the legislative, executive, and supreme judicial powers of government, ought to be forever separate and distinct from each other."); (2) Maryland, 1776 Constitution, Declaration of Rights, sec. VI, Poore, Constitutions, p. 818 ("That the legislative, executive, and judicial powers of government, ought to be forever separate and distinct from each other."); (3) New Hampshire, 1784 Constitution, Bill of Rights, sec. XXXVII, Poore, Constitutions, p. 1283 (the "essential powers" of the "legislative, executive and judicial, ought to be kept [] separate from and independent of each other. . . .").

Both department and powers: Virginia, 1776 Bill of Rights, sec. 5, Poore, Constitutions, p. 1909 ("[T]he legislative and executive powers of the State should be separate and distinct from the judiciary"); and Virginia, 1776 Constitution (para. 2), Poore, Constitutions, p. 1910 ("The legislative, executive, and judiciary department, shall be separate and distinct, so that neither exercises the powers properly belong to the other. . . .").

51. Poore, Constitutions, pp. 378, 960, 1910.

52. Poore, Constitutions, pp. 960, 968.

53. Max Farrand, *The Framing of the Constitution of the United States*, pp. 3–4 (1913). See also Hamilton, *Federalist Papers* # 22, p. 108 (noting the "want of a judiciary power" in the Articles of Confederation).

54. See *The Documentary History of the Ratification of the Constitution* (all dates are 1788): Vol. XV, p. 512 (Jan. 31); Vol. XVI, p. 72; p.120; p. 172; p. 255; p. 328; p. 431 (Feb. 7, 14, 21, 28, Mar. 6, 20, respectively) (hereafter "Documentary History").

55. Hamilton, *Federalist Papers* ## 78–81, pp. 395–420; # 78, p. 396 ("least dangerous").

56. Jonathan Elliott, *The Debates of the Several State Conventions on the Adoption of the Federal Constitution*, Vol. 4, pp. 257–58 (2d ed. 1859) (hereafter "Elliott's Debates").

57. Although the Federalist Papers were tendentious documents that did not necessarily reflect the views of the convention or those who ratified the Constitution, they provide some evidence of how the political community used language and, therefore, how it thought about government. See Cohens v. Virginia, 19 U.S. 264, 418 (1821) (Marshall, C.J.) (Federalist Papers are of "great authority" because of their "intrinsic merit" and the part that "two of its authors performed" during the ratification process).

58. Madison, *Federalist Papers* ## *47, 48,* pp. 245–56.

59. Madison, *Federalist Papers* # 47 (discussing New York, p. 249, Pennsylvania, p. 250, South Carolina, p. 251, and New Jersey, p. 250).

60. Documentary History, Vol. XV, pp. 512, 515 (Jan. 31); Vol. XVI, p. 120 (Feb. 14).

61. Documentary History, Vol. XV, p. 513 (Jan. 31); Vol. XVI, p. 174 (Feb. 21).

Madison also used the word "judicial" as an institutional reference, just as others may have used "judiciary" to refer to a judicial power. Documentary History, Vol. XV, p. 513 (Jan. 31) ("power to the general judicial"; "vest the judicial with a power"); Vol. XVI, p. 174 (Feb. 21) and p. 256 (Feb. 28) ("power of the judicial"); Vol. XVI, p. 328 (Mar. 6) ("power in the supreme judicial of the United States"). And he also used the word "judicial" to refer to a judicial department in his failed "separation of powers" constitutional amendment. Casper, Essay, p. 221 ("The powers delegated by this constitution, are appropriated to the departments to which they are respectively distributed: so that the legislative department shall never exercise the powers vested in the executive or judicial; nor the executive exercise the powers vested in the legislative or judicial; nor the judicial exercise the powers vested in the legislative or executive departments.").

62. Documentary History, Vol. II, p. 342. According to Thomas Lloyd, Wilson said (at Documentary History, Vol. II, p. 353): "[T]he United States exhibit[s] to the world, the first instance, . . . of a nation . . . deliberating fully, and deciding calmly, concerning that system of government, under which they would wish that they and their posterity live."

63. Warren, Making, pp. 739–40.

64. Abram Chayes, "How Does the Constitution Establish Justice?" 101 *Harv. L.Rev.* 1026, 1026, 1028 (1988).

65. Bank of United States v. Deveaux, 9 U.S. 61, 85 (1809).

66. 2 U.S. 419, 466 (1793).

67. Martin v. Hunter's Lessee, 14 U.S. 304, 329 (1816) (Story, J.).

68. 5 U.S. 137, 177 (1803) (Marshall, C.J.).

69. 14 U.S. at 329.

70. U.S. v. Hudson and Goodwin, 11 U.S. 32, 33 (1812) (Johnson, J.). See also Calder v. Bull, 3 U.S. 386, 398 (1798) (Iredell, J.).

71. Vile, Constitutionalism, p. 173.

NOTES TO CHAPTER 3

1. See Charles M. Cook, *The American Codification Movement* (1981).

2. This is illustrated by Chief Justice Marshall's opinions for the Court up-

holding Congress's power to create a national bank and preventing states from impairing contracts (McCulloch v. Maryland, 17 U.S. 316 [1819] [national bank]; Dartmouth College v. Woodward, 17 U.S. 518 [1819] [Contract Clause]; Sturges v. Crowninshield, 17 U.S. 122 [1819] [Contract Clause]); and by Justice Story's development of a uniform federal admiralty and commercial law (De Lovio v. Boit, 7 F. Cas. 418, 443 [C.C.D. Mass. 1815] [Admiralty law]; Swift v. Tyson, 41 U.S. 1 [1842] [federal commercial law]).

3. 5 U.S. iii (1803); 14 U.S. v–vi (1816).

4. Alexander Hamilton, *Federalist Papers # 78*, p. 396 (Max Beloff ed., 2d ed. 1987).

5. John P. Kelsh, "The Opinion Delivery Practices of the United States Supreme Court, 1790–1945," 77 *Wash. U. L.Q.* 137 (1999) (hereafter "Kelsh, Opinion"). See also Charles Warren, *The Supreme Court in United States History*, Vol. I, p. 653 (rev. ed. 1926).

6. Kelsh's data specify "approximately" 63 decisions; Kelsh, Opinion, p. 140. The seven cases I omitted are: 2 U.S. 401 (3d case) (1792); 2 U.S. 409 (1792); 2 U.S. 411 (1792); 3 U.S. 369 (1797); 3 U.S. 410 (1799); 4 U.S. 6 (1st case) (1799); 4 U.S. 6 (2d case) (1799).

7. 3 U.S. 357; 3 U.S. 411; 3 U.S. 415.

8. References to a unanimous opinion appear in 3 U.S. 6; 3 U.S. 42; 3 U.S. 188; 3 U.S. 344. Reference to a majority opinion appears in 3 U.S. 121.

9. 3 U.S. 6 (Chief Justice Jay mentioned by name); 3 U.S. 121; 3 U.S. 297; 3 U.S. 308; 3 U.S. 320. In addition, Justice Wilson is described as delivering an "opinion of the court" in 3 U.S. 344.

10. Cases referring to Chief Justice Ellsworth as author of an opinion of the court are: 3 U.S. 365; 3 U.S. 401; 3 U.S. 415; 3 U.S. 425; 4 U.S. 1; 4 U.S. 8. Cases referring to an unnamed Chief Justice as author of an opinion of the court are: 3 U.S. 302; 3 U.S. 308; 3 U.S. 321; 3 U.S. 331.

11. Cases referring to Chief Justice Ellsworth as author of the opinion, without describing it as an opinion of the court, are: 3 U.S. 319; 3 U.S. 321.

The idea of the Court speaking as an institutional body is also conveyed by references to a unanimous court in five additional cases (2 U.S. 401; 3 U.S. 184; 3 U.S. 285; 3 U.S. 378; 3 U.S. 384). And that is also the implication in several other cases where the report states "we are of opinion," "the Court were of opinion," and the "court delivered their opinion" (3 U.S. 1; 3 U.S. 382; 4 U.S. 3).

12. *The Documentary History of the Supreme Court of the United States*, Vol. I, Part I (Appointments and Proceedings), pp. 117–18 (Maeva Marcus ed., 1985) (hereafter "History, Supreme Court").

13. William R. Casto, *The Supreme Court in the Early Republic*, p. 110 (1995) (hereafter "Casto, Supreme Court").

14. The most thorough recent study suggests that Dallas omitted about 110–120 opinions, while publishing about 60 opinions; see Craig Joyce, "The Rise of the Supreme Court Reporter: An Institutional Perspective on Marshall Court Ascendancy," 83 *Mich. L.Rev.* 1291, 1303 n.74 (1985) (hereafter "Joyce, Rise").

15. *The Works of Thomas Jefferson,* Vol. XII, pp. 246, 250 (hereafter "Jefferson, Works") (letter to William Johnson, Oct. 27, 1822). See also id., pp. 213, 216 (letter to James Pleasants, Dec. 26, 1821).

16. 4 U.S. at p. 41.

17. Practices regarding lawyers' arguments varied. Wheaton claimed to present nothing more than a "faithful outline" of lawyers' arguments; 14 U.S. iii (1816). Peters was unsure what to do. When Peters considered issuing *two* volumes of reports for the 1830 term (made necessary in part by the inclusion of lawyers' arguments), he asked Marshall's advice. Marshall assured him that lawyers' arguments were important in shedding understanding on what the Court did, warranting a second volume. Frank D. Wagner, "The Role of the Supreme Court Reporter in History," 26 *J. Supreme Court History* 9, 16 (2001) (hereafter "Wagner, Role"). The reporter Black omitted some lawyers' arguments "when it was found that room could not be made for them"; 67 U.S. 3 (1863) (prefatory note).

18. Erwin Surrency, *A History of American Law Publishing,* pp. 44–45 (1990) (hereafter "Surrency, History").

19. Farmers' Bank v. Burchard, 33 Vt. 346, 393–94 (1860).

20. Kelsh, Opinion, p. 139.

21. 2 U.S. 415.

22. 3 U.S. 336.

23. 3 U.S. 401.

24. Compare 4 U.S. 33, 35 with 5 U.S. 1, 44. See also 25 U.S. 117, where the Supreme Court concluded that a Tennessee state court's judgment was part of the record on appeal, but the court's opinion was not, even though at the time of the Tennessee decision state law required the opinions to be in writing.

25. *Reports of Cases Adjudged in the Superior Court of the State of Connecticut, from the Year 1785, to May 1788* (hereafter "Kirby's Reports").

26. Francis Hopkinson's *Judgements in Admiralty in Pennsylvania* is sometimes said to be the first of the state law reports (in 1789), beating out Kirby's Connecticut Reports by one month, but Hopkinson's volume contained only six cases. Frederick Hicks, *Materials and Methods of Legal Research,* p. 132 n.4 (3d ed. 1942).

27. Kirby's Reports, pp. 118, 119, 139, 150.

28. Kirby's Reports, pp. 22, 27, 127, 134.

29. Casto, Supreme Court, p. 110.

30. 1 N.J.L. 19, 24 (1790).

31. 1 N.Jy. 54 ("We"); 1 N.Jy. 67, 125 ("I"); 1 N.Jy. 19, 83, 111, 274 (both "I" and "we" in same opinion).

32. Volume I of Johnson's unofficial New York Reports for 1799 to 1800 (hereafter "Johnson, Reports") (cases beginning on pp. 110, 120, 123, 127, 147, 156, 162, 231, 240).

33. See Johnson, Reports (cases beginning on pp. 17, 169, 310).

34. See Johnson, Reports (cases beginning on pp. 142, 153, 163).

35. See, for example, 1 U.S. 491.

36. See, for example, 1 U.S. 443, 447, 451, 453, 459, 464.

37. 2 Bay's Rep. 11, 17; 2 Bay's Rep. 115, 116; 2 Bay's Rep. 237, 242.

38. N. Chipman, *Reports of Cases Determined in the Supreme Court*, Book I, pp. 4–5 (1792) (hereafter "Chipman, Reports").

39. See, for example, Chipman, Reports, pp. 19, 58.

40. See Chipman, Reports, pp. 86–87.

41. See, for example, 1 Wash. 8,11; 4 Call 213, 217, 221, 234, 357.

42. See, for example, 1 Wash. 9, 10.

43. See, for example, 1 Wash. 260, 262; 2 Call 198.

44. Leonard Baker, *John Marshall, A Life in Law,* pp. 414–15 (1974) (Marshall experienced Pendleton's use of a single opinion of the court while arguing before the Virginia court).

45. David Mays, *Edmund Pendleton, 1721–1803,* p. 263 (1952).

46. Jefferson, Works, Vol. XII, pp. 246, 248–49 (letter to William Johnson, Oct. 27, 1822). See also "Letter from Jefferson to Johnson," Mar. 4, 1823, id. at 277, 279–80 (importance of seriatim opinions).

Pendleton's opinion of the court practice in the late 18th Century was not securely established and evoked a "seriatim" reaction. The reporter Francis Gilmer complained that his reports were enlarged beyond his "expectation or control" by the "number and length of seriatim opinions." Francis W. Gilmer, *Preface to Reports of Cases Decided in the Court of Appeals for 1820–1821,* Preface, p. 786 (in Virginia Reports Annotated, Vol. I).

47. See especially, Kelsh, "The Opinion Delivery Practices of the United States Supreme Court, 1790–1945," 77 *Wash. U. L.Q.* 137 (1999); G. Edward White, "The Working Life of the Marshall Court, 1815–1835," 70 *Va. L.Rev.* 1 (1984) (hereafter "White, Working Life"); Karl L. ZoBell, "Division of Opinion in the Supreme Court: A History of Judicial Disintegration," 44 *Cornell L.Rev.* 186 (1959) (hereafter "ZoBell, Division").

48. ZoBell, Division, p. 194.

49. Talbot v. Seaman, 5 U.S. 1, 26 (1801).

50. Wilson v. Mason, 5 U.S. 45, 87 (1801) (the second opinion of the court after Marshall became Chief Justice).

51. The first full opinion in Volume 6 of the U.S. Reports began "Marshall,

262 | Notes to Chapter 3

C.J. after stating the facts of the case, delivered the opinion of the court"; Faw v. Marsteller, 6 U.S. 10, 22 (1804).

52. Kelsh, Opinion, p. 144; ZoBell, Division, p. 194.

53. White, Working Life, pp. 38–39.

54. ZoBell, Division, p. 193 n.41; Kelsh, Opinion, p. 149.

55. ZoBell, Division, p. 194.

56. Kelsh, Opinion, pp. 146–47.

57. McIntire v. Wood, 11 U.S. 504, 505 (1813).

58. Kelsh, Opinion, p. 148.

59. White, Working Life, p. 40.

60. See Jefferson, Works, Vol. XII, pp. 246, 277 (Jefferson letters to William Johnson, Oct. 27, 1822 and Mar. 4, 1823); id. at 135 (to Spencer Roane, Sept. 6, 1819, impeachment a "scarecrow"); id. at 213 (to James Pleasants, Dec. 26, 1821); id. at 295, 296 (to James Madison, June 13, 1823, "proper restraint by their being compelled to explain publicly the grounds of their opinions"). See also Donald Morgan, *Justice William Johnson, The First Dissenter*, p. 171 (1954) (hereafter "Morgan, Johnson") (discussing pro-seriatim views of Roane and Madison).

61. Jefferson, Works, Vol. XII, p. 248 (Jefferson letter to William Johnson, Oct. 27, 1822) (divided judgment has less weight as precedent).

62. Morgan, Johnson, p. 171 n.11.

63. An important exception was Ogden v. Saunders, 25 U.S. 213 (1827), which was also Marshall's only dissent in a constitutional case.

64. Talbot v. Seaman, 5 U.S. 1, 43 (1801).

65. 7 U.S. 267 (1806) ("has," "understands," "does"); 17 U.S. 255, 291 (1819) ("considers").

66. Mandeville v. Holey, 26 U.S. 136, 137 (1828) ("The Court are satisfied"); Soulard v. U.S., 29 U.S. 511, 511 (1830) ("The Court have"); U.S. v. Robertson, 30 U.S. 641, 660 (1831) ("The court are divided"); Brown v. Swann, 33 U.S. 435, 435 (1834) ("the court are of opinion"); Ex Parte U.S., 33 U.S. 700, 700 (1834) ("The court are unanimous").

67. White, Working Life, pp. 34–35, 39–42; see also id. pp. 41–42 (Nov. 10, 1831 letter from Marshall to Story expressing concern that the scattering of Justices would lead to more seriatim opinions).

68. Briscoe v. Commonwealth's Bank, 33 U.S. 118, 121 (1834) (two justices absent). See also Mayor v. Miln, 34 U.S. 85, 85 (1835) (Supreme Court will not take up cases involving constitutional issues unless the Court is at full strength).

69. U.S. v. Gooding, 25 U.S. 460, 478 (1827).

70. See www.ourcivilisation.com/smartboard/shop/gowerse/complete/chap904 .htm; www.alt-usage-english.org/groupnames.html.

71. See Norman Blake, *A History of the English Language*, Ch. 9 (1996); Manfred Gorlach, *English in Nineteenth-Century England* (1999); George

Krapp, *Modern English: Its Growth and Present Use,* pp. 243, 257–59 (Marckwardt rev. ed., 1969); Sterling Leonard, *The Doctrine of Correctness in English Usage, 1700–1800,* Ch. 12 (1929).

72. G. H. McKnight, *Modern English in the Making,* pp. 527–30 (1928).

73. For plural references to the United States, see, for example, 7 U.S. 73, 81; 17 U.S. 316, 345; 20 U.S. 283, 292. I am aware of one such reference *after* the Civil War; U.S. v. Perryman, 100 U.S. 235, 236 (1879).

74. I conducted the Westlaw search for the time periods specified in the text, using five databases: SCT-OLD (before 1945), SCT, ALLSTATES-OLD (before 1945), ALLSTATES, and LAW-RPTS (for English cases).

PLURAL: (("court are" +5 "of opinion") or ("court were" +5 "of opinion")) % {but not} minority or majority or member or district or both or justices or judges +5 (("court are" +5 "of opinion") or ("court were" +5 "of opinion"))

SINGULAR: (("court is" +5 "of opinion") or ("court was" +5 "of opinion")) % {but not} minority or majority or member or district or justices or judges +5 (("court is" +5 "of opinion") or ("court was" +5 "of opinion"))

For the U.S. Supreme Court, the "Before 1801" cases excluded Pennsylvania cases by adding "% {but not} co(pa.)" to the Westlaw search.

The "+5" in the middle of the phrase "court is {was, are, were} of opinion" identifies cases in which one or more adverbs, such as "clearly" or "unanimously" appeared within the phrase.

The "% {but not} minority or majority or member or justices or judges +5" excludes cases in which the Court said something like "a majority of the court are," which would not have been a case where the Court spoke with a single voice; "% {but not} district" excludes cases in which the Court stated that a district court was of a particular opinion.

The search had several shortcomings. First, a case could include quotes from older opinions; this probably overstates the plurals, because more recent cases probably quote older cases where the plural was more likely. Second, references in lawyers' arguments were not excluded. Third, there were probably some false positives (as in "if this court were," which indicates mood, not plural number).

75. The following summary of the evolution of the U.S. Supreme Court reporting system is based primarily on the following sources: J.C. Bancroft Davis, *Appendix to the Reports of Decisions of the Supreme Court of the United States,* 131 U.S. at pp. lxiv–ccxxxiv (1889); Morris Cohen & Sharon O'Connor, *A Guide to the Early Reports of the Supreme Court of the United States* (1995); Gerald T. Dunne, "Early Court Reporters," *Supreme Court Historical Society* (Yearbook 1976); Dwight Jessup, *Reaction and Accommodation: The United States Supreme Court and Political Conflict, 1809–1835* (1978); Craig Joyce, "The Rise of the Supreme Court Reporter: An Institutional Perspective on Marshall Court Ascendancy," 83 *Mich. L.Rev.* 1291 (1985); Erwin Surrency, "Law Reports in the United States," 25 *Am. J. Leg. Hist.* 48 (1981); Erwin

Surrency, *A History of American Law Publishing,* Ch. 5 (1990); Frank D. Wagner, "The Role of the Supreme Court Reporter in History," 26 *J. Supreme Court History* 9 (2001); G. Edward White, "The Working Life of the Marshall Court, 1815–1835," 70 *Va. L.Rev.* 1 (1984).

See also the following material in the Oliver Wendell Holmes Devise, *History of the Supreme Court of the United States: Julius Goebel, Jr.,* Ch. XV, "The Supreme Court—Appellate Practice," in Vol. I, *Antecedents and Beginnings to 1801,* pp. 662–721 (1971); G. Edward White, Ch. VI, "The Reporters: Henry Wheaton, Richard Peters and Wheaton v. Peters," in Volumes III–IV, *The Marshall Court and Cultural Change, 1815–1835,* pp. 384–426 (1988); George Lee Haskins & Herbert A. Johnson, *A History of the Supreme Court of the United States,* Vol. II, *Foundations of Power: John Marshall, 1801–1815* (1981) (passim).

76. This chapter does not deal with reports of federal judicial opinions below the Supreme Court level. The use of juries in the lower federal courts with the power to declare law might have made law reports less important, although the decline of jury lawmaking as the 19th Century progressed would alter that equation. Chapter 4, dealing with state law reports, considers a possible relationship between jury lawmaking and the importance of law reports.

77. 1 Stat. 73 (1789).

78. Henry Wheaton, "Reports of Cases Argued and Adjudged in the Supreme Court of the United States, February Term, 1818," 8 *N. Am. Rev.* 63 (1818).

79. Act of Mar. 3, 1817, 3 Stat. 376, Ch. 63 (1817).

80. Ron Chernow, *Alexander Hamilton,* p. 289 (2004).

81. The 1817 law had a three-year life and was renewed in 1820, 1823, and 1827. Annual congressional appropriations provided for payment to the reporter during the 1830s, when there was no authorization law in effect. Note, "American Reports and Reporters," 22 *Am. Jurist* 108, 110–11 (1839).

82. See John H. Langbein, "Chancellor Kent and the History of Legal Literature," 93 *Colum. L.Rev.* 547 (1993).

83. 33 U.S. at pp. 619–20.

84. Peters's Condensed Reports of selected cases, decided before he became the reporter, omitted lawyers' arguments and were apparently a "roaring success"; Joyce, Rise, pp. 1364–65, 1369. Curtis's 22-volume 1856 edition of all prior Supreme Court cases was issued without lawyers' arguments and won considerable praise; Morris Cohen & Sharon O'Connor, *A Guide to the Early Reports of the Supreme Court of the United States,* pp. 83–84 (1995) (hereafter "Cohen & O'Connor, Guide").

85. 25 U.S. 611, 614, 640–43 (1827).

86. One piece of evidence is a comparison of manuscript copies of the Iredell

and Wilson opinions in Chisholm v. Georgia with Dallas's version. The differences are primarily stylistic (for example, omitting "the"; "perfectly convinced" vs. "decidedly of opinion") or the result of hearing a word differently ("precaution" vs. "position"; "controversies" vs. "consequences"). See History, Supreme Court, Vol. V, pp. 164–86 (Iredell), pp. 193–214 (Wilson). The most substantive difference I could find was the absence of the word "national" before "judiciary" in Wilson's manuscript, in contrast to Dallas's inclusion of the word.

87. Cohen & O'Connor, Guide, pp. 84–85 (discussing the reporter Howard, who succeeded Peters in 1843).

88. 28 U.S. 397 (1830).

89. 33 U.S. at p. vii (1834).

90. 42 U.S. xxxv (1843) (rule no. 42, issued in 1835).

91. Pub. L. No. 272, 67th Cong., Ch. 267, sec. 226, 42 Stat. 816 (1922) ($8,000 payment as full compensation). Compare Pub. L. No. 475, 61st Cong., Ch. 231, sec. 226, 36 Stat. 1152, 1153 (1911), where a dollar compensation was fixed but the reporter could still enjoy profits from sale to the public, albeit at a price fixed by Congress.

92. Wagner, Role, p. 16. The last report of an opinion to include lawyers' arguments was 315 U.S. 521 (1942).

93. Wagner, Role, pp. 9–10.

94. Wagner, Role, pp. 12–13. The duties of the U.S. Reporter are described in 28 U.S.C. sec. 673.

95. No official reports have ever been issued for the opinions of the federal circuit courts of appeals or district courts, Surrency, History, p. 71, although the authorization for the Attorney General to purchase the Federal Reporter (Act of March, 1911, sec. 229, 36 Stat. 1155) provides an indirect federal subsidy for private reports.

96. History, Supreme Court, Vol. V, p. xxiv.

97. 131 U.S. at pp. xv–xvi.

98. Joyce, Rise, p. 1310 n.110.

99. Joyce, Rise, pp. 1374, 1378.

100. Joyce, Rise, pp. 1357–58.

101. R. Kirkland Corzine, "The Emergence of Written Appellate Briefs in the Nineteenth-Century United States," 38 *Am. J. Leg. Hist.* 482, 485–98 (1994).

102. See also 28 U.S.C. sec. 411(a), which requires the opinions to be printed, bound, and distributed in the U.S. Reports.

103. Ch. 74, sec. 10, 27 Stat. 434, 436, Feb. 9, 1893. Tucker's preface to Volume 1 of the App.D.C. series (pp. iii–iv, dated May 15, 1894) states that he received manuscript copies of opinions handed down from the bench. An 1894 law repeated the writing requirement; Ch. 172, sec. 10, 28 Stat. 160, July 30, 1894.

NOTES TO CHAPTER 4

1. See generally Denis P. Duffy, "Genre and Authority: The Rise of Case Reporting in the Early United States," 74 *Chi.-Kent L.Rev.* 263 (1998) (hereafter "Duffy, Genre").

2. Henry Wheaton, William Johnson, & Dudley Atkins Tyng, "Law Reports," 18 *N. Am. Rev.* 371, 372–73 (1824) (hereafter "1824 NAR") (U.S. Supreme Court not successor to another court; appears in "naked simplicity" and encounters "immense obstacles").

3. Vermont v. New Hampshire, 289 U.S. 593, 608 (1933).

4. Francis R. Aumann, "American Law Reports: Yesterday and Today," 4 *Ohio St. L.J.* 331, 341 n.39 (1938).

5. Anton-Hermann Chroust, "The Dilemma of the American Lawyer in the Post-Revolutionary Era," 35 *Notre Dame L.Rev.* 48, 48–50, 66–68 (1959) (hereafter "Chroust, Dilemma").

6. See, for example, the discussion of state struggles over judicial authority in North Carolina and Massachusetts in the following articles: Walter F. Pratt, Jr., "The Struggle for Judicial Independence in Antebellum North Carolina: A Tale of Two Judges," 4 *L. & Hist. Rev.* 129 (1986); Samuel Shapiro, "The Conservative Dilemma: The Massachusetts Constitutional Convention of 1853," 33 *New Eng. Q.* 207 (1960).

7. Alexis de Toqueville, *Democracy in America,* Vol. I, p. 298 (Barnes & Co. 1858).

8. E. Lee Shepard, "Lawyers Look at Themselves: Professional Consciousness and the Virginia Bar, 1770–1850," 25 *Am. J. Leg. Hist.* 1, 19 (1981) (reports give lawyers material for argument and "sense of professionalism").

9. Charles Sellers, *The Market Revolution,* p. 47 (1991). See also *Lawyers and the Rise of Western Political Liberalism,* p. 2 (Terence C. Halliday & Lucien Karpik eds., 1997) (lawyers secure their own class position and serve modern capitalist economy).

10. Another and even clearer manifestation of the interaction between judicial and professional concerns in the early 19th Century involved the prevention of codification of judicial law through legislation. See Elijah Pane, "Reports of Cases Argued and Determined in the Circuit Court of the United States, for the Second Circuit," 27 *N. Am. Rev.* 167, 172 (1828) (hereafter "1828 NAR"). See generally Charles M. Cook, *The American Codification Movement* (1981); Robert W. Gordon, "Book Review of Cook, *The American Codification Movement,*" 36 *Vand. L.Rev.* 431 (1983).

As Robert Gordon explains, despite an "obsession" with codification among legal commentators from 1820 to 1850 (nearly every issue of the periodical American Jurist at this time contained some discussion of codification), real codification never stood much of a chance. Gordon, supra, at pp. 431, 433–36.

Bentham was viewed as too radical and his offers to assist American governments in codifying the law were generally spurned. Livingstone, the codifier of Louisiana law, seemed to be Bentham's only active U.S. admirer. See H.L.A. Hart, *Essays on Bentham,* pp. 76–78 (1982). Consequently, the debate about codification paid modest attention to Bentham's proposals to codify the common law, and the bench and bar were successful in focusing attention on the more professionally oriented efforts to consolidate the statute books—what was known as "revision" of the law. See "A Notice of the Most Recent Revisions, Digests, and Collections, of the Statute Laws of the United States, and of the Several States," 18 *Am. Jurist* 227, 230–53 (1837).

More drastic codification of the common law was also discouraged by the authoring of treatises, such as those by Chancellor Kent of New York and Justice Story. Kent's *Commentaries on American Law* were published in 1826. Story's eight private law treatises appeared between 1832 and 1845; R. Kent Newmyer, *Supreme Court Justice Joseph Story,* p. 281 (1985). These treatises helped to demonstrate that legal expertise could organize and develop indigenous common law legal doctrine without necessarily resorting to statutory codification. See also Morton J. Horwitz, *The Transformation of American Law, 1780–1860,* pp. 257–58 (1977).

11. Clark v. Herring, 5 Binn. 33, 38 (1812) (Pennsylvania); Lawrence M. Friedman, *A History of American Law,* pp. 111–15 (2d ed. 1985) (mentioning New Jersey and Kentucky; New Jersey repealed its prohibition in 1819); John H. Langbein, "Chancellor Kent and the History of Legal Literature," 93 *Colum. L.Rev.* 547, 568 n.106 (1993) (New York).

12. Chroust, Dilemma, p. 63; "Law Reporting," 8 *Alb. L.J.* 1, 2 (1873–74).

13. "The Boston Review" (March 1806), located at http://www.sjchs-history .org/review1806.html.

14. See Dale A. Oesterle, "Formative Contributions to American Corporate Law by the Massachusetts Supreme Judicial Court from 1806 to 1810" in *The History of the Law in Massachusetts: The Supreme Judicial Court, 1692–1992* (Russell Osgood ed., 1992).

15. 1828 NAR, pp. 179–80.

16. Note, "American Reports and Reporters," 22 *Am. Jurist* 108, 108 (1839) (hereafter "1839 AMJUR"). See also 1824 NAR, p. 377 (by 1824, 15 states had published law reports, eight of which were "adopted and commissioned by the public authority"). One observer even argued that the law reports were worthy of study by "scholars of taste and general literature"; 1828 NAR, p. 183. Another commentator says that official reports became universal after the 1840s and 1850s; Frederick G. Kempin, Jr., "Precedent and Stare Decisis: The Critical Years, 1800 to 1850," 3 *Am. J. Leg. Hist.* 28, 35–36 (1959) (hereafter "Kempin, Precedent").

17. Frederick C. Hicks, *Materials and Methods of Legal Research,* p. 137

(3d ed. 1942) (hereafter "Hicks, Materials"); Michael Swygert & Jon Bruce, "The Historical Origins, Founding, and Early Development of Student-Edited Law Reviews," 36 *Hastings L.J.* 739, 748–51 (1985); Erwin Surrency, *A History of American Law Publishing,* p. 39 (1990) (hereafter "Surrency, History") ("With independence, American lawyers strove to create a distinctively American body of law.").

18. See also Wilfred J. Ritz, *American Judicial Proceedings First Printed before 1801: An Analytical Bibliography* (1984).

19. See William E. Nelson, *Americanization of the Common Law,* Ch. 9, pp. 165–74 (1975); Renee B. Lettow, "New Trial for Verdict against the Law: Judge-Jury Relations in Early Nineteenth-Century America," 71 *Notre Dame L.Rev.* 505, 508, 518–19 (1996); Note, "The Changing Role of the Jury in the Nineteenth Century," 74 *Yale L.J.* 170 (1964).

20. Surrency, History, p. 92 (all but Pennsylvania).

21. Surrency, History, pp. 82–89.

22. 1839 AMJUR, p. 108. Cf. 1828 NAR, p. 179 (law reporting is "the promulgation of the laws").

23. Surrency, History, p. 41.

24. See generally Thomas J. Young, Jr., "A Look at American Reporting in the 19th Century," 68 *Law Library J.* 294, 298–99, 303 (1975) (hereafter "Young, Look").

25. Connecticut—see, for example, Peck v. Smith, 1 Conn. 103, 105 (1814); Georgia (often when the opinion was not unanimous)—see, for example, 20 Ga. 804 (1856); 23 Ga. 536 (1857); Maryland—see, for example, 2 H. & G. 1 (1827); 4 H. & J. 450 (1819); Massachusetts—see, for example, 4 Mass. 245 (1808); 8 Mass. 162 (1811); Michigan—see, for example, 4 Mich. 27 (1852); New Jersey—see, for example, 15 N.J.L. 155 (1835); North Carolina (often when divided in opinion)—see, for example, 15 N.C. 197 (1833); Pennsylvania —see, for example, Eakin v. Raub, 12 Serg. & Rawle 330 (1825); 4 Yeates 399 (1807); South Carolina—see, for example, 3 S.C.L. 115 (1802); Virginia—see, for example, 22 Va. 172 (1822); 20 Va. 328 (1819); Wisconsin—see, for example, 3 Wis. 157 (1854).

26. William R. Casto, *The Supreme Court in the Early Republic,* p. 110 (1995) (Connecticut's 1784 requirement not followed, with judges instead writing majority and dissenting opinions).

27. Similarly, Louisiana required seriatim votes by statute in 1821, commencing with the junior member, but this requirement was repealed one year later and was, in any event, satisfied in form by the statement "I concur in the opinion for the reasons adduced." Joe W. Sanders, "The Role of Dissenting Opinions in Louisiana," 23 *La. L.Rev.* 673, 677 (1963).

28. See Robert C. Berring & Elizabeth A. Edinger, *Finding the Law,* pp. 23–

24 (11th ed. 1999) (hereafter "Berring & Edinger, Finding"); 1828 NAR, pp. 179–80.

29. Caleb Nelson, "A Re-Evaluation of Scholarly Explanations for the Rise of the Elective Judiciary in Antebellum America," 37 *Am. J. Leg. Hist.* 190 (1993).

30. 1828 NAR, p. 180; 1839 AMJUR, p. 108; Hicks, Materials, p. 136; Surrency, History, pp. 42–43.

31. See George Lee Flint, Jr., "Secured Transactions History: The Northern Struggle to Defeat the Judgment Lien in the Pre-Chattel Mortgage Act Era," 20 *N. Ill. L.Rev.* 1, 7 n.24 (2000). See also Lewis L. Laska, *Tennessee Legal Research Handbook*, p. 81 (1977) (since 1829, Tennessee Supreme Court required to write opinions, whether or not opinions reported).

32. "American Law Periodicals," 2 *Alb. L.J.* 445, 447 (1870) (until 1843, "western" states lacked good legal periodicals; Western Law Journal started in Cincinnati to do for the West what the American Jurist had done for the East).

33. Evan Haynes, *The Selection and Tenure of Judges*, pp. 99–100 (1944) (hereafter "Haynes, Selection").

34. Max Radin, "The Requirement of Written Opinions," 18 *Calif. L.Rev.* 486 (1930) (hereafter "Radin, Requirement").

35. Frederick Judson, "The Procedure in Our American Judicial System," 46 *Am. L.Rev.* 865, 874 (1912).

36. Radin, Requirement, p. 491 n.15 (Florida, Kansas, Maryland, Missouri, Nebraska, West Virginia). See, for example, McCalls Ferry Power Co. v. Price, 69 A. 832, 838 (Md. 1908) (requirement that written opinions be filed within three months was directory). See also Note, "The Written-Opinion Statutes," 5 *Ill. L.Rev.* 233 (1910–1911) (arguing that these laws were not obligatory).

37. Houston v. Williams, 13 Calif. 24 (1859) (legislatures could no more require judges to give reasons than judges could force legislatures to give reasons, citing Coke's argument that setting down reasons could take judges away from "necessary service of the commonwealth"); Vaughan v. Harp, 49 Ark. 160 (1887); State v. District Court, 105 Pac. 721 (Mont. 1909).

38. Andrew A. Bruce, "Judicial Buncombe in North Dakota and Other States," 88 *Central L.J.* 136, 137 (1919).

39. Haynes, Selection, pp. 112, 115, 124, 127.

40. Duffy, Genre, p. 273.

41. In two instances, state law specified someone who held a particular judicial office to be the reporter (Delaware in 1830 and 1831) or named a specific individual to be the reporter (Kentucky in 1810 and 1822).

42. 33 U.S. 591 (1834). See also Banks v. Manchester, 128 U.S. 244 (1888).

43. Callaghan v. Myers, 128 U.S. 617, 647 (1888).

44. Unofficial reporters had also expressed concern about inadequate com-

pensation—a Georgia reporter said that the reports would have come out earlier but for too few subscribers; a Vermont reporter said that expense might prevent continuation of the reports; and a Kentucky reporter had insufficient sales to recoup expenses.

45. Richard Priest Dietzman, "The Kentucky Law Reports and Reporters," 16 *Ky. L.J.* 16, 25 (1927) (hereafter "Dietzman, Kentucky").

46. Kempin, Precedent, p. 35.

47. Morris L. Cohen & Paul C. Seeman, "A Man without Qualities: Ephraim Williams, First Reporter of the Supreme Court," 9 *Mass. Leg. Hist.* 137, 147 (2003); John H. Moore, "One Hundred Fifty Years of Official New York Reporting and the Courts in New York," 6 *Syr. L.Rev.* 273, 275 (1955).

48. See Duffy, Genre, pp. 273–75 (rise of written opinion crowding out lawyers' arguments).

49. John B. West, "A Symposium of Law Publishers," 23 *Am. L.Rev.* 396, 400, 403–05 (1889) (hereafter "West 1889").

50. West 1889, p. 404 ("The opinions are printed from compared and certified copies of the original, furnished in most cases by the clerk himself, or other custodian. . . .").

51. Hicks, Materials, p. 154.

52. Surrency, History, p. 49.

53. Banks v. Manchester, 128 U.S. 244, 253 (1888). See generally Patterson & Joyce, "Monopolizing the Law: The Scope of Copyright Protection for Law Reports and Statutory Compilations," 36 *UCLA L.Rev.* 719 (1989).

54. Hicks, Materials, p. 151.

55. Young, Look, pp. 305–06. The contemporary debate over whether to publish *all* opinions is consistent with the demise of the reporter's discretion, because the publication decision rests with the court.

56. Berring & Edinger, Finding, pp. 24–25; Robert C. Berring, "Legal Research and Legal Concepts: Where Form Molds Substance," 75 *Cal. L.Rev.* 15, 21 (1987) (hereafter "Berring, Research").

57. West's commitment to completeness did not go unchallenged. See James E. Briggs, "A Symposium of Law Publishers," 23 *Am. L.Rev.* 407 (1889), for a defense of selective publication of judicial opinions.

58. "The National Reporter System," 1 *Docket* 648, 649 (1912).

59. West 1889, p. 401. See also Surrency, History, p. 28 (by the close of the 19th Century, lawyers evaluated publication by timeliness).

60. Report of the Special Committee on Reports and Digests," 2 *Am. Bar Assoc. J.* 618, 622 (1916) (hereafter "1916 ABA Report").

61. Report of the Committee on Law Reporting," 18 *A.B.A. Rep.* 343 (1895) (hereafter "1895 ABA Report"). See also John F. Dillon, "Paper Prepared at Request of the Committee on Judicial Administration and Remedial Procedure," 9 *A.B.A. Rep.* 257 (1886) (entitled "Law Reports and Law Reporting").

62. 1916 ABA Report, p. 622.

63. Alden I. Rosbrook, "The Art of Judicial Reporting," 10 *Cornell L.Q.* 103, 106 (1925).

64. Berring, Research, pp. 18–19, 20.

65. Dietzman, Kentucky, p. 27.

66. 1916 ABA Report, p. 621.

67. 1916 ABA Report, pp. 625–56. Sometimes state law eliminated the reporter's power to determine which opinions should be published. See, for example, Act of June 12, 1878, No. 232, 1878 Pa. Laws 201, stating that "[t]he court shall cause to be reported such of its decisions . . . as determine any theretofore unsettled, or new and important, or modify any theretofore settled, question of law . . . , or that give construction to a statute of ambiguous or doubtful import, together with such other of its decisions as may be deemed by the court of public interest and importance."

68. 1916 ABA Report, pp. 632–33 (Illinois), p. 642 (New York). Official state reporters also usually published all of what the judge wrote, not just selected passages of an opinion. The 1916 ABA Report indicated that in only two states did the reporter have some choice about how much of the opinion to report (p. 636 [Maine]; p. 653 [South Dakota]), and the South Dakota correspondent suggested that the court should make this decision.

69. Leah F. Chanin, "A Survey of the Writing and Publication of Opinions in Federal and State Appellate Courts," 67 *Law Library J.* 362, 367, 370, 372 (1974) (Arkansas, Kansas, Maine, New York). The current Arkansas statute (Ark. Code Ann. sec. 16-11-203 [Michie 1987]) states that the reporter does not have to report unimportant cases if the Chief Justice concurs in this decision. But see Mass. Gen. Laws Ch. 221, sec. 64 (1999) ("[The reporter] shall in his discretion report the several cases more or less at large according to their relative importance, so as not unnecessarily to increase the size or number of the volumes of reports.").

70. Ga. Code of 1861, pt. I, tit. 5, Ch. 2, Art. III, sec. 222, p. 53.

71. Dietzman, Kentucky, p. 25.

72. 1895 ABA Report, p. 364.

73. 1916 ABA Report, p. 627 (Arizona); p. 635 (Kansas).

74. 1916 ABA Report, p. 626 (Alabama); p. 644 (Ohio); pp. 631–32 (Georgia); p. 638 (Minnesota).

75. See *The Bluebook: A Uniform System of Citation*, tbl T.1 (Columbia Law Review Ass'n et al., eds., 18th ed. 2005); John William Wallace, *The Reporters*, pp. 570–91 (1882).

76. Leah F. Chanin, Pamela J. Gregory, & Sarah K. Wiant, *Legal Research in the District of Columbia, Maryland and Virginia*, p. 379 (Virginia section) (2d ed. 2000); Surrency, History, p. 45. See also Berring & Edinger, Finding, p. 24.

77. "Law Reports," 9 *Alb. L.J.* 230, 230 (1874).

78. See, for example, the brief biographical sketches of Kentucky reporters in Dietzman, Kentucky, p. 27.

79. 1916 ABA Report, p. 623.

80. According to the "Bluebook," cited in note 75, *supra*, the following 21 states adopted the West National Reporting System as their official reports for opinions from their highest court; the year of adoption is in parentheses: Alabama (1976); Alaska (1960); Colorado (1980); Delaware (1966); Florida (1948); Indiana (1981); Iowa (1968); Kentucky (1951); Louisiana (1972); Maine (1965); Minnesota (1977); Mississippi (1966); Missouri (1956); North Dakota (1953); Oklahoma (1953); Rhode Island (1980); South Dakota (1976); Tennessee (1971); Texas (1962); Utah (1974); Wyoming (1959). The copyright notices in the official state reports specify that five additional states reprint copies of the West reports as their official state reports (Arizona, Hawaii, Idaho, New Mexico, West Virginia).

Seven of the 26 states relying on West still designate a reporter: one reporter (Alabama, Colorado, and Florida); one individual as both reporter and clerk (Idaho and Maine); the Attorney General and the reporter are the same official (Tennessee); the Attorney General is the ex officio reporter (West Virginia). Information about whether a state makes use of a "reporter" appears in http:// arjd.washlaw.edu/ARJD2004final.htm; for Tennessee, see Tenn. Const., Art. 6, sec. 5; for West Virginia, see West Va. Const., Art. 7, sec. 1 (for West Virginia).

81. The copyright notice in the Montana law reports specifies that the copyright is in the "State Reporter," which is a publishing company (currently Lexis/ Nexis).

82. See, for example, Conn. Gen. Stat. sec. 51-216a(f) (Supp. 2004) (Commission on Official Legal Publications, an agency of the judicial branch, "shall . . . cause official legal publications to be copyrighted . . . for the benefit of the people of the state"); Ga. Code Ann. sec. 50-18-34 (2002) (reports shall be copyrighted and copyright belongs to the state); 705 Ill. Comp. Stat. secs. 65/1, 65/5 (1999) (copyright regarding non-opinion material is in the court and the reporter for benefit of the state); Kan. Stat. Ann. sec. 20-206 (1995) (reporter to obtain copyright in volumes for the state); Mich. Comp. Laws sec. 26.6 (1994) (copyright for the state); Neb. Rev. Stat. sec. 24-212 (1995) (copyright of each volume shall be entered by the reporter for the benefit of the state); Wash. Rev. Code sec. 2.32.160 (2004) (creating Commission on Supreme Court Reports; copyright notice in reports indicates that the copyright is in the Commission). In Vermont, the copyright notice in the law reports specifies that the copyright is in the "Court Administrator, State of Vermont," and neither the reporter nor the court administrator enjoys any profits from the copyright; Lexis/Nexis is the publisher of the reports and is responsible for the editorial work.

83. See, for example, N. H. Rev. Stat. Ann. sec. 505:9-10 (1997) (reporter may dispose of copyright as deems expedient and pay proceeds to state); N. Y. Jud. Ct. Acts Law secs. 434(13), 436 (McKinney 1983 & Supp. 2004) (denying reporter any pecuniary interest in reports); Va. Code Ann. sec. 2.2-2822 (Michie 2001) (all potentially copyrightable material developed by state employee shall be property of the state).

84. Conversations with court administrators in Arkansas, Massachusetts, and North Carolina.

85. Note, "Carter v. Helmsley-Spear, Inc.: A Fair Test of the Visual Artists Rights Act," 28 *Conn. L.Rev.* 877, 885 (1996).

86. Callaghan v. Myers, 128 U.S. 617 (1888).

87. No role: Mich. Comp. Laws secs. 26.2, 26.8 (1994) (reporter shall deliver decisions, syllabus, etc. to person having contract to publish them; board of state auditors solicits contract bids for publication of reports); Mont. Code Ann. secs. 3-2-603, 18-7-101 (2003 & Supp. 2004) (government department can contract for printing); N. C. Gen. Stat. sec. 7A-6 (2000) (reporter prepares opinions for publication; Administrative Officer of the Court shall contract for printing reports, or the Supreme Court may designate commercial publisher's reports as official reports); S. C. Code Ann. secs. 14-3-120, 14-3-820 (Law. Co-op. 1977) (reporter appointed by Supreme Court, but a committee of four appointed by Speaker of House, President of Senate, and Chief Justice makes contract for publication of reports); Vt. Stat. Ann. tit. 4, sec. 17, tit. 29, sec. 1191 (2000) (justices of Supreme Court appoint a reporter, but court administrator contracts with publisher for printing and editing of law reports); Va. Code Ann. sec. 17.1-322 (Michie 2003) (reporter delivers manuscript reports to printer chosen by Comptroller).

88. One of a panel: Cal. Gov't Code sec. 68903 (1997) (contract to publish entered into by Chief Justice, Secretary of State, Attorney-General, President of State Bar, and Reporter); Conn. Gen. Stat. sec. 51-216a(b) (Supp. 2004) (commission on official legal publications, an agency of judicial department with the reporter as one member, publishes official law reports and can contract with publisher).

89. Reporter contracts with approval: Ga. Code Ann. secs. 15-4-2(2), 15-18-21 to -30 (2001) (reporter has a duty to publish reports in accordance with state printing law requiring reporter to make a contract with the publisher, with Governor's approval); Idaho Code sec. 1-506 (1998 & Supp. 2003) (reporter contracts to publish with court approval); 705 Ill. Comp. Stat., sec. 65/2 (1999) (reporter contracts to publish with court approval); Md. Code Ann., Cts. & Jud. Proc. sec. 13-204 (2002) (reporter, under court direction, lets contract for publication).

90. State printer: Kan. Stat. Ann. sec. 20-205 (1995) (reporter delivers opin-

ions to state director of printing); Nev. Rev. Stat. secs. 2.330, 2.340, 2.380 (1998) (reporter shall have opinions printed, apparently by state printer; printer gives proofs of advance sheets to reporter to examine; superintendent of state printing division causes quality printing); Ohio Rev. Code Ann. sec. 2503.21 (Anderson 2001) (reporter to deliver report in manuscript to superintendent of purchases and printing; also, with approval and under direction of court, reporter may contract to publish reports); Wash. Rev. Code sec. 2.32.100, sec. 2.32.120 (2004), sec. 43.78.070(1) (1998) (reporter's duties include giving proofs to judges who supervise publication; public printer may print reports for publisher under contract approved by Governor).

91. Reporter contracts: Ark. Code Ann. secs. 16-11-205 to -209 (Michie 1999) (reporter superintends and certifies printing job by contractor, who delivers reports to Administrative Office of the Courts, which results in payment by state auditor); Mass. Gen. Laws Ch. 221, sec. 64A (1999) (reporter to obtain contract bids for publication); Neb. Rev. Stat. sec. 24-212 (1995) (reporter causes opinions to be printed and bound); N.H. Rev. Stat. Ann. sec. 505:7 (1997) (reporter shall publish reports); N.Y. Jud. Ct. Acts Law sec. 434(1),(2) (McKinney 1983 & Supp. 2004) (contract with publisher made under direction of reporter); W. Va. Code sec. 5A-3-23 (2003) (reporter to contract with publisher).

92. It is certainly hard to imagine a modern court holding, as a 19th-Century Michigan court did, that reporters could not constitutionally be divested of their syllabus-writing authority. In re Headnotes to Opinions, 8 N.W. 552 (Mich. 1881) (requiring judges to prepare the syllabus would unconstitutionally deprive the reporter of performing an essential duty, in effect abolishing the reporter's office by reducing him to an "ordinary proofreader"). See also In re Griffiths, 20 N.E. 513 (Ind. 1889) (cannot require court to keep syllabus; that is the reporter's job).

93. Southern Pacific Co. v. Jensen, 244 U.S. 205, 222 (1917) (Holmes, J., dissenting).

NOTES TO CHAPTER 5

1. See J.G.A. Pocock, *The Ancient Constitution and the Feudal Law: A Study of English Historical Thought in the Seventeenth Century* (1987).

2. William Blackstone, *Commentaries on the Laws of England,* Vol. I, p. 84.

3. David Lieberman, *The Province of Legislation Determined: Legal Theory in Eighteenth-Century Britain,* pp. 232–35 (1989). See also Gerald J. Postema, *Bentham and the Common Law Tradition* (1986) (hereafter "Postema, Bentham").

4. H.L.A. Hart, *The Concept of Law,* pp. 94–95, 100–10 (2d ed. 1994).

5. Charles Fried, "Revolutions?" 109 *Harv. L.Rev.* 13, 26 n.66 (1995).

6. See Morton J. Horwitz, "The Constitution of Change: Legal Fundamentality without Fundamentalism," 107 *Harv. L.Rev.* 30, 57–65 (1993).

7. See Laurence H. Tribe, "The Puzzling Persistence of Process-Based Constitutional Theories," 59 *Yale L.J.* 1063 (1980) (critiquing John Hart Ely, *Democracy and Distrust* (1980) for failing to develop a theory of substantive rights).

8. See Guido Calabresi, *A Common Law for the Age of Statutes* (1982) (legal landscape); William D. Popkin, *Statutes in Court* (1999) (hereafter "Popkin, Statutes") (background considerations).

9. See John F. Manning, "The Absurdity Doctrine," 116 *Harv. L.Rev.* 2387, 2389 (2003).

10. Popkin, Statutes, pp. 49–50, 73–80.

11. McCulloch v. Maryland, 17 U.S. 316, 407 (1819).

12. Philip P. Frickey, "Marshalling Past and Present: Colonialism, Constitutionalism, and Interpretation in Federal Indian Law," 107 *Harv. L.Rev.* 381, 409 (1993); William Michael Treanor, "The Original Understanding of the Takings Clause and the Political Process," 95 *Colum. L.Rev.* 782, 857–58 (1995).

13. Antonin Scalia, "Assorted Canards of Contemporary Legal Analysis," 40 *Case W. Res. L.Rev.* 581, 594–96 (1989–1990), lists the misunderstanding of McCulloch v. Maryland as one of the canards of modern judging.

14. Roper v. Simmons, 543 U.S. 551, 589, 605 (O'Connor, J., dissenting).

15. Poe v. Ullman, 367 U.S. 497, 542 (1961) (Harlan, J., dissenting).

16. Chisom v. Roemer, 501 U.S. 380 (1991).

17. Republican Party of Minnesota v. White, 536 U.S. 765 (2002).

18. 531 U.S. 98 (2000).

19. Act of Feb. 3, 1887, Ch. 90, 24 Stat. 373.

20. Gore v. Harris, 773 So.2d 524, 528–29 (Fla. 2000) (Shaw, J., concurring).

21. Bush v. Gore, 531 U.S. 1046, 1047 (2000) (Scalia, J., concurring).

22. Chevron, U.S.A. Inc. v. Natural Resources Defense Counsel, Inc., 467 U.S. 837 (1984). See Thomas W. Merrill & Kristin E. Hickman, "Chevron's Domain," 89 *Geo. L.J.* 833 (2001).

23. United States v. Mead Corp., 533 U.S. 218 (2001). In National Cable & Telecommunications Ass'n v. Brand X Internet Services, 545 U.S. 967, 1003 (2005), Justice Breyer's concurring opinion rejected Justice Scalia's view that the Mead case required some degree of formal rulemaking before Chevron-deference, arguing that Scalia had "wrongly characterized the Court's opinion in [Mead Corp.]."

24. Regions Hospital v. Shalala, 522 U.S. 448 (1998).

25. Food and Drug Administration v. Brown & Williamson Tobacco Corp., 529 U.S. 120 (2000).

26. 539 U.S. 558 (2003); 543 U.S. 551 (2005).

27. 539 U.S. at 576–77; 543 U.S. at 561.

28. Seminole Tribe of Florida v. Florida, 517 U.S. 44, 69 (1996); Kaiser Aluminum & Chemical Corp. v. Bonjorno, 494 U.S. 827, 857 (1990) (Scalia, J., concurring).

29. Benjamin N. Cardozo, *The Nature of the Judicial Process* (1921).

30. See, for example, Richard A. Posner, *Economic Analysis of Law* (6th ed. 2003).

31. Hale compares the common law to "the Argonauts' Ship [which] was the same when it returned home, as it was when it went out, tho' in the long Voyage it had successive Amendments, and scarce came back with any of its former Materials," quoted in Postema, Bentham, p. 6.

32. Popkin, Statutes, Ch. 7. See also Aharon Barak, *Purposive Interpretation in Law* (2005).

33. For a recent discussion of institutional style in Australian courts, see Matthew Groves & Russell Smyth, *A Century of Judicial Style: Changing Patterns in Judgment Writing on the High Court, 1903–2001*, pp. 255, 275–78 (2004).

34. Karl L. ZoBell, "Division of Opinion in the Supreme Court: A History of Judicial Disintegration," 44 *Cornell L.Q.* 186, 203 (1959) (hereafter "ZoBell, Division").

35. John P. Kelsh, "The Opinion Delivery Practice of the United States Supreme Court, 1790–1945," 77 *Wash. U. L.Q.* 137, 175–77 (1999). See also David O'Brien, "Institutional Norms and Supreme Court Opinions: On Reconsidering the Rise of Individual Opinions," in *Supreme Court Decision-Making* (Cornell W. Clayton & Howard Gillman eds., 1999) (discussing history of shift away from consensus norms); Kevin M. Stack, "The Practice of Dissent in the Supreme Court," 105 *Yale L.J.* 2235 (1996).

The practice of writing majority opinions with layers of sections and subsections was originally intended to simplify understanding of complex decisions, but it has enhanced the Justices' ability to write separately because it is now easy to disagree with a portion of the majority opinion without refusing to join most of what a majority has to say; B. Rudolph Delson, "Typography in the U.S. Reports and Supreme Court Voting Protocols," 76 *N.Y.U. L.Rev.* 1203 (2001).

36. In one such opinion, Justice Washington in 1805 stressed that he "owe[d] it in some measure to myself and to those who may be injured by the expense and delay to which they have been exposed to shew at least that the opinion was not hastily or inconsiderately given." United States v. Fisher, 6 U.S. 358, 398 (1805). This suggests that Jefferson's emphasis on judicial reputation as a reason for favoring seriatim opinions did in fact operate as an incentive for some judges to write separately.

37. Charles Evans Hughes, *The Supreme Court of the United States: Its Foundations, Methods, and Achievements,* p. 68 (1928).

38. Graves v. New York ex rel O'Keefe, 306 U.S. 466, 487 (1939) (Frankfurter, J., concurring).

39. Posner provides data on separate opinions as a percentage of total opinions (rather than cases with separate opinions as a percentage of total cases). See Richard A. Posner, *The Federal Courts: Crisis and Reform,* pp. 357–59 (1996) (hereafter "Posner, Federal Courts"). His data show the following percentages of separate opinions: 8.7% in 1895 (18 out of 206, all dissents); 5.6% in 1915 (16 out of 288, 14 dissents and two concurrences); and 10.3% in 1935 (18 out of 174, 14 dissents and four concurrences). As late as 1935 only 10% of U.S. Supreme Court opinions were separate opinions, but the number rose to 43% in 1955, and 57% in 1995. The increase in concurring opinions is very large—2% (1935), 11% (1960), 24% (1982), 35% (1994), 25% (1995).

40. Robert Jackson, *The Supreme Court in the American System of Government,* p. 16 (1955).

41. Morton J. Horwitz, *The Transformation of American Law, 1870–1960,* p. 169 (1992) (hereafter "Horwitz, Transformation").

42. The most notable dispute occurred in an exchange between Pound and Llewellyn about whether Pound should be admitted into the Legal Realist pantheon. See Karl. N. Llewellyn, "A Realistic Jurisprudence—The Next Step," 30 *Colum. L.Rev.* 431 (1930); Roscoe Pound, "The Call for a Realist Jurisprudence," 44 *Harv. L.Rev.* 697 (1931); Karl N. Llewellyn, "Some Realism about Realism—Responding to Dean Pound," 44 *Harv. L.Rev.* 1222 (1931). Horwitz discusses this dispute at Horwitz, Transformation, pp. 170–80. See also Thomas C. Grey, "Modern American Legal Thought," 106 *Yale L.J.* 493, 499, 501 (1996) (review of Neil Duxbury, *Patterns of American Jurisprudence* (1995) (drawing a sharp distinction between Progressives and Realists)).

43. Oliver Wendell Holmes, Jr., *The Common Law,* p.1 (1881).

44. John F. Dillon, "Paper Prepared at Request of the Committee on Judicial Administration and Remedial Procedure," 9 *A.B.A. Rep.* 257, 260 (1886).

45. Roscoe Pound, "The Need of a Sociological Jurisprudence," 31 *A.B.A. Rep.* 911 (1907).

46. See Laura Kalman, *Legal Realism at Yale, 1927–1960* (1986).

47. Jerome Frank, *Law and the Modern Mind* (1930).

48. Act of Feb. 13, 1925, Ch. 229, 43 Stat. 936 (Judges Bill).

49. Thomas G. Walker, Lee J. Epstein, & W.J. Dixon, "On the Mysterious Demise of Consensual Norms in the United States Supreme Court," 50 *J. Pol.* 361, 364–66 (1988) (hereafter "Walker, Mysterious"). See also Stacia L. Haynie, "Leadership and Consensus on the U.S. Supreme Court," 54 *J.*

Pol. 1158 (1992); Lee J. Epstein, Jeffrey A. Segal, & Harold J. Spaeth, "The Norm of Consensus on the U.S. Supreme Court," 45 *Am. J. Pol. Sci.* 362 (2001).

50. Walker, Mysterious, pp. 366–68.

51. Walker, Mysterious, pp. 378–84. But see Louis Lusky, "Fragmentation of the Supreme Court: An Inquiry into Causes," 10 *Hofstra L.Rev.* 1137 (1982).

52. Alpheus Thomas Mason, *Harlan Fiske Stone: Pillar of the Law,* pp. 589, 789 (1956) (hereafter "Mason, Stone").

53. William O. Douglas, "Chief Justice Stone," 46 *Colum. L.Rev.* 693, 695 (1946).

54. Mason, Stone, pp. 790–91.

55. Mason, Stone, pp. 575, 639.

56. Mason, Stone, pp. 574, 580.

57. Mason, Stone, p. 606. One observer suggested that decision day resembled congressional debates; Mason, Stone, p. 794.

58. Mason, Stone, p. 483.

59. Mason, Stone, pp. 639, 793–94.

60. Mason, Stone, p. 939 n.†.

61. The practice of writing separately was made easier by an expansion in the number of law clerks. The Justices had one law clerk in 1930s, got a second in 1947, a third in 1970, and a fourth in 1978; Posner, Federal Courts, pp. 139, 357.

62. Gregory A. Caldeira & Christopher J.W. Zorn, "Of Time and Consensual Norms in the Supreme Court," 42 *Am. J. Pol. Sci.* 874, 900 (1998) (hereafter "Caldeira & Zorn, Norms").

63. Mason, Stone, pp. 98, 133, 135. See also Young B. Smith, "Harlan Fiske Stone: Teacher, Scholar, and Dean," 46 *Colum. L.Rev.* 700, 705–06 (1946).

64. Mason, Stone, pp. 121–22; Herbert F. Goodrich, "The Story of the American Law Institute," 3 *Wash. U. L.Q.* 283, 283–84 (1951).

65. Mason, Stone, pp. 120, 123–24, 209, 302, 364, 434–35.

66. Mason, Stone, pp. 120 (evolving), 629 (nonformulaic), 799 (candor).

67. Mason, Stone, pp. 303, 446, 591, 796–97.

68. Harlan F. Stone, "Dissenting Opinions Are Not without Value," 26 *J. Am. Judicature Society* 78 (1942).

69. Mason, Stone, pp. 251–61, 464, 550.

70. Mason, Stone, p. 783 (quoting Konefsky).

71. See United States v. American Trucking Ass'ns, Inc., 310 U.S. 534 (1940); Gregory v. Helvering, 69 F.2d 809 (2d Cir. 1934) (Hand, Learned, J.), affirmed, 293 U.S. 465 (1935).

72. United States v. Hutcheson, 312 U.S. 219 (1941) (later law implicitly repeals prior law).

73. Gregory v. Helvering, 69 F.2d 809 (2d Cir. 1934) (Hand, J.) (plain purpose of tax law did not include transaction), affirmed, 293 U.S. 465 (1935).

74. United States v. Carolene Products Co., 304 U.S. 144, 152 n.4 (1938). See Learned Hand, "Chief Justice Stone's Conception of the Judicial Function," 46 *Colum. L.Rev.* 696, 698 (1946) (criticizing Stone's approach).

75. Steven A. Peterson, "Dissent in American Courts," 43 *J. Pol.* 412, 430 (1981). See also Caldeira & Zorn, Norms, p. 875 (norms not directly observable).

76. Scott D. Gerber & Keeok Park, "The Quixotic Search for Consensus on the U.S. Supreme Court," 91 *Am. Pol. Sci. Rev.* 390, 405 (1997).

77. Quoted in Lisa L. Milord, *The Development of the ABA Judicial Code,* p. 137 (1992).

78. Mason, Stone, pp. 589, 607–09, 797.

79. See Learned Hand, *The Bill of Rights,* p. 72 (1958) ("disunity cancels the impact of monolithic solidarity on which the authority of a bench so largely depends"); ZoBell, Division, p. 209 ("respect for, and willing obedience to, the dictates of the Court will be more easily earned" if there are fewer cases with disagreement). See also Charles Johnson & Bradley Canon, *Judicial Policies: Implementation and Impact,* pp. 168–71 (2d ed. 1999) (hereafter "Johnson, Judicial") (suggesting that the size of the judicial majority can affect the public response to judicial decisions but citing studies that question whether that is true). See also Ruth Bader Ginsburg, "Remarks on Writing Separately," 65 *Wash. L.Rev.* 133 (1990).

80. E. Wayne Thode, *Reporter's Notes to Code of Judicial Conduct,* p. 50 (1973).

81. John Hart Ely, "Another Such Victory: Constitutional Theory and Practice in a World Where Courts Are No Different from Legislatures," 77 *Va. L.Rev.* 833, 842–54 (1991).

82. See Gregory A. Caldeira, "Neither the Purse nor the Sword: Dynamics of Public Confidence in the Supreme Court," 80 *Am. Pol. Sci. Rev.* 1209 (1986); Dean Jaros & Robert Roper, "The U.S. Supreme Court: Myth, Diffuse Support, Specific Support, and Legitimacy," 8 *Am. Pol. Q.* 85 (1980); Walter F. Murphy & Joseph Tanenhaus, "Explaining Diffuse Support for the United States Supreme Court: An Assessment of Four Models," 49 *Notre Dame L.Rev.* 1037 (1974).

83. See Deborah R. Hensler, "Do We Need an Empirical Research Agenda on Judicial Independence?" 72 *S. Cal. L.Rev.* 707, 711–12 (1999).

84. Herbert Kritzer, "The Impact of *Bush v. Gore* on Public Perceptions and Knowledge of the Supreme Court," 85 *Judicature* 32 (2001). The article cautions that its data do not measure long-term effects.

85. Vincent Price & Anca Romantan, "Confidence in Institutions before, during, and after 'Indecision 2000,'" 66 *J. Pol.* 939 (2004).

86. James L. Gibson, Gregory A. Caldeira, & Lester Kenyatta Spence, "Measuring Attitudes toward the United States Supreme Court," 47 *Am. J. Pol. Sci.* 354 (2003).

87. Bush v. Gore, 531 U.S. 98, 157–58 (2000) (Breyer, J., dissenting).

88. See Valerie J. Hoekstra, *Public Reaction to Supreme Court Decisions,* pp. 113–24, 145–46, 154–55 (2003).

89. Another example of a unanimous opinion by the Chief Justice in a sensitive racial desegregation case is Swann v. Charlotte-Mecklenburg Bd. of Educ., 402 U.S. 1 (1971) (busing remedy available to desegregate schools).

See also United States v. Nixon, 418 U.S. 683 (1974), where Chief Justice Burger wrote for a unanimous Court in the Nixon Tapes case to require the President to turn various documents over to a special prosecutor. The Justices did not adopt Justice Brennan's suggestion that the Court use the Cooper v. Aaron approach, where all the Justices signed a single opinion; see Bob Woodward & Scott Armstrong, *The Brethren: Inside the Supreme Court,* pp. 296, 309–10 (1979).

90. Cooper v. Aaron, 358 U.S. 1 (1958).

91. A similar desire to project judicial authority seems to have impelled the District of Columbia Court of Appeals to issue an unusual *per curiam* opinion on behalf of all seven named judges after an *en banc* review in U.S. v. Microsoft Corp., 253 F.3d 34 (D.C. Cir. 2001).

A *per curiam* opinion may also be issued by the Court in contentious cases when time constraints force a quick decision and the judges do not have the time to hammer out a single majority opinion; no single judge takes responsibility for the opinion and no judge yields pride of authorship to another. There are three major examples: (1) the Pentagon Papers case—N.Y.Times Co. v. U.S., 403 U.S. 713 (1971) (*per curiam* opinion followed by six concurring opinions and three dissenting opinions); (2) the campaign finance case—Buckley v. Valeo, 424 U.S. 1 (1976) (*per curiam* opinion followed by five opinions, joining in part and dissenting in part from the *per curiam* opinion); and (3) the 2000 Presidential election case—Bush v. Gore, 531 U.S. 98 (2000) (*per curiam* opinion with one concurring opinion by Chief Justice Rehnquist writing for three Justices, and four dissents).

See generally Laura Krugman Ray, "The Road to Bush v. Gore: The History of the Supreme Court's Use of the *Per Curiam* Opinion," 79 *Neb. L.Rev.* 517 (2000); Richard Lowell Nygaard, "The Maligned *Per Curiam*: A Fresh Look at an Old Colleague," 5 *Scribes J. Legal Writing* 41 (1994–1995).

92. Lucas A. Powe, *The Warren Court and American Politics,* p. 45 (2000). Some observers thought Nixon meant a unanimous decision; Earl M. Maltz, *The Chief Justiceship of Warren Burger, 1969–1986,* p. 42 (2000).

93. See, for example, Garcia v. San Antonio, 469 U.S. 528 (1985) (overruling 5–4 decision in National League of Cities v. Usery, 426 U.S. 833 [1976]).

94. Alden v. Maine, 527 U.S. 706, 814 (1999) (Souter, Stevens, Ginsburg, and Breyer, J.J., dissenting).

95. See, for example, KP Permanent Make-Up, Inc. v. Lasting Improvement I, Inc., 543 U.S. 111, 113 n* (2004) (joining majority opinion except for two footnotes); Intel Corp. v. Advance Micro Devices, Inc., 542 U.S. 241, 267 (2004) (concurring in judgment).

96. Chief Justice William Rehnquist, *2004 Year-End Report on the Federal Judiciary* (2005).

97. See, for example, unpassed House Resolution 468 in the 108th Congress, 1st Sess. (2003), objecting to Supreme Court references to foreign law, undoubtedly prompted by recent Court decisions striking down capital punishment for the mentally retarded and invalidating a sodomy statute. Although these were "liberal" decisions, the appeal to the jurisprudence of other nations is also common for "conservative" judges: see, for example, Seminole Tribe of Florida v. Florida, 517 U.S. 44, 69 (1996) (Rehnquist, C.J., for the Court) ("[The decision on state sovereign immunity] found its roots not solely in the common law of England, but in the much more fundamental jurisprudence in all civilized nations."); Kaiser Aluminum & Chemical Corp. v. Bonjorno, 494 U.S. 827, 855 (1990) (Scalia, J., concurring) ("The principle that the legal effect of conduct should ordinarily be assessed under the law that existed when the conduct took place has timeless and universal human appeal. It was recognized by the Greeks, by the Romans, by English common law, and by the Code Napoleon.").

98. Frank I. Michelman, "Traces of Self-Government," 100 *Harv. L.Rev.* 4 (1986).

99. I am aware of a few state-specific studies that compiled state court data on nonunanimity rates. (1) California—Uelmen, http://itrs.scu.edu/instructors/uelmen/research.htm; (2) Indiana—Kevin W. Betz et al., "An Examination of the Indiana Supreme Court Docket," in Volumes 26–36 of the *Indiana Law Rev.* (1992–2003); (3) Delaware—Randy J. Holland & David A Skeel, "Deciding Cases without Controversy," 5 *Del. L.Rev.* 115 (2002) (hereafter "Holland, Deciding"); (4) Washington—Charles H. Sheldon, "The Incidence and Structure of Dissensus on a State Supreme Court" in *Supreme Court Decision-Making* (Cornell W. Clayton & Howard Gillman eds., 1999) (hereafter "Sheldon, Incidence"); (5) Tennessee—Note, "Judicial Decision Making: A Statistical Analysis of the Tennessee Supreme Court—1992 Term," 24 *Memphis St. U. L.Rev.* 325 (1994) (hereafter "Tennessee").

100. The remaining six states were Delaware, Iowa, Montana, New Hampshire, New York, and Rhode Island.

A minor indicator of a tilt toward separate opinions is repeal of a prior prohibition on publication of dissents. I am aware of two states where this occurred: Pennsylvania—Act of Apr. 11, 1845, 1845 Pa. Laws 374, sec. 2 (repealed

1951); and Louisiana—see Joe W. Sanders, "The Role of Dissenting Opinions in Louisiana," 23 *La. L.Rev.* 673, 678 (1963) (1898 prohibition of official publication of dissents revoked in 1921).

101. Henry R. Glick & George W. Pruet, Jr., "Dissent in State Supreme Courts: Patterns and Correlates of Conflict," in *Judicial Conflict and Consensus: Behavioral Studies of American Appellate Courts*, Ch. 9 (Sheldon Goldman & Charles H. Lamb eds., 1986) (hereafter "Glick & Pruet, Dissent"). This study finds an increase in the average dissent rate over the following five time periods: 8.9% (1916); 11.7% (1941); 12.3% (1966); 14.91% (1974–75); 18.4% (1980–81). The study also records an increase in the number of states with dissent rates over 25% (though none reaches the 60% level)—specifically: two in 1916, five in 1941, seven in 1966, eight in 1974–75, and 13 in 1980–81. In addition, 38 states showed an increase in dissent rates from 1966 to 1980–81, while ten showed a decrease.

102. See G. Alan Tarr, "Rethinking the Selection of State Supreme Court Justices," 39 *Willamette L.Rev.* 1445, 1446–60 (2003). See also Frances Kahn Zemans, "The Accountable Judge: Guardian of Judicial Independence," 72 *S. Cal. L.Rev.* 625 (1999); "Symposium on Judicial Election, Selection, and Accountability," 61 *S. Cal. L.Rev.* 1555–2073 (1988).

103. Glick & Pruet, Dissent, pp. 203, 208–12 (presence of an intermediate appellate court was the most significant factor influencing dissent rates for 1980–81). See also Paul Brace & Melinda Gann Hall, "Neo-Institutionalism and Dissent in State Supreme Courts," 52 *J. Pol.* 54, 65 (1990) (hereafter "Brace & Hall, Dissent"); Sheldon, Incidence, pp. 118–20 (separate opinions increased in the Washington Supreme Court after the establishment of an intermediate court of appeals in 1969, at which time all cases became subject to discretionary review in the Supreme Court, except for mandatory review of all death cases); Holland, Deciding, pp. 123–24 (suggesting that mandatory appeals produces less dissent).

104. For example, in Tennessee, ten of 11 dissenting votes in criminal cases in the 1992 term were in death penalty cases; Tennessee, p. 340.

105. Brace & Hall, Dissent, p. 65.

106. Sheldon, Incidence, p. 118 (separate opinions increased in Washington after shift to *en banc* nine-member review instead of two five-member panels); Holland, Deciding, pp. 120–21 (smaller panels might help to explain fewer dissents).

107. Brace & Hall, Dissent, pp. 57–58.

108. See Johnson, Judicial, pp. 168–71; Laura Langer, Jody McMullen, Nick Ray, & Dan Stratton, "Recruitment of Chief Justices on State Supreme Courts: A Choice between Institutional and Personal Goals," 65 *J. Pol.* 656, 656 (2003).

109. The limited data available for the U.S. Courts of Appeals (which is

an intermediate court of appeals below the U.S. Supreme Court) suggest that smaller panels (usually three persons) and less difficult cases (because of a mandatory right of appeal from the U.S. District Courts) will produce a lower rate of separate opinions. One study found a very low rate of dissent overall during the time period studied (1953–1975); Donald R. Songer, "Factors Affecting Variation in Rates of Dissent in the U.S. Court of Appeals," in *Judicial Conflict and Consensus: Behavioral Studies of American Appellate Courts,* pp. 117–20 (Sheldon Goldman & Charles H. Lamb eds. 1986) (finding an average dissent rate of 7% and 8.3% in criminal and labor law cases, respectively). See also Harry T. Edwards, "The Effects of Collegiality on Judicial Decision Making," 151 *U. Pa. L.Rev.* 1639, 1651–52 (2003) (arguing that the Supreme Court's frequent practice of issuing multiple opinions is inappropriate and noting a trend in the D.C. Circuit toward fewer dissents).

110. There is at least one striking example of a state in which attitudes toward judging appear to dominate any influence that operational factors might have on a judge's inclination to write separately, although it was in the direction of *more* unanimity. New York, which had an intermediate court of appeals and seven judges on its highest court throughout the study period, was the only state in the study in which nonunanimity rates in the latter three years were all *lower* than nonunanimity rates in the earlier three years, even though an intermediate appellate court and a larger number of judges is usually hypothesized to increase nonunanimity rates. New York's singular pattern may have resulted from pride in a commitment to consensus; see "Court of Appeals' Key Rulings Still Show Unity, Collegiality," *New York Law Journal,* July 30, 2003, p. 1.

111. Alabama, California, Georgia, Illinois, Indiana, Louisiana, Missouri, New Jersey, New York, Ohio, Tennessee, and Texas (both civil and criminal).

112. Delaware, Maine, Montana, Nevada, New Hampshire, Rhode Island, South Dakota, Vermont, West Virginia, and Wyoming. One state (North Dakota) had a temporary intermediate court of appeals in 1990 but not in 2000.

113. There might have been other jurisdictional rule changes, such as withdrawal of mandatory high court jurisdiction, which could have increased the difficulty of cases reaching the highest court of the state. I do not have information about such changes for states generally, although I am aware that Indiana reduced mandatory Supreme Court jurisdiction in 2001, and one study has suggested that this led to less unanimity; Kevin W. Betz & P. Jason Stephenson, "An Examination of the Supreme Court Docket, Dispositions, and Voting in 2001," 35 *Ind. L.Rev.* 1117, 1118 (2002). As Appendix 3A indicates, several states had dramatic changes in workload unrelated to the introduction of an intermediate appellate court that could have been the result of jurisdictional changes—for example, New Mexico, Oklahoma (criminal), Louisiana, and New York.

114. An increase in the nonunanimity rate occurred after temporary adop-

tion of an IAC in 1990, as compared to the prior four years in the study, but there was a drop to one-third of the 1990 rate in 2000 when there was no longer an IAC.

NOTES TO CHAPTER 6

1. Richard A. Posner, "Judges' Writing Styles (And Do They Matter?)," 62 *U. Chi. L.Rev.* 1421, 1422 (1995) (hereafter "Posner, Writing Styles").

2. See Francis-Noel Thomas & Mark Turner, *Clear and Simple as the Truth,* pp. 3, 10 (1994).

3. 12 Coke's Reports 63, 65.

4. Quoted in Hans W. Baade, "The *Casus Omissus:* A Pre-History of Statutory Analogy," 20 *Syr. J. Int'l L. & Comm.* 45, 84 (1994).

5. 218 F.2d 547, 553 (2d Cir. 1914). See also Learned Hand's observations in Commissioner v. Ickelheimer, 132 F.2d 660 (2d Cir. 1943) (Hand, J., dissenting) ("[T]he colloquial words of a statute have not the fixed and artificial content of scientific symbols; they have a penumbra, a dim fringe, a connotation, for they express an attitude of will, into which it is our duty to penetrate. . . .").

6. 252 U.S. 189 (1920).

7. Benjamin N. Cardozo, *The Nature of the Judicial Process,* p. 11 (1921) (hereafter "Cardozo, Nature"). See also Richard A. Posner, *Law and Literature: A Misunderstood Relation,* p. 290 (1988) (hereafter "Posner, Law/Lit") (Marshall as magisterial).

8. Cardozo, Nature, p. 11.

9. Cardozo, Nature, pp. 25–26.

10. See, for example, Calder v. Bull, 3 U.S. 386, 388 (1798) (Chase, J.) ("An ACT of the Legislature (for I cannot call it a law) contrary to the great first principles of the social compact, cannot be considered a rightful exercise of legislative authority."); Fletcher v. Peck, 10 U.S. 87, 133 (1810) (Johnson, J., concurring) ("[T]here are certain great principles of justice, whose authority is universally recognized, that ought not to be entirely disregarded.").

11. 25 U.S. 213, 344–47 (1827) (Marshall, C. J., dissenting).

12. 17 U.S. 316, 403–04 (1819) (Marshall, C.J., for the Court).

13. 5 U.S. 137, 177–78 (1803).

14. Panhandle Oil Co. v. Mississippi, 277 U.S. 218, 223 (1928) (Holmes, J., dissenting).

15. Jacobellis v. Ohio, 378 U.S. 184, 197 (1984) (Stewart, J., concurring). For a discussion of Stewart's opinion, see Paul Gewirtz, "On 'I Know It When I See It,'" 105 *Yale L.J.* 1023 (1996).

16. Brown v. Allen, 344 U.S. 443, 540 (1953) (Jackson, J., concurring).

17. Terminiello v. Chicago, 337 U.S. 1, 37 (1949) (Jackson, J., dissenting).

18. Richard A. Posner, "The Jurisprudence of Skepticism," 86 *Mich. L.Rev.* 827, 874 (1988) (hereafter "Posner, Skepticism").

19. Bank One Chicago, N.A. v. Midwest Bank & Trust Co., 516 U.S. 264, 278 (1996) (Stevens, J., concurring).

20. Albertson's Inc. v. Commissioner, 42 F.3d 537, 540 (9th Cir. 1994).

21. 815 F.2d 1090 (7th Cir. 1987).

22. See, for example, Western Union Telegraph Co. v. Lenroot, 323 U.S. 490 (1945), where a predominantly textualist majority opinion asserts that legislative intent is a shaky basis for interpreting a statute, but then ends the opinion with a statement that the policy implications of a contrary decision are so adverse for the economy and the nation that the legislature is unlikely to have intended such a result.

23. Learned Hand, *The Spirit of Liberty,* p. 130 (Irving Dilliard ed., 3d ed. 1977) (hereafter "Hand, Spirit of Liberty").

24. Gerald Gunther, *Learned Hand: The Man and the Judge,* p. 592 (1994) (hereafter "Gunther, Hand").

25. Gunther, Hand, p. 592.

26. 154 F.2d 785 (2d Cir. 1946).

27. 60 F.2d 737 (2d Cir. 1937).

28. Frederick Schauer, "Opinions as Rules," 62 *U. Chi. L.Rev.* 1455 (1995).

29. See, for example, Exacto Spring Corp. v. Commissioner, 196 F.3d 833, 835 (7th Cir. 1999) ("like many other multi-factor tests, [this one is] redundant, incomplete, and unclear."). See also Prussner v. United States, 896 F.2d 218, 224 (7th Cir. 1990) ("Multifactored tests can be difficult to apply."). Rules that sound clear but give little guidance come in for similar criticism; Donovan v. Fall River Foundry Co., Inc., 696 F.2d 524, 526 (7th Cir. 1982) ("[W]e are unwilling to decide [the issue] simply by reference to a maxim of statutory construction," quoting Rehnquist's statement that "generalities about statutory construction help us little."). Posner is also dubious about using dictionaries; Joy v. Hay Group, Inc., 403 F.3d 875, 877 (7th Cir. 2005) ("Dictionaries give a range of linguistic possibilities; rarely do they help a court decide which one the drafter of the contract or statute in question intended. . . .").

30. Patricia M. Wald, "A Reply to Judge Posner," 62 *U. Chi. L.Rev.* 1451, 1453 (1995).

31. Weisberg argues that bad judicial style correlates with an opinion's fragility; Richard Weisberg, *Poethics: and Other Strategies of Law and Literature,* pp. 7–33 (1992) (badly crafted opinion will lose its future power). But it seems hard to demonstrate that fragile opinions are more heavily represented in the category of badly crafted rather than well-crafted opinions.

32. Posner, Skepticism, pp. 879–80.

33. Posner, Writing Styles, p. 1432.

34. Cardozo, Nature, pp. 18, 19, 21.

35. 281 U.S. 111 (1930).

36. Abner J. Mikva, "For Whom Judges Write," 61 *S. Cal. L.Rev.* 1357, 1363–69 (1988) ("In our age of legal complexity . . . a purely Holmesian approach is untenable"; but the author pleads for a return to his brevity and focus.).

37. 2 U.S. 419 (1793).

38. Alden v. Maine, 527 U.S. 706, 721 (1999).

39. Morton J. Horwitz, "The Constitution of Change: Legal Fundamentality without Fundamentalism," 107 *Harv. L.Rev.* 30, 61–65 (1993).

40. Laura Krugman Ray, "Judicial Personality: Rhetoric and Emotion in Supreme Court Opinions," 59 *Wash. & Lee L.Rev.* 197, 199–201 (2002) (hereafter "Ray, Rhetoric").

41. Ray, Rhetoric, pp. 227–29.

42. See, for example, Kaiser Aluminum & Chemical Corp. v. Bonjorno, 494 U.S. 827, 857 (1990) (Scalia, J., concurring).

43. See Planned Parenthood of Southeastern Pa. v. Casey, 505 U.S. 833, 996 (1992) (Scalia, J., concurring and dissenting).

44. For an argument against judges attempting to replicate Chief Justice Marshall's magisterial (or prophetic) style, see Lewis Henry LaRue, "How Not to Imitate John Marshall," 56 *Wash. & Lee L.Rev.* 819 (1999).

45. Richard A. Posner, *Law, Pragmatism, and Democracy* (2003); Richard A. Posner, *Cardozo: A Study in Reputation*, pp. 33–57, 125–43 (1990); Richard A. Posner, *The Federal Courts: Crisis and Reform*, pp. 107–15, 230–36 (1985); Richard A. Posner, "A Political Court," 119 *Harv. L.Rev.* 31 (2005); Richard A. Posner, "Judges' Writing Styles (And Do They Matter?)," 62 *U. Chi. L.Rev.* 1421 (1995); Richard A. Posner, "Goodbye to the Bluebook," 53 *U. Chi. L.Rev.* 1343 (1986).

46. See generally Robert F. Blomquist, "Playing on Words: Judge Richard A. Posner's Appellate Opinions, 1981–82—Ruminations on Sexy Judicial Opinion Style during an Extraordinary Rookie Season," 68 *U. Cinc. L.Rev.* 651 (2000); Robert F. Blomquist, "Dissent, Posner-Style: Judge Richard A. Posner's First Decade of Dissenting Opinions, 1981–1991—Toward an Aesthetic of Judicial Dissenting Style," 69 *Mo. L.Rev.* 73 (2004).

47. Milner v. Apfel, 148 F.3d 812, 814 (7th Cir. 1998) (laws dealing with masturbation, fornication, sodomy, etc.).

48. 680 F.2d 42, 45.

49. Buck v. Bell, 274 U.S. 200, 207 (1927).

50. The same cautious simplification occurs when complex legal issues are reduced to a quantitative formula for ease of presentation and as a help in organizing thought. Thus: "[The Learned Hand] formula is a valuable aid to clear thinking about the factors that are relevant to a judgment of negligence and

about the relationship among those factors"—683 F.2d 1022, 1026; "Quantification will rarely be possible but expressing mathematically the relationship between the value of the interest and the probability of its erroneous destruction may assist in thinking about the tests"—672 F.2d 644, 645.

51. 241 F.3d 609, 611; 144 F.3d 1060, 1062; 135 F.3d 457, 458; 37 F.3d 321, 323; 998 F.2d 513, 516; 842 F.2d 180, 182–83; 678 F.2d 716, 717.

52. Richard A. Posner, *The Federal Courts: Crisis and Reform*, pp. 352–53 (1996) (hereafter "Posner, Federal Courts"). Others have expressed a similar aversion to footnotes: Abner J. Mikva, "Goodbye to Footnotes," 56 *U. Colo. L.Rev.* 647 (1985); "A Footnote Has No Place," *N.Y. Times*, July 28, 1995, at B18 (explaining why Justice Breyer does not employ footnotes in his opinions). See also Gunther, Hand, pp. 528–29 (Learned Hand's objection to Judge Frank's use of footnotes because it converted judicial opinions into mini-treatises).

53. Posner, Federal Courts, pp. 352–53.

54. 249 F.3d 667,672 (discussing "moral hazard"); 174 F.3d 862, 867 (discussing "economic loss" doctrine).

55. 156 F.3d 771, 778 (Posner, J., concurring):
It is a matter of judgment whether to base a decision of an appeal on a broad ground, on a narrow ground, or on both, when both types of ground are available. If the judges are dubious about the broad ground, then they will do well to decide only on the narrow ground; but if they are confident of the broad ground, they should base decision on that ground (as well as on the narrow ground, if equally confident of it) in order to maximize the value of the decision in guiding the behavior of persons seeking to comply with the law. One of the most important things that appellate courts do is to formulate rules of law. They would formulate very few rules, and leave the law in a state of considerable and avoidable uncertainty, if they always chose to decide a case on the narrowest possible ground. It is true that the broader the ground, the more likely it is to sweep in cases that the judges cannot perfectly foresee, and this argues for caution in deciding cases on broad grounds, because there is a greater risk for error. . . . But I think we could prudently have gone further in this case than the majority does to clarify the law. . . .

56. "The place to start in rethinking the proper standard is with the purpose, so far as it can be discerned, of exempting tiny employers from the antidiscrimination laws."—166 F.3d 937, 940; "This interpretation is more sensible than National's because it tracks the purpose of [the law]. . . ."—144 F.3d 1125, 1128; "We should think about the purpose of the home office deduction and why it is so limited. . . . With the purpose behind the home office deduction and its limitations in mind, we examine the application [of the statute to the facts]."—919 F.2d 1273, 1274–75; "Words are not plain in themselves. They

are plain only by virtue of a context that includes not only minimum cultural and linguistic competence but also, in the case of words that are intended to convey a command . . . , any other clues to the speaker's or writer's intentions. . . . The Tax Court's interpretation is both consistent with the purposes of Congress in enacting the statute (so far as those purposes can be reconstructed) and unlikely to cost the Treasury substantial revenue."—842 F.2d 180, 183–84; "Our suggested interpretation [of the tax law] may not be inevitable as a textual matter, but considerations of legislative purpose reinforce it."—692 F.2d 1129, 1132; "But we cannot stop here. Having regard to the purpose and not merely the language of section 16(b), we must consider whether the [statutory] words . . . should be read more broadly. . . ."—682 F.2d 643, 645; "The issue does not lend itself to decision by verbal talismans. The intelligent decision of particular cases requires instead a sensitivity to the purposes of both the 30-day limitation and its judicially engrafted exception."—668 F.2d 962, 966.

57. 144 F.3d 1056, 1060; 37 F.3d 321, 323–24; 972 F.2d 869, 871; 956 F.2d 703, 707; 695 F.2d 1086, 1093 (dissent from denial of *en banc* hearing); 691 F.2d 1213, 1215.

58. West Virginia U. Hospitals, Inc. v. Casey, 499 U.S. 83, 101 (1991).

59. Richard A. Posner, " 'What Am I, a Potted Plant?' The Case against Strict Constructionism," in *Judges on Judging*, p. 182 (David M. O'Brien ed., 1997). Posner first used this phrase in the *New Republic*, Sept. 28, 1987, p. 23.

60. See, for example, 162 F.3d 491, 494; 147 F.3d 631, 632; 68 F.3d 1006, 1009.

61. 471 U.S. 84 (1985), discussed in Posner, Law/Lit, p. 256.

62. For state court judges, see: Shirley S. Abrahamson, "Judging in the Quiet of the Storm," 24 *St. Mary's L.J.* 965 (1993) (Wisconsin); Judith S. Kaye, "The Human Dimension in Appellate Judging: A Brief Reflection on a Timeless Concern," 73 *Cornell L.Rev.* 1004 (1988) (New York); Robert A. Leflar, "Some Observations Concerning Judicial Opinions," 61 *Colum. L.Rev.* 810 (1961) (Arkansas); Stewart G. Pollock, "The Art of Judging," 71 *N.Y.U. L.Rev.* 591 (1996) (New Jersey); Walter V. Schaefer, "Precedent and Policy," 34 *U. Chi. L.Rev.* 3 (1966) (Illinois); Albert Tate, Jr., "The Law-Making Function of the Judge," 28 *La. L.Rev.* 211 (1968) (Louisiana); Roger J. Traynor, "Reasoning in a Circle of Law," 56 *Va. L.Rev.* 739 (1970) (California).

For federal judges, see: Ruggero J. Aldisert, "The Role of Courts in Contemporary Society," 38 *U. Pitt. L.Rev.* 437 (1977) (3d Cir.); Charles E. Clark, "The Limits of Judicial Objectivity," 12 *Am. U. L.Rev.* 1 (1963) (2d Cir.); Frank N. Coffin, "Judicial Balancing: The Protean Scales of Justice," 63 *N.Y.U. L.Rev.* 16 (1988) (1st Cir.); Joseph C. Hutcheson, Jr., "The Judgment Intuitive: The Function of the 'Hunch' in Judicial Decision," 14 *Cornell L.Q.* 274 (1928) (S.D. Tex.); Irving R. Kaufman, "The Anatomy of Decisionmaking," 53 *Fordham*

*L.Rev.*1 (1984) (2d Cir.). See generally Shirley S. Abrahamson et al., "Judges on Judging: A Bibliography," 24 *St. Mary's L.J.* 995 (1993).

63. The characterization of the judge as Hercules comes from Ronald Dworkin, *Law's Empire* (1986).

64. Frederick Schauer, "Giving Reasons," 47 *Stan. L.Rev.* 633 (1995).

65. PMC, Inc. v. Sherwin-Williams Co., 151 F.3d 610, 620. See generally Michael Taggart, "Should Canadian Judges Be Legally Required to Give Reasoned Decisions in Civil Cases?" 33 *U. Toronto L.J.* 1 (1983).

66. Frank I. Michelman, "Traces of Self-Government," 100 *Harv. L.Rev.* 4, 23, 29, 33 (1986). See also Christopher J. Peters, "Adjudication as Representation," 97 *Colum. L.Rev.* 312 (1997).

67. See G. Edward White, "The Chancellor's Ghost," 74 *Chi-Kent L.Rev.* 229, 236 (1998).

68. 98 Eng. Rep. 201 (1768).

69. 98 Eng. Rep. at pp. 222, 248.

70. 98 Eng. Rep. at pp. 250–51.

71. Fyodor Dostoevsky, *Brothers Karamazov,* Part II, Book V, Ch. V, p. 301 (Modern Library College 1950) (hereafter "Dostoevsky, Brothers"). See also id. at pp. 303, 305 (people want "miracle, mystery and authority").

72. See U.S. v. Vasen, 222 F.2d 3, 11 (7th Cir. 1955) ("Laymen everywhere quickly discern differences between actions and words. Our theory of government and law will quickly rot and wither planted among shallow applications of basic tenets in empty ceremonies."); Christopher E. Smith, "Law and Symbolism," 1997 *Mich. St. L.Rev.* 935, 948 (disappointed public can lead to loss of faith in the law).

73. See Tony Mauro, " 'In Other News . . .': Developments at the Supreme Court in the 2002–2003 Term That You Won't Read About in the U.S. Reports," 39 *Tulsa L.Rev.* 11, 13–15, 24–25 (2003).

74. See Bradley C. Canon & Charles A. Johnson, *Judicial Policies: Implementation and Impact,* pp. 168–71 (2d ed. 1999) (questioning whether even size of majority affects implementation of opinion by lower courts; clarity and persuasiveness of opinions are even harder to correlate with the decision's impact); Posner, Skepticism, pp. 874–75 (judges remembered for exercise of power, not style).

75. See Valerie J. Hoekstra, *Public Reaction to Supreme Court Decisions* (2003); and materials cited in William D. Popkin, "An 'Internal' Critique of Justice Scalia's Theory of Statutory Interpretation," 76 *Minn. L.Rev.* 1133, 1179–80 (1992).

76. Will Durant, *Epilogue to Caesar and Christ: A History of Roman Civilization and of Christianity from Their Beginnings to A.D. 325,* p. 665 (1944).

77. Dostoevsky, Brothers, pp. 308, 310.

78. Compare Scott Altman, "Beyond Candor," 89 *Mich. L.Rev.* 296 (1990) (awareness of discretion loosens bounds) with Richard A. Posner, *Law, Pragmatism, and Democracy,* p. 96 (2003) (hereafter "Posner, Pragmatism") (judges less power hungry if they know that they are exercising discretion). See also Nicholas S. Zeppos, "Judicial Candor and Statutory Interpretation," 78 *Geo. L.Rev.* 353 (1989).

79. Posner, Pragmatism, pp. 351–52.

80. See Posner, Skepticism, pp. 865, 873 (need to maintain judicial authority may explain why a pretense of certainty in judicial opinions prevails over uncertain judicial reasoning).

81. Posner, Pragmatism, pp. 91–92 (suggesting that the bulk of the legal academy would have applauded a decision citing such criteria as reasons for upholding separate but equal schools). See also *What* Brown v. Board of Education *Should Have Said* (Jack M. Balkin ed., 2002), containing nine opinions by legal scholars, rewriting the Brown opinion.

82. Joseph Goldstein, *The Intelligible Constitution,* p. 58 (1992).

83. See Robert A. Ferguson, "The Judicial Opinion as Literary Genre," 2 *Yale J. L. & Human.* 201, 206–07 (1990) ("The one thing a judge never admits in the moment of decision is freedom of choice."); Hand, Spirit of Liberty, p. 131 (judicial opinion sweeps all the chessmen off the board); Walter V. Schaefer, "Precedent and Policy," 34 *U. Chi. L.Rev.* 3, 9 (1966) (judge becomes an advocate when writing an opinion); Dan Simon, "The Double-Consciousness of Judging: The Problematic Legacy of Cardozo," 79 *Or. L.Rev.* 1033, 1070–71 (hereafter "Simon, Cardozo") (collecting recent authorities); Charles M. Yablon, "Are Judges Liars? A Wittgensteinian Critique of Law's Empire" in *Wittgenstein and Legal Theory,* p. 261 (Patterson ed., 1992) (judges do not describe internal thought processes, they make arguments). See generally Jan Gillis Wetter, *The Styles of Appellate Judicial Decisions* (1960).

84. See Ray, Rhetoric, pp. 194, 222; Posner, Federal Courts, pp. 145–51; Richard A. Posner, "What Do Judges and Justices Maximize? (The Same Thing Everybody Else Does)," 3 *Sup. Ct. Econ. Rev.* 1 (1993) (hereafter "Posner, Maximize") (most judges cede opinion writing to law clerks because they believe that the core judicial function is deciding, not articulating, grounds of decision). But see Richard A. Posner, "Legal Writing Today," 8 *Scribes J. Legal Writing* 35, 38 (2002) (urging judges to write their own opinions).

85. Simon, Cardozo, p. 1065.

86. See generally Dan Simon, "A Psychological Model of Judicial Decision Making," 30 *Rutgers L.J.* 1, 8–11 (1998) (noting the Realist attacks on certainty in judicial opinions and the persistence of certainty despite the attacks); id at p.12 n.58 (also noting that an expression of uncertainty by Justice Breyer evoked a reaction that it was "disturbing"); Dan Simon, "Freedom and Constraint in Adjudication: A Look through the Lens of Cognitive Psychology," 67

Brook. L.Rev. 1097, 1136 nn. 95–96 (2002) (example of concern about judge expressing doubt in Delaware case).

87. Purpose—Muscarello v. United States, 524 U.S. 125, 132 (1998); Lewis v. United States, 523 U.S. 155, 160 (1998); Legislative history—F. Hoffman-La Roche Ltd. v. Empagran S.A., 542 U.S. 155, 163 (2004). Breyer has authored one of the leading articles on judicial use of legislative history; Stephen Breyer, "On the Uses of Legislative History in Interpreting Statutes," 65 *S. Cal. L.Rev.* 845 (1992).

88. *New York Times,* July 28, 1995, at B18.

89. Denver Area Educational Telecommunications Consortium, Inc. v. F.C.C., 518 U.S. 727, 750, 757 (1996).

90. Linda Greenhouse, *New York Times,* Week in Review, July 14, 1966, at p. 5, col. 1.

91. Brown v. Pro Football, Inc., 518 U.S. 231, 242 (1996).

92. Metro-North Commuter Railroad Co. v. Buckley, 521 U.S. 424, 436 (1997).

93. Mobil Oil Exploration & Producing Southeast, Inc. v. U.S., 530 U.S. 604, 607 (2000).

94. Stogner v. California, 539 U.S. 607, 628–29 (2003).

95. Stenberg v. Carhart, 530 U.S. 914, 923 (2000).

96. Sometimes a judge will adopt an authoritative tone in his or her opinions but a personal voice in his or her extrajudicial writings. See Elizabeth Roth, "The Two Voices of Roger Traynor," 27 *Am. J. Leg. Hist.* 269, 300 (1983) ("official style is severe, orderly, and persuasive . . . [lacking] the playful . . . passages which ornament his extrajudicial writing. . . .").

97. Posner, Maximize, pp. 29–30.

NOTES TO THE POSTSCRIPT

1. See generally Tom Ginsburg, *Judicial Review in New Democracies: Constitutional Courts in Asian Cases* (2003).

2. See R.P. Anand, "The Role of Individual and Dissenting Opinions in International Adjudication," 14 *Int'l & Comp. L.Q.* 788, 788–89, 796 (1965) (hereafter "Anand, Role") (providing data and referring to Article 57 of the Statute creating the International Court of Justice, permitting separate opinions).

3. Anand, Role, p. 706.

4. Harold Hongju Koh, "On American Exceptionalism," 55 *Stan. L.Rev.* 1479, 1506 (2003).

5. John Ferejohn & Pasquale Pasquino, "Constitutional Adjudication: Lessons from Europe," 82 *Tex. L.Rev.* 1671, 1692–1700 (2004).

6. Donald P. Kommers, *The Constitutional Jurisprudence of the Federal Republic of Germany,* pp. 21, 26 (1997).

7. See generally Carl Baudenbacher, "Judicialization: Can the European Model Be Exported to Other Parts of the World?" 39 *Tex. Int'l L.J.* 381 (2004); Gerda Kleijkamp, "Comparing the Application and Interpretation of the United States Constitution and the European Convention on Human Rights," 12 *Transnational L. & Cont. Prob.* 307 (2002).

8. P. van Dijk & G.J.H. van Hoof, *Theory and Practice of the European Convention on Human Rights,* App. VI, p. 832 (3d ed. 1998).

9. *Collected Edition of the "Travaux Preparatoires" of the European Convention on Human Rights,* Vol. IV, p. 154 (1977).

10. See generally Kurt H. Nadelman, "Judicial Dissent: Publication v. Secrecy," 8 *Am. J. Comp. L.* 415 (1959).

Index

personal voice, 153; rely on wisdom of ages, 112
Scarman, Lord, 25, 28
Schauer, Frederick, 150
Schenck v. U.S., 146
Separate opinions (states): Alabama, 135; Alaska, 135; Arizona, 135; Arkansas, 135; California, 136; Colorado, 136; Connecticut, 136; Delaware, 136; Florida, 136; Georgia, 136; Hawaii, 136; Idaho, 136; Illinois, 137; Indiana, 137; Iowa, 137; Kansas, 137; Kentucky, 137; Louisiana, 137; Maine, 137; Maryland, 137; Massachusetts, 138; Michigan, 138; Minnesota, 138; Mississippi, 138; Missouri, 138; Montana, 138; Nebraska, 138; Nevada, 138; New Hampshire, 139; New Jersey, 139; New Mexico, 139; New York, 139; North Carolina, 139; North Dakota, 139; Ohio, 139; Oklahoma-Civil, 139; Oklahoma-Criminal, 140; Oregon, 140; Pennsylvania, 140; Rhode Island, 140; South Carolina, 140; South Dakota, 140; Tennessee, 140; Texas-Civil, 140; Texas-Criminal, 141; Utah, 141; Vermont, 141; Virginia, 141; Washington, 141; West Virginia, 141; Wisconsin, 141; Wyoming, 141
Separate opinions (states, in general), 127–141: articles on specific states, 281n99; effect of intermediate appellate court, 131–133; effect of number of judges, 133–134; effect of operational rules, 129–134; effect of workload, 130; increase since 1950, 127–128; and Legal Realism, 128–129; less often than for U.S. Supreme Court, 127–128; sanction for writing separately (mundane and political), 129–130; summary data on effect of operational rules (Appendix 3), 241–244; summary data on separate opinions (Appendix 2), 237–238. *See also* Separate opinions (states)
Separate opinions (U.S.), 114–126: analogy to deliberative democracy, 126; arguments for and against, 122–126; and Chief Justice Stone, 119–121; and discretion to hear cases, 118; explanations for, 116–122; historical antecedents,

115–116; increase in U.S. Supreme Court after 1940, 114, 117; influence on evolution of judicial law, 125; and judicial authority, 122–125; and Legal Realism, 116–122; Marshall Court, 71–72; pre-Marshall Court, 62–68; reduce value of precedent, 72; reflect judicial diversity, 126; and workload, 119. *See also* Seriatim opinions
Separation of powers, three meanings, 43–44; in France, 43; Montesquieu, 45–47; in state constitutions, pre–1787, 47–51; U.S. Constitution's approach (shared power; independence), 44, 55
Seriatim opinions: in Connecticut, 68, 91–92; in England, 10, 30–33; in Georgia, 91–92; Jefferson favors, 66, 72, 91–92; Madison favors, 72; in Marshall Court, 71, 72; in Maryland, 91; in Massachusetts, 91; in modern practice, 114; in New Jersey, 91; in North Carolina, 91; in Pennsylvania, 69, 91; in pre-Marshall Court, 62–68; in South Carolina, 69, 91–92; in states, 91–92; in Vermont, 69, 92; in Virginia, 91–92. *See also* Separate opinions *various entries*
Shelley's Case, 22
Sources of judicial law, 2, 4; in England, substantive common law, 8–9, 11, 13, 16, 108; institutional, 2, 4; institutional and substantive sources of law, 4, 10, 106, 108–114; judicial voice, relates to source of law, 3, 143; legal science, 112; natural law, 112; substantive, 2, 4; tradition, 113; whether derived from the people, 44, 94, 108, 109, 145, 152
State constitutions, pre–1787: Connecticut, 48; Delaware, 48; Georgia, 49, 54; judicial role, 47–51; Maryland, 49; Massachusetts, 47, 49, 52, 54; New Hampshire, 47, 49, 50, 51; New Jersey, 48; New York, 48; North Carolina, 49; Pennsylvania, 48–49; Rhode Island, 48; separation of powers, 47–51; South Carolina, 49; Virginia, 49, 52, 54
Statutory interpretation (U.S.): and equitable interpretation, 13–14, 23–24, 47; judicial discretion after Revolution, suspicion of, 50; judges rely on substantive

About the Author

William D. Popkin is Walter W. Foskett Professor Emeritus of Law, Indiana University School of Law at Bloomington. He is author of *Statutes in Court: The History and Theory of Statutory Interpretation, Materials on Legislation,* and *Fundamentals of Federal Income Tax Law.*

CPSIA information can be obtained
at www.ICGtesting.com
Printed in the USA
LVHW090158110121
676189LV00021B/195

9 780814 767269